On Krishnamurti's Teachings
The Collected Writings, Talks and Classroom
Discussions of Allan W. Anderson on
the Teachings of J. Krishnamurti

Allan W. Anderson

Karina Library Press
discover the unexpected

On Krishnamurti's Teachings: The Collected Writings, Talks and Classroom Discussions of Allan W. Anderson on the Teachings of J. Krishnamurti

ISBN-13: 978-1-937902-00-1 (trade paper)
ISBN-13: 978-1-937902-01-8 (ebook edition)

Karina Library Press
Michael Lommel, publisher

www.karinalibrary.com

PO Box 35
Ojai, California
93024

All sources quoted herein used by permission or under fair use. See 'Works Cited'.

Also by Allan W. Anderson

Reflections on the I Ching

Self-Transformation and the Oracular

A Wholly Different Way of Living (Dialogues with Krishnamurti)

Songs from the Mifflinger Sea and a little cove of Nonsense

www.allanwanderson.com

To the spirit of Krishnamurti's teaching

From the unreal
lead me to the real
From the darkness
lead me to the light
From death
lead me to immortality.

—Bṛhadarāṇyaka Upaniṣad [1.3.28]

Contents

Editor's Preface xi
Foreword xiii
On Krishnamurti's Teaching: An Ongoing Personal Response xv

PART I: WRITINGS AND TALKS 1
On the Significance of Krishnamurti's Teachings 3
Introduction to *Total Freedom* 13
Address on the Inauguration of the Krishnamurti Center 19
Liberation: Secular and Ultimate 27
On Non-Attachment: Some Aspects of Asian Thought 37
What is Sacred? 45
Preface to *Under the Pepper Tree* 53

PART II: CONFERENCE PAPERS 59
Human Transformation Independent of Knowledge and Time 61
   Knowledge and Time 66
   Understanding and Timelessness 69
   Not to Misunderstand and Timing 73
Inner Transformation and Bearing 77
   Bearing and Understanding 81
   Not to Misunderstand and Bearing 93

Awareness, Consciousness and Bearing 97
    Awareness 98
    Awareness and Consciousness 103
    Bearing 106
Primal Intuition and Bearing 111

Part III: University Lectures 123
Lectures on the video series, 'A Wholly Different Way of Living'
Knowledge and the Transformation of Man 125
Knowledge and Conflict in Human Relationships 131
What is Communication with Others? 139
What is a Responsible Human Being? 147
Order Comes From the Understanding of Our Disorder 155
The Nature and Total Eradication of Fear 163
Does Pleasure Bring Happiness? 171
Sorrow, Passion, and Beauty 181
The Art of Listening 189
Being Hurt and Hurting Others 199
Love, Sex and Pleasure 205
A Different Way of Living 211
Death, Life and Love Are Indivisible—the Nature of Immortality 221
Religion, Authority and Education—Part I 229
Meditation and the Sacred Mind 235

Works Cited 239

Index 243

Editor's Preface

In 1974 Professor Allan W. Anderson was invited by the Krishnamurti Foundation of America to interview Krishnamurti for the purpose of documenting Krishnamurti's teachings in the round. The conversations were wide-ranging and fascinating. They were later published under the title *A Wholly Different Way of Living*. While the two men came from vastly different backgrounds, they met on the common ground of a meditative inquiry into human nature. In subsequent years Professor Anderson continued to develop themes touched upon in those earlier conversations. He wrote several papers and gave a number of talks on aspects of Krishnamurti's teachings. He also taught a seminar on Krishnamurti at San Diego State University. His papers, talks and a transcription of that most unique seminar are collected here for the first time.

We are immensely grateful to Evelyne Blau for contributing the Foreword to this volume and to Mark Lee and the Krishnamurti Foundation of America for granting permission to include papers that have previously appeared in their various publications. Many thanks also to Barbara Asaro for her invaluable assistance with proof reading the manuscript.

Bruce Hanson, Ph.D.

Foreword

This seminal collection of works by Allan Anderson expresses his deep concern with vital matters that are shared by all of humanity. His exploration into questions that profoundly affect people of every race and gender, from every quarter of the globe, are brought into focus in his discerning questions posed to J. Krishnamurti. In 1974 he held 18 one hour conversations with the philosopher, teacher and author Krishnamurti, who was perhaps the most noted iconoclast of his day. One who spoke on a wide range of topics, often focusing on 'what is', as he put it. His teaching pointed again and again to not being hobbled by the influence of others, be they those we look up to such as Gurus, Priests and Masters but, also the culture into which we are born, with its deep impact on our conditioned mindset. Our admiration can also include Rulers, Kings or Dictators whose iron hand can impose a sense of order into the confusion and disorder of our lives.

Our beliefs, the rules set out by our conditioned past, can prevent us from direct observation and true insight.

As a teacher Krishnamurti did not offer comfort or consolation, but rather asked that we take direct responsibility for our actions and to our relationship with others.

As the interviews continued under the challenging exploration of both Anderson and Krishnamurti, the topics plumb depths that could only be achieved by those who are able to interact with direct responsiveness.

The universality of the topics, ranging in part from questions regarding Fear, Desire, Death, Religion and Authority and lastly

Meditation, to offering the widest scope for those willing to face essential questions.

The rapport with which the two men interact, the open minded approach to serious issues, indicate not only the depth and passion of their concern but the ability to really listen. Each responding to the other, not as if from across the ravine of pre-held positions, but each looking afresh at every issue as it arises.

Lastly, the awakening of that supreme intelligence which does not depend on any authority and which is beyond all thought can only come about from the well-spring of direct perception. Each man, in his own way, makes clear that such perception is possible.

Evelyne Blau
June, 2011

Introduction
On Krishnamurti's Teaching: An Ongoing Personal Response[1]

Great teachers are rare. This statement is a commonplace and, as a truism, it hardly draws notice. However, such usual inattention in no way alters the fact that the obvious conceals the most salient significances. Sages over millennia have stressed this to virtually no avail. The pre-Socratic thinker, Heraclitus, wrote that nature loves to hide and that unless one expects the unexpected he will not find it for it is difficult and hard to come by. In the same vein, the seminal Spanish thinker, Ortega y Gasset, contemplated this theme with his statement that masks surround us.

It is one of the characteristics of our human species that we can entertain these remarks cerebrally and even dilate upon them intellectually, yet without meeting them viscerally or being touched by them emotionally. Such a bloodless relation to the obvious has through technology given us great material power over our physical environment. Unhappily, it has done nothing to generate or to advance self-inquiry. Without self-inquiry human nature cannot reach its essential promise which is to become free of self-misunderstanding.

As a species we deform ourselves when we apply a sheerly abstract measure for our conduct whether from memory, dogma, ideology, self-image or a collapse into another's authority. Imagination itself,

---

[1] Introduction written by Allan Anderson for *Krishnamurti: 100 Years* by Evelyne Blau.

which since the Romantic era continues to enjoy the wildest praise, is no less an abstract guide. Unlike Nature, imagination is not its own rule. This want of inherent self-correction is imagination's Achilles' heel. The overweening confidence in imagination is depth psychology's chief liability and until it shifts its center of gravity it will go on failing the promise touted for it in the early days of Freud and Jung. Important as it is to recognize a thing's constant tendency or essence (whether represented mathematically or literarily) this intellectual abstraction cannot stand in for the thing's existence which is fraught with incalculable changes in the give and take of its career.

A philosophical grasp of this distinction between essence and existence is still an abstraction unless with Socrates one regarded philosophy as concerned in wisdom. Unfortunately, academic philosophy in our time shows little if any interest in the wisdom tradition as such and on that account many gifted students shy away from it who otherwise might contribute with distinction to this discipline.

These matters held my attention for many years before I met Krishnamurti. I was privileged to be invited to share twenty dialogues with him, eighteen of which comprise the book, *A Wholly Different Way of Living*. These video-tapes and transcriptions pursue the theme of the transformation of man independent of knowledge and time. He made a profound impression upon me and was the single most decisive influence of any living teacher I had personally encountered. His approach to self-inquiry was lucid, unwavering and correcting. I owe him a debt impossible to repay.

From the moment we began our conversations I was struck by his quality of attention. There was nothing contrived about it nor was it based on a muscular effort of the will to attend. It might be likened, on a different level, to the dynamic of balance as when one rides a bicycle, drives a car or simply walks. Unless there is a disturbance in the inner ear or other impediment, normal walking is unselfconscious yet not unconscious. Beyond strength and skill, it entails knack, which is a gift. Since most of us walk there doesn't seem to be much, if anything, of a gift about it. Yet, without knack our walking would be unspontaneous, graceless, sheerly mechanical and wooden-puppet-like. Krishnamurti's listening was knackful. It had the simplicity and openness of a child with the alertness of a warrior. It combined the harmlessness of the dove with the wisdom of the serpent. [Mt 10:16]

This way of being taught me much about education and teaching. It brought home to me why so many gifted students are lost to higher education—their chief complaint being that it all seems unreal, there being no relation shown between thinking one's life and living it.

I know of no other way of meeting this objection than through inviting the student to look at his or her conflict of motives through a pure act of attention, not as positive effort but as a negative one; negative, that is, since "In attention there is no exclusion, no resistance, and no effort. And therefore no frontier, no limits."[2] Negative again, in that a pure act of attention does not open out upon a positive understanding. Rather it discovers the astonishing sufficiency within just *not misunderstanding*. Suddenly the distance between the striver and the goal no longer obtains for no time elapses between the act of attention and the healing already taking place. Here, timeliness is exact.

This negation is not undertaken in order to attain to something better. Krishnamurti puts it precisely: "Negation is to deny what is false not knowing what is truth. [It is] to see the false in the false and to see the truth in the false, and it is the truth that denies the false. You see what is false, and the very seeing of what is false is the truth."[3]

During our conversations over the span of those eighteen dialogues, another feature of attention as negation (in the above sense) began to disclose itself to me. The dialogues were entirely unrehearsed yet proceeded as from an order intrinsic to them. Many persons who saw and heard them from beginning to end

---

[2] Krishnamurti/Anderson, *A Wholly Different Way of Living*, p. 153.
[3] Krishnamurti, *Total Freedom*, p. 271.

have remarked this to me and in some cases the remark generated a dialogue between us that moved in like fashion provided that an uncontrived act of attention prevailed.

Literally, process is a going forward. Going forward means movement from a source. A complete process entails a beginning, a middle and an end and these structural nodes are susceptible to derangement if not held together by an ordering principle. As noted above, this principle is present with an uncontrived act of attention. Uncontrivance means that there is no preconceived set-up imposed upon the act of attention.

As the dialogues progressed it became clearer to me from Krishnamurti's statements that, as he put it, "the first step is the last step."[4] It is this first step that at the outset either subverts the process or calls its flowering into being. Further, this first step cannot be one step among the others that follow. Rather, it is the one step that must inform all steps if the process is to remain sound throughout or, to put it remedially, if healing and health are to prevail. In that sense we never get beyond square one, nor is there any need to.

This first step is the seeing of the false in the false and this seeing of the false is the truth. How different this is from the egoic notion that one can look on truth, goodness and beauty, bare. In the strict sense there is no I here who makes a pure act of attention upon an object over there. Thus there is no contradiction between subject and object—the contradiction that has since time out of mind generated endlessly tiresome debates over how we know that we know and the conundrum of free will. Life lived genuinely meditatively, i.e., with an abiding pure act of attention is not embarrassed by such questions since even upon entertaining them it is lived free from a conflict of motives.

It is some twenty years since Krishnamurti and I conversed together and after the conclusion of our dialogues it was not my good fortune to see him again but our discussions continue to abide with me in spirit as freshly as they did two decades ago.

---

[4] Krishnamurti/Anderson, op. cit., p. 172.

In pondering these things since then, one question in particular has grown in importance for me. What resource have we for making as well as abiding in an uncontrived act of attention? This question has the most poignant significance for anyone who asks, "What is the relation between thought which is goal oriented and life lived meditatively or without a why?"[5]

During one of our dialogues called "Hearing and Seeing" Krishnamurti made the remarkable statement that hearing is not letting anything interfere with seeing. This remark renewed my passion for Socrates' claim that he had a daimon within that always told him what not to do and this divine voice attended him constantly. I have thought to give this resource the name, primal intuition. By intuition here I do not mean one of Jung's four functions of the psyche, a function chiefly concerned in insight. Primal intuition, on the contrary, has no content and acts simply as a warning. Primal intuition lies below the threshold of personality and the psychic self. It is not co-opted by archetypes nor is it subject to the suasions of will and feeling. However, when these latter are ineptly related to primal intuition, as the voice that tells one what not to do, this voice becomes muffled or even quite unheard. It seems that wild creatures receive it purely—especially those that continue to survive our human atrocities upon their domains. Perhaps it is allied with what the Hindus call *Ātman*, the Buddhists, Suchness and Christians, the Holy Spirit.

I believe this resource enables the serious self-enquirer to keep unconfused the natural function of goal oriented linear, calculative thinking and life lived meditatively, a way of being that is satisfied by its own exercise, a living without a why. Calculative thinking which is bent on a goal that lies outside the means taken to reach it is necessarily time-bound. Some have misunderstood Krishnamurti as denigrating thought of this order. This has caused them to look askance upon, even reject technology. This is a misreading. It is

---

[5] Reiner Schürmann provides an excellent discussion of Meister Eckhart's "living without a why" in *Meister Eckhart Mystic and Philosopher,* p. 63-64.

not technology, thought and knowledge that Krishnamurti inveighs against but their misuses.

Calculative and meditative thinking are opposed only in thought which has not yet penetrated to their reciprocal operation. A pure act of attention is not prejudiced by any practical undertakings. On the contrary, without the meditative attitude that is open to primal intuition, practice of any kind is hostage to any number of fixations and aberrated notions. Imagination, for all its essential service to creativity, all too easily subserves the vagaries of chaotic emotion.

The sound relation between calculative and meditative thinking is not a coincidence of opposites but their co-operation. In this relation thought and existence reciprocate, the work of the world gets done while one lives without a why. Lao Tzu and Krishnamurti seem at one in Lao Tzu's line: "Tao does nothing, yet nothing is left undone."[6]

I am deeply grateful for the instruction I received through my conversations with Krishnamurti for they remain an inexhaustible font of inspiration, suggestion and nourishment. They open out upon the boundless.

La Jolla,
1994

---

[6] Lao Tzu, *Tao Te Ching*, chap. 37.

Abbreviations

Old Testament		New Testament	
Gen	Genesis	Mt	Matthew
Ps	Psalms	Mk	Mark
Prov	Proverbs	Lk	Luke
Eccl	Ecclesiastes	Jn	John
Jer	Jeremiah	Rom	Romans
Ez	Ezekiel	Cor	Corinthians
		Gal	Galatians
		Phil	Philippians
		Heb	Hebrews
Other			
Gītā	*Bhagavad Gītā*		

Part I
Writings and Talks

On the Significance of Krishnamurti's Teachings[1]

It is the highest honor and privilege to have been asked to make these opening remarks on this unique occasion, the one hundredth year of Krishnamurti's birth. This occasion is not unique because it is a commemoration, even a centenary. In our time when gatherings, commemorations, centenary celebrations come and go with a careless speed, we are apt to take them in as thoughtlessly as we are quick to forget them. As we say, they simply come and go.

This particular centenary is unique for us because for ourselves present it is both the first and the last of its kind. It is unlikely that any of us here expects to be in the land of the living in the year 2095; at that time some future generation will celebrate the second Krishnamurti Centenary in our absence provided that we as a species have not destroyed ourselves physically or spiritually between now and then.

This opening talk falls under the rubric keynote address which means that its task is to set forth both the topic and its tone for the duration of our gathering's dialogues. When Mark Lee, our Foundation's Director, invited me to this task I asked him what topic he felt suitable. He replied, "How about the significance of Krishnamurti's teachings?" I agreed. How easy to agree; how difficult to ponder.

I use the word ponder here rather than the word think since the word think does not immediately convey whether it is calculative thinking or meditative thinking that is meant. Calculative thinking computes, meditative thinking ponders. Calculative thinking strides

---

[1] Keynote Address for the Krishnamurti Centenary, Ojai, May 6, 1995.

through the world in seven league boots ever in faster pursuit of whatever lies outside the means it uses to reach it. It is eminently useful in the practical order; it satisfies our material needs and wants and, as for wants, it even invents them. Yet, it is ever restless and cannot come to peace and even when it most satisfies our material needs, let alone our wants, it can do so only intermittently. In the material order we necessarily move from hunger to hunger, shelter to shelter, vacation to vacation since all things pass and nothing stays. However, calculative thinking is absolutely necessary for our material survival; yet, ironically, in our time, the misuse and abuse of it and of technology has engendered a rapacity that seeks to devour the very world itself which means our own extinction.

How can things have come to such a pass? Very simply. More and more of us are coming to believe and practice, and the young now are even taught so, that calculative thinking is the only way of thinking. Unless calculative thinking is restored to its healthy role, the next century, which is less than five years away, will see the beginning of a fatal denaturing of our human being. This is because our human nature is essentially a meditative one and, further, unless meditative thinking can still be restored to a reciprocal relation with healthy calculative thinking our current spiritual disease which is life-threatening is bound to become wholly fatal and the prophecy just mentioned—indeed, not mine alone—is bound to come to pass.

We are now in a position to see the beginning of an answer to the question: What is the significance, the meaning, the importance of Krishnamurti's teachings? They are of supreme importance since they are nothing if not meditational in the deepest and proper sense of that word. As such the teachings draw us to return to our origin, our essential nature by which I do not mean some theory of our prehistoric ancestry. Such theories are biologically and psychologically interesting but spiritually inept. They are spiritually inept because they reduce our nature to a seed once cradled in the dark womb of matter which on coming to flower cannot raise us to a contemplation of the boundless but only to a calculation of our material horizons.

Krishnamurti's teachings, if lived, and that is an immense *if*, restore us to an intuition of our original nature, our natural state, our original innocence none of which is a private possession. On our awaking from the illusion that these are our private possessions we realize an absolute freedom of spirit which is love, and love is the source of creation and the point from which genuine meditation and self-inquiry can authentically begin.

We have, now, one of the answers to the question of the significance of Krishnamurti's teachings which is that they are genuinely meditational in the deepest and proper sense of that word. As such they recall us to our natural state which is not a private possession. This is the state of our original nature, a nature given to us in advance with our being as human.

To speak of original nature in the possessive, as *our* own, is very apt to mislead. It seems to indicate that it is something we "have." The truth of the matter is otherwise. Rather, being-as-human disposes that original nature has us. It has us *freely* not coercively. If it had us coercively we should be unable to indulge in self-betrayal; also, we should be unable to fall into self-misunderstanding. These disorders, these conditions are functional only and will yield to remedy; nevertheless their momentum is such that they can afflict one's person for a whole lifetime.

Awaking to it, that original nature has us rather than our having it as a personal and private possession, goes far to clarify why Krishnamurti consistently refused to be treated as a personality figure or to pose as an authority crutch for followers. Awaking to the impersonal character of original nature further clarifies why Krishnamurti refused to establish his teachings upon the twin pillars of depth psychology, namely, experience and personality. The vagaries of so called "lived experience" are ephemeral and as inconstant as the states of consciousness. His statement that consciousness is its content is exact. Consciousness is tied to change and therefore cannot measure itself. Only awareness can specify the true character of each change in the content of consciousness.

The pure act of attention within awareness is not subject to a conflict of motives and so is able to negate totally the false in the false and to see the truth in the false. It does not measure the truth by a proposition on the strength of which it gives itself airs that it knows the truth in advance. This most common self-misunderstanding reveals its absurdity when one awakes to it that one cannot have the truth but only *be* it. A pure act of attention secures itself against the humbug of the self-misunderstanding that imagines one can have the truth in advance. It secures itself in this way: While it is seeing what is false it is upon the self-same present instant seeing what is truth and in this seeing both seer and seen fall away. The persona of the seer and the abstraction from the seen are not actors in the play. There is only seeing in the presence of the present. This seeing manifests itself not in a psychological explanation but in action which is death and creation upon the same instant.

On awaking to awareness and its pure act of attention Krishnamurti's statement that perception is the action becomes lucidly intelligible. This suggests a second significance of the teachings, namely, awareness as the choiceless watcher of the vagaries of consciousness is what puts self-inquiry on a firm footing. Here self-inquiry, that rarest of human acts, though the only saving one among them, is freed from the modern subjectivist view of it as an internal motion of the psyche.

On pondering further what puts self-inquiry on a firm footing, watching choicelessly the erratic movements of consciousness, one asks: What is the significance of thought in the teachings? This question is crucial for a balanced contemplation of the teachings. I am sure I am not alone in coming across person after person, each having the mistaken and curious notion that the teachings hold that there is something intrinsically wrong with thought as such.

Now, if pondering is to rest upon a firm footing it must include thought functionally since there is no pondering without thinking.

This issue concerned me deeply during the course of our eighteen dialogues which are now published under the title, *A Wholly Different Way of Living*. During the thirteenth dialogue I felt it timely to bring the matter before us so as to give Krishnamurti the opportunity to make himself completely clear. I shall quote from the text. My statements are preceded by the letter A and Krishnamurti's by the letter K. The transcript follows:

> A. ....One of the things that has concerned me in this series of dialogues is that someone would feel that in our discussions of thought and knowledge what we have been saying is that there is some dysfunction in thought and in knowledge which relates to their own nature, the nature of thought and the nature of knowledge, which could very well give the impression that thought is a disease or that knowledge is a disease, rather than giving the impression, as I have understood from you, that thought and knowledge have their proper uses.
>
> K. Of course.
>
> A. Their natures are not corrupt as such.
>
> K. Certainly not, it is the usage of them.[2]

There is no need to quote further. This is eminently clear. The nature of thought is not corrupt. We corrupt it by misusing it. When this clarification of the nature of thought is brought into relation with the profound statement Krishnamurti made in his *Notebook* that "There's a 'thinking' born out of the total emptiness of the mind..."[3] everything is present to place pondering on a firm footing. Calculative and meditative thought are each given their due. But it is well to remember that whereas meditative thought can put calculative thought in checkmate this is not the case conversely.

---

[2] Krishnamurti/Anderson, *A Wholly Different Way of Living*, p. 186.
[3] Krishnamurti, *Krishnamurti's Notebook*, p. 127.

When this is grasped adequately, one intuits how choiceless awareness and thought's role in self-inquiry reciprocally reinforce each other. Their union in love opens out upon that emptiness which lies beyond thought and the vagaries of consciousness while somehow abiding in them, nearer than hands and feet. This is a second significance of the teachings.

Perhaps this intuition of the unconditioned lay at the heart of Krishnamurti's enigmatic pronouncement that no one had understood him. Happily, however, he added that if the teachings are lived one might touch that focus of understanding and energy that were his.

This enigmatic claim that no one had understood him is not without precedent. In the *Tao Te Ching* Lao Tzu says, "My teachings are easy to understand, easy to practice but no one understands them and no one practices them."[4] He then goes on to point out that his teachings are sourced in Nature and his deeds destined by Tao; further, he says that since people don't understand this, they don't understand him.

Confucius[5] stated that no one knew him except Heaven. Jesus said to his disciples, "There are many things I would have told you but you cannot bear them." [Jn 16:12-13] When the acid test of the cross obtained only one man stood with him and a few women. The women showed infinitely more courage than the rest of the men who failed to appear.

One of my most vivid memories of my few informal conversations with Krishnamurti occurred during a break between our dialogues. He stood up, shrugged his shoulders, and said, "I've been saying these things for fifty years" and then fell silent. His meaning was patently clear. He felt he had not succeeded in communicating what he was all about.

These four teachers stand together in at least one respect. They refused to denature their teachings so as to please and make comfortable those who heard them. One is reminded of Plato's

---

[4] Lao Tzu, *Tao Te Ching*, ch. 70.
[5] Confucius, *Analects*, XIV.37

point that the proper use of rhetoric is not to persuade but to speak the true.[6]

These teachers were not purveyors of ideas, theories, visions and cosmic explanations. If I have understood anything whatsoever of their teachings it is this: They taught what it is to exist in what one understands. Please let me repeat this. They taught what it is to exist in what one understands. This is a third significance of Krishnamurti's teachings. He taught what it is to exist in what one understands. An event in his life will bring these words precisely into their own. On August 2, 1929, he dissolved the Order of the Star of the East of which he was the Head. Momentous as this was for the organization and the whole Theosophical movement it must have been as nothing contrasted with what it was for himself.[7] Please do not misunderstand. I am not here speaking for Krishnamurti. That is absurd and patently impossible. I speak only as one who has some acquaintance with the price of self-inquiry. Authentic self-inquiry begins inevitably at a point of no return, an either/or which, unless one bolts from it, entails a psychological death which is also a creation.

If one has undergone that death which is also a creation it is not difficult to resonate empathically to another's like ordeal by which I do not mean the conjuring of fanciful images of the other's psyche and all that rubbish but the sober recognition that for oneself and the other that point of no return is here to stay. Isn't this what Krishnamurti meant when he said "The first step is the last step"?[8] And isn't this step the step into what he called the vacant mind? Surely this mind must be the mind which is not limited by its own essence.

On pondering this further, the question arises, "If the point of no return is here to stay, how is it the case that the first step is the last step?" This is because every year, month, day, hour, minute, second, indeed every instant is a point of no return. Since it belongs

---

[6] Plato, *Phaedrus*, 277b-d.
[7] Krishnamurti, *Total Freedom*, p. 1.
[8] Krishnamurti/Anderson, op. cit., p. 172.

to the instant, the point of no return is without duration, unlike the second, minute and hour. Yet instants follow upon each other and it is this apparent continuity that invites a self-misunderstanding. On one hand the instant is on the side of the timeless since it is without duration and on the other hand since instants succeed one another they seem to be a matter of time.

This felt difficulty vanishes when one perceives that each present instant has within it the unprecedented. The teachings bear witness to this. Krishnamurti's *Notebook* states repeatedly that the death of yesterday is the complete uncertainty of tomorrow, that love and death have no continuity; further, that the totality attends to the fragment even though the fragment cannot understand the whole.

This helps our pondering to a happy issue. The unprecedented in every present instant opens on the eternal yet the fragments of time are continuous. Intellect finds this contradiction unsolvable. But intelligence is not embarrassed by it. Intelligence discovers the solution on awaking to the *timely* and the fitting which primal intuition reveals upon the instant. This timeliness abides between the timeless and time.

More significant than his words alone is Krishnamurti's life as he described it in his address on dissolving The Order of the Star. He said, "I have made this decision. It is not from a momentary impulse. I have not been persuaded to it by anyone. I am not persuaded in such things. For two years I have been thinking about this, slowly, carefully, patiently, and I have now decided to disband the Order, as I happen to be its Head. You can form other organizations and expect someone else. With that I am not concerned, nor with creating new cages, new decorations for those cages. My only concern is to set men absolutely, unconditionally free."[9]

Note how that he said "For two years I have been thinking about this, slowly, carefully, patiently...." Now patience, unlike endurance has no agenda. Unlike endurance which is a matter of time, patience abides through time without being *of* it. The beautiful Greek word

---

[9] Krishnamurti, *Total Freedom*, p. 7.

for patience, *hypomonē* means, literally, to stay behind, to stay under. It has the closest relation to one of the great words in our English tongue, namely, understand. What is it that we stand under when we understand? It is a pressure from above that gently weights us down into ever greater depth toward our original nature, our original innocence which is not a private possession but that emptiness without a centre, that silence "in which and from which all things flow and have their being."[10]

Could it be that such a standing under is the beginning of living out the teachings, the beginning of the first step which is the last step? This question, like the teachings themselves, is not addressed to the crowd, indeed cannot be so. The significance of the teachings is not available to the collective but to the single self only, the one alone in one's *un*-lonely aloneness, in the deepest depth beneath the ephemeral flux of personality; this only one with ears to hear and eyes to see who *listens* and perceives. Such a one, like Krishnamurti, stands patiently under the suasion of the eternal, listening in the valley of the timely between the peaks of the timeless and time yet upon each instant, is absolutely at one with that emptiness without a centre, the silence "in which and from which all things flow and have their being."

And so the first step is the last step into the pathless land of the true, into the fullness of the peace that passeth understanding, for the former things have truly passed away.

As a single self, a friend in dialogue with single selves and friends, I thank you for listening.

---

[10] Krishnamurti, *Krishnamurti's Notebook*, p. 100.

Introduction to *Total Freedom*[1]

When first privileged to meet Krishnamurti, I was deeply struck by the intensity of his quietude. The intensity bespoke great energy and his quietude expressed a settled tranquility. Such a combination is rare; indeed, so rare that on encountering it nothing can be taken for granted.

Our meeting was, as we say loosely, accidental. It was in a sound studio. I had neither met him before nor read any of his books. Yet, amazingly, he invited me on the spot to undertake a video-taped dialogue with him. He seemed not in the least concerned that, in the ordinary sense, he did not know me from Adam. I inferred that he was either a great gambler or so attuned to the present instant that his action was exact, a paragon of timeliness. There was something profoundly impersonal in that invitation without his being aloof or indifferent.

The next shock came with his asking me, "What would you like to talk about?" I replied, "How about hearing and seeing?" He accepted the topic joyously. And so immediately began, impromptu, a conversation on inward hearing and inward seeing. Two years later, again utterly unexpectedly for me, he invited me to undertake a series of dialogues that would encompass the kernel of his teaching. Though years before, I had been in radio broadcasting—announcing and news casting—and so had some professional acquaintance with studio programming, none of that experience was decisive for the movement of the dialogues. They developed out of their own germ,

---

[1] Introduction to *Total Freedom: The Essential Krishnamurti* by Jiddu Krishnamurti.

without any rehearsal, prearrangement, contrivance or hands-on fashioning. Both his ease and intensity of focus were amazing.

Krishnamurti was an exact embodiment of his doctrine of "choiceless awareness." Here, the word "choiceless" might suggest only a mode of subjectivity. On the contrary, choiceless awareness while reflected in the persona, is in no way reducible to it and so eludes a psychological reduction. Choicelessness is the mind's equivalent of the silence out of which intelligible utterance arises, of "that emptiness in which the things of the mind can exist but the things are not the mind… that emptiness has no centre and so is capable of infinite movement. Creation is born out of this emptiness but it is not the creation of man putting things together. That creation of emptiness is love and death."[2] This last sentence points directly and immediately to the character of the instant for both self-awakening and self-misunderstanding. Unless there is a psychological death to our self-identification with memory and upon the same instant a total understanding of need, we remain collapsed into the content of thought and a timely response to the instant eludes us.

"When there is a total understanding of need, the outward and the inner, then desire is not a torture. Then it has a quite different meaning, a significance far beyond the content of thought and it goes beyond feeling, with its emotions, myths and illusions. With the total understanding of need, not the mere quantity or the quality of it, desire then is a flame and not a torture. Without this flame life itself is lost. It is this flame that burns away the pettiness of its object, the frontiers, the fences that have been imposed upon it. Then call it by whatever name you will, love, death, beauty. Then it is there without an end."[3]

Some might think it untoward to begin a short introduction to sagely works with a personal anecdote. One thinks of Krishnamurti's repeated caution to his audiences: "The speaker is unimportant." Then there is Chuang Tzu's: "The Perfect man has

---

[2] Krishnamurti, *Total Freedom*, p. xi.
[3] Ibid., p. xii.

no self; the Holy man has no merit; the Sage has no fame."[4] (All three being the same.) True enough and almost never pondered, let alone embodied. Yet to find in such words an invitation to ignore the personal presence of a great teacher (whether in the flesh or remembered) betrays a shallow readiness to try to go beyond where one has not begun. Krishnamurti admonishes us that "Meditation is not something different from daily life... it is the seeing of what is and going beyond it."[5] If one has not seen what is, how can one go beyond it?

Unfortunately, academic practice shows little or no understanding of "seeing what is" in the context of genuine self-inquiry. Rather, academic life is a journey through the forest of abstractions. Experimental science has the advantage of requiring laboratory demonstration of its theoretical conclusions. Even so, this procedure is pursued within the dual structure of perceiver and perceived. Perception without the perceiver, as in meditation is unheard of. "This perception is entirely different from seeing an object without an observer, because in the perception of meditation there is no object and therefore no experience... What meaning has such meditation? There is no meaning; there is no utility. But in that meditation there is a movement of great ecstasy... It is the ecstasy which gives to the eye, to the brain, and to the heart the quality of innocency. Without seeing life as something totally new, it is a routine, a boredom, a meaningless affair. So meditation is of the greatest importance. It "opens the door to the incalculable, to the measureless."[6]

This ecstatic pointer of Krishnamurti's so escapes our contemporary mind-set as to be practically unintelligible. Yet it is supremely intelligent. How so? Because it implies a radical distinction between consciousness and awareness. In our time, philosophy and depth psychology have virtually absolutized consciousness. They fail to discern that consciousness is not self-

---

[4] Chuang Tzu, *Basic Writings*, p. 32.
[5] Krishnamurti, *Total Freedom*, p. xiii.
[6] Ibid., p. xii.

correcting. How can it be so since as consciousness of, it is ever tied to change? It is only as awareness has an object that consciousness comes into play. In itself awareness is independent of objects and changeless. On that account it is the door to the incalculable and measureless.

Krishnamurti invites us to begin the most radical self-inquiry since it opens out upon the infinite space of awareness. Self-inquiry begins by asking not what am I but what am I not? Such a no-nonsense question has no need of theoretical structures, the conceptual paraphernalia of our depth psychologies, philosophies and theologies and belief systems. The question is astonishingly yet frighteningly simple; frightening because it entails the deepest sense of aloneness since none but oneself can ask the question nor answer it. Yet, with the patience, courage and radical trust to hang in there without bolting from it one discovers the unlonely aloneness of that "meditation which is absolutely no effort, no achievement, no thinking, the brain is quiet, not made quiet by will, by intention, by conclusion and all that nonsense; it is quiet. And, being quiet, it has infinite space."[7]

In this short introduction, I have deliberately avoided taking an academic approach to Krishnamurti's teaching. To have done so would have falsified his spirit and quite missed the mark of his message. He was not concerned in the career of ideas and the ongoing palaver that is believed to express the finest examples of the life of the mind. In his last talk (January 1986) he put the matter cogently and succinctly: "It would be useless for you and the speaker to listen to a lot of words, but if we could together take a very long journey, not in terms of time, not in terms of belief or conclusions or theories, but in examining very carefully the way of our lives, fear, uncertainty, insecurity and all the inventions that man has made, including the extraordinary computers. If we take a long journey into this, where are we at the end of two million years? Where are we going, not as some theory, not what some wretched book says,

---

[7] Ibid., p. xiii.

however holy it is, but where are we all going? And where have we begun? They're both related to each other: where we are going, where we begin. The beginning may be the ending. Don't agree. Find out."[8]

Right away, one hears the cry: "How, how find out?!" The very word, how, betrays a belief in the power of process and procedure to produce an effect; and indeed, they do in the material order. But here, the directive to find out addresses a different sphere, the sphere of one's misrelation to oneself. The attempt to impose upon this disorder any discipline according to a pattern only hardens the misrelation, binding it further to time, belief, conclusions and theories. There is no how to making a pure act of attention to what is at hand. There is nothing mysterious about this. In fact, in the normal course of daily living we make, perhaps, a few such acts but quickly fall out of them. Why? The answer to that question comes only through self-examination—not through theories of the unconscious or from learned disquisitions on the nature of man. The pure act of attention is spontaneous and free; the hearer and the heard, the perceiver and perceived drop away leaving only listening and seeing. "Only when the mind is blissful, quiet, without any movement of its own, without projection of thought, conscious or unconscious—only then does the eternal come into being."[9]

During this century we have taken in with our mother's milk the enervating dogma that the hallmarks of human nature are anxiety (angst) and estrangement, a secularized version of the dogma of original sin. But through meditation, as Krishnamurti revealed it, and self-inquiry, one discovers one's original nature, original innocence and the natural state. Is this, then, the heart of the matter? Yes, since the heart of the matter is a matter of the heart.

---

[8] Ibid., p. xiii.
[9] Ibid., p. xiv.

Address on the Inauguration of the Krishnamurti Center
Ojai, California. December 5, 1998.

I am most honored and grateful for your invitation to address with Evelyne Blau, Mary Zimbalist and Alan Kishbaugh the founding of the Krishnamurti Center.

The founding of the Center is an occasion for double rejoicing. Broadly speaking, it expands access to Krishnamurti's spoken and written legacy. Speaking essentially, though, the Center's academic role invites the contemplation of Krishnamurti's teachings on human transformation independent of knowledge and time. These days I hardly dare use the words academic and contemplative in the same breath. Western culture has, since the 18th century, suffered a steady and increasing estrangement from genuine contemplation as the ancients and medievals recognized it—though it never attracted most persons even then.

The eighteenth century saw the rise of socially organized, experimental scientific inquiry. Experimental science for good and ill brought a vast deal of raw nature under so called human control. This activity continues to hold such theatrical sway upon our titanic imaginations that we tend now to look upon evil as basically a nuisance which must, in time, yield to our experimental cleverness, finally to be eliminated. This naïve presumption persists despite our killing more people and species in the 20th century than in all others.

There has always been a trickle of sageliness through this wasteland, though experimental science with its dependence upon knowledge and time has not a prayer of being able to account for it. How is it then, that extremely few drink from this stream of sageliness? Ironically, thousands make handsome livings from professing to drink from it but, comically, they don't transform into sages. Nothing has changed. Clearly, this matter lies deeper than we know.

These words might well appear to some as unduly pessimistic and unfitting on this happy occasion of celebrating the birth of a new housing for Krishnamurti's legacy. I quite understand such a sentiment. Yet if we should find ourselves among that number, we can never have pondered the law of compensation which secures that every advance contains the seeds of retreat and if these seeds are not anticipated and met timely, firmly and flexibly the advance itself will not prevail. Such seeds are not anticipated through probability theory or rational empiricism. They can be intuited only through what Krishnamurti called the total emptiness of the mind which is the foundation of genuine meditation without ceasing.

Now I come directly to the point. We cannot employ this Center justly if we do not take with utmost seriousness Krishnamurti's statement that no one had understood him. Happily, he added a condition. He said one might come to understand the teachings through living them out.

Once, during a 15 minute break between our video-taping two dialogues of the eighteen fold series with the title, "A Wholly Different Way of Living," he stood up, turned his back three quarters to me and, with a slight droop to his shoulders, said quietly, "I've been saying these things for fifty years...." He did not need to speak the rest. It was plain from his tone and body language that he most likely would have added: "And all to no effect."

Many persons have thought that, given the time it was my privilege to spend with him during our twenty hours of video-taped conversations, surely I must have understood him—at least in some degree. But his last words on the matter during his final days many years later should put to rest any notion that I must have understood him. I am content with that both with respect to our video-taped dialogues and now.

Perhaps someone since then and now has come to understand him by thoroughly living out the teachings. Yet, if so, how would such a one or we validate that since Krishnamurti is no longer with us physically to determine it? In any case, were he still here and willing to make such a determination he would not make it as an authority over against the person to be measured. To do so would be in contradiction with himself who consistently refused such a role. Further, it would be unnecessary since self-inquiry, deeply engaged as he taught it, is self-validating. One's way of life is totally changed, not in degree but in kind and nothing could be more tranquilly evident to oneself. Yet, such evidence is not arguable nor publicly verifiable.

This is precisely why Krishnamurti is not accepted at the university. In the KFA's Newsletter, Fall 1998, Raymond Martin, Professor of Philosophy at the University of Maryland, writes a lucid article on the question "Why isn't Krishnamurti accepted at the University?" He writes, "A large part of the answer, I think, is that academics, in their official capacities as academics are theorists... Krishnamurti went out of his way to discourage people from regarding what he had to say as a contribution to theory. Rather, he encouraged them to regard it as an invitation to meditation." In noting Krishnamurti's statement, "the observer is the observed" as a truth statement, he comments: "From an academic point of view, when someone claims verbally to be revealing the truth, he or she is proposing a theory. So, whatever Krishnamurti's intentions, it would seem that he and the academics are both partly in the same 'business' of proposing theories... Academics are interested in considering theories only for the purpose of evaluating them, and at the university the only sort of evaluation of theories that counts is based not on meditation but on argument and public evidence. Krishnamurti did not provide these to back up what he had to say."

Professor Martin goes on to point up what he takes to be a resemblance between the 18th century British empiricist David Hume's critique of the concept of self and Krishnamurti's. He concludes with the hope that some in academe will work up

Krishnamurti's topics into theory and then, in the standard academic way, assess these theories.

Now one must ask whether such a program can, if undertaken, promote an understanding of Krishnamurti. What if the statement, "the observer *is* the observed" is not a view, let alone one view among others? What if it is just a simple operational invitation to that quality of meditation that opens out on "observing without the observer"? In that case Krishnamurti was not in the business of proposing theories and therefore had no need to back up what it was he had to say.

What if, with respect to the problem of being understood he was in same case with Lao Tzu, the ancient Chinese sage, who said in the *Tao Te Ching*, "My teaching is easy to understand yet no one understands it; my practice is easy to practice yet no one practices it"?[1] It is inconceivable that Lao Tzu imagined that argument or public verification would disclose an understanding of him or his practice.

Please do not infer that I am opposed to academic inquiry, on the contrary. However, in all my decades of university teaching of philosophy and religious studies rare, indeed, was it to find anyone interested in genuine self-inquiry or meditation as Krishnamurti taught it which, as different from depth psychology, is not ensconced in theories.

I applaud Professor Martin's concern and effort to introduce Krishnamurti to the academic community and that he sees, in his own words, that "Theorizing is one thing, meditating a wholly different thing, perhaps even an antithetical thing. They are like oil and water... and theory and meditation do not mix."

If we are to take this matter with utmost seriousness in its relation to the founding of the Krishnamurti Center we must penetrate it a step further. It is always helpful and sometimes useful to see the difference between things. It is quite another thing to discern in what the difference consists. For our present concern, it consists in

---

[1] Lao Tzu, *Tao Te Ching*, ch. 70.

that truth abides in two different spheres. Truth and falsity are both in thought and in things outside of thought, which is to say that there is both cognitive and existential truth and the infinite gap between them is a truly perilous pass. Meditating, as Krishnamurti taught it, requires navigating this pass. It is a characteristic of our human condition that we have little if any stomach for this act. Either we navigate this pass or we don't and no amount of amiable theorizing on 'both/and' rather than facing the 'either/or' can lessen the terror of this act. It cannot even touch it. Krishnamurti is a genuine free-flying wild goose and cannot be domesticated to run along the ground with tame geese who just talk about talk.

This brings me full circle to the question of understanding Krishnamurti and how it is that I am content with it that I do not understand him. Many are familiar with our series of dialogues and how they concluded with my thanking him and confessing that throughout them I had been undergoing a transformation. He replied with his last words in the series. Please note, as I quote them, his crucial omission: "Because you are willing enough to listen, good enough to listen. Most people are not, they won't listen. You took the time, the trouble, the care to listen."[2] He did not add that on that account I had understood him. From these words it does not follow logically that I had or had not understood him. I preferred to infer that I had not understood him and that openhearted listening was not enough.

I have only one claim. For the last quarter of a century since we conversed I have unflaggingly attempted not to misunderstand him. With that statement made, the lexicographers, grammarians and rhetoricians will object that since the word misunderstand is the antonym of understand and two negatives express an affirmative I must be affirming that I understand. Now within the sphere of truth and falsity of statement their objection carries.

At last we have come to the heart of the matter. In claiming the ongoing attempt not to misunderstand Krishnamurti, I am

---

[2] Krishnamurti/Anderson, *A Wholly Different Way of Living*, p. 269.

using words to express a matter within the sphere of the truth and falsity of existence. This entails existing in what one has understood and there, only being what one is, is true. Everyone of normal intelligence knows the meaning of the words "be true to yourself, don't let yourself down." Not to misunderstand is to stand sure in the perilous pass between truth of statement and truth of being. Given that every succeeding instant bears within it the unexpected, no theoretical understanding, based as it is upon semantic memory, can dictate the timely and fitting response to each moment, each bearing the ultimate moment of truth.

It is for this reason that during another of our breaks between video-tapings I asked Krishnamurti about his repeated statement that perception is the action. Did that statement mean that perception coerces the action or is it not the case that there is an intemporal pause within which one stands or bolts from facing what is at hand? "Oh, yes sir," he affirmed.

Let me quote from our last conversation, the eighteenth dialogue, "Meditation and the Sacred Mind." In the transcript K stands for Krishnamurti and A for me:

> A: But that very statement: 'I am the world and the world is me' sounds as you have said so often, so absurd that one starts to bolt again.
>
> K: I know.
>
> A: To panic again.
>
> K: That means one has to be very, very serious. It isn't a thing that you play with.
>
> A: No, it's not what's called these days a 'fun thing.'
>
> K: No sir!

A: In no sense. The discussion you have undertaken concerning meditation is so total. It isn't a thing that you do among other things.

K: Meditation means attention, care. That's part of it... all of this comes down to a sense of deep, inward seriousness, and that seriousness itself brings about attention, care and responsibility, and everything that we have discussed... the ending of suffering means the observation, the seeing of suffering. Not to go beyond it, refuse it, rationalize it or run away from it, just to see it. Let it flower. And as you are choicelessly aware of this flowering, it comes naturally to wither away. I don't have to do something about it.[3]

It should be clear from these words that none of this is theoretical or based on theories nor can it be made into a theory. Meditation starts with the confession 'I do not know what meditation is.' As the act obtains there is always the critical possibility, through inattention, of falling out of it. No concept can function as a net beneath this high wire. The great Danish thinker, Kierkegaard, noted similarly on the act of faith that even if we could reduce the whole of it to a concept one still would not know how it got into one or how one got into it.

I have not meant to discourage academic activity for the Center. There is a deal of textual sifting that needs to be undertaken to rescue Krishnamurti's talks and writing from the absurd misunderstanding on the part of many of his readers that thought and words are intrinsically defective and hopelessly misleading. It is their abuse not their use that he inveighs against. He is not a prophet of voidness nor an advocate of forms.

If the Center can house not only his archival legacy but the activity of students who approach his work with that deep inward seriousness that brings about attention, care and responsibility, the Center will be truly meditational and not let him down. And, from

---

[3] Krishnamurti/Anderson, op. cit., p. 268-269 © Victor Gollancz, 1991.

his standpoint, infinitely more importantly, they will not have let themselves down but will have returned to themselves.

Poetry comes more easily to me than prose so I shall, with your indulgence, tie off these remarks with a quatrain that bubbled up for me not long ago:

> Driftwood returns to the abandoned shore
> Transfigured, stark and lone;
> Those who venture seas unthought
> Come back as spirit's own.

Liberation: Secular and Ultimate[1]

Abstract

Secular and ultimate liberation are presented not as opposed logically or dialectically but as the incomplete to the complete. Secular liberation is shown to be tied to the modern idea of progress. This idea is found to be illusory and therefore frustrating. Ultimate liberation is liberation from self-misunderstanding. It is liberation into the standpoint of non-duality in which *samsāra* is *nirvāna* and *nirvāna* is *samsāra* in absolute selfhood.

When Professors Charles Fu and Sandra Warytko presented me with the title for this topic, I was delighted by the coupling of the words secular and ultimate. The words imply a distinction but not on that account do they suggest a mutual exclusion.

If, instead of secular and ultimate, the two words chosen had been secular and sacred, a mutual exclusion might well have been implied. The adjective, secular, is derived from Late Latin *saeculāris*, meaning 'worldly, profane.' The opposition between profane and sacred is obvious and common knowledge. Still, there is another anterior meaning in the word secular deriving from Latin *saeculum*, a generation, then in Late Latin it finally refers to humankind, the world of human beings. This is the meaning I wish to bring forward for this meditation.

We have now shrunk our boundary since by secular I do not mean nature as opposed to the divine or the profane in contradistinction

---

[1] A paper presented to the International Society for Philosophy and Psychotherapy at Shi Lai Buddhist Temple, Los Angeles, July 13, 1996. It is included in this volume as it is concerned in a topic of central concern to Krishnamurti.

to the sacred. With this narrowing of focus, the first half of our title, secular liberation, refers to liberation in terms of the world of human thought word and deed or, if you will, the world of the human body-mind.

This expression in no sense reduces human nature to biology. It is not meant to diminish but to specify, to single out our human world of cultures and their products, our human world of bearings, undergoings, sorrows and joys, despairs and hopes. On the other hand our second adjective, ultimate, includes beatitude where we awaken to that most profound Buddhist disclosure that *nirvāna* is *samsāra* and *samsāra* is *nirvāna,* that we apprehend *nirvāna as quite samsāra* and *samsāra as quite nirvāna*. Indeed, with that disclosure totally viscerally undergone we realize the locus of our human nature, our residence of no residence, situated precisely upon and within that '*as quite*' in awaking to *samsāra as quite nirvāna* and *nirvāna as quite samsāra.*

Let us imagine just anyone asking me my name. I should have to answer "Allan" and drop it. Yet, if a Buddhist who had fully realized *nirvāna* is *samsāra* and *samsāra* is *nirvāna* asked me I could answer, "Allan, as quite." And when he or she, puzzled, raised an eyebrow and I tried to explain, wouldn't he or she begin to smile knowingly and beatifically; and wouldn't we begin to walk together sharing our beatitudes, in playful seriousness and serious playfulness?

Our English word, ultimate, drives from the old and archaic Latin preposition, *uls* meaning beyond, that which is over there complementing this which is here and present. Literally, ultimate means the far side. Religious thought, in various traditions, speaks of the far side symbolically, poetically, as the other shore which the spiritual traveler is crossing toward, the far side that consummates the long and arduous journey from this world to the next. The image is familiar to both Buddhist and Christian. The Negro spiritual "Deep River" sighs most poignantly for the far side: "Deep river, my home is over Jordan/ I want to cross over into camp ground," i.e., I want to reach the other shore where the saints dwell together in the joy and peace that passeth understanding.

This consummation reflects the other meaning of our word, ultimate, which signifies coming to an end and the reaching of finality. Ultimate liberation is liberation that is finished, full, complete and perfect beyond comparison. Just what this is, insofar as it lends itself to words at all, we shall try to contemplate together later in this meditation. In the meantime we must return to the first half of our title, secular liberation, and note briefly how such a thought, historically, exploded into human consciousness.

The concept of secular liberation is a western idea that we count on which means that we take it for granted rather than ponder it consciously as a task for thought. It arose tied to the idea of collective human progress. The idea of progress for humanity as a whole is only about two hundred years old. Previous to that progress was thought to be largely an individual matter depending on one's gifts and luck. Everyone of normal intelligence was expected to advance from naïve childhood to the wisdom of old age. It was commonly believed that the human condition had historically changed for the worse. The golden age was taught to be in the past and not expected in the future. Even the Greeks who looked upon liberation as a cultural achievement did not imagine it for humanity at large but only for themselves within the walls of their city states. If the human condition was to be liberated from its vale of tears it would have to be by divine supervention and fiat which would bring the worldly world to a cataclysmic end.

Modern western societies no longer hold that view. Instead it is expected that our children's future will be better than our present and made possible through our collective ingenuity, i.e., through socially organized scientific inquiry.

Whereas the ancients looked to the past for their models of wisdom believing that sageliness did not come down with the last shower, the late seventeenth century spawned the notion that veneration of one's wise forefathers and mothers put the cart in front of the horse and so crippled the possibility of a true advance upon the funded wisdom of the past. The new idea was that experimental science was not properly subject to received authority as were matters of theology where the proper approach was to contemplate what religious authority disclosed.

During the nineteenth century confidence in experimental science was further radicalized. Now it was claimed that the methods of experimental science should be applied to all fields from physics to the history of religions. Now social, moral and religious authority were no longer exempt from the judgment of experimental science.

This attitude of socially organized scientific inquiry has entered into every aspect of our human condition, that is to say, every known aspect which is subject to measure. We owe experimental science great respect and abiding gratitude for liberating us from the dead hands of social, moral and religious authoritarianisms. Yet, on giving socially organized scientific inquiry the full respect due it we must not overlook that it did nothing to prevent this century's two catastrophic world wars and the lesser wars following upon them. We have killed more human beings during this century than at any other period of history to say nothing of our continuing depredations upon our natural environment and these senseless spoilings all in the name of progress.

Still, while bearing these cautions in mind it would be ungrateful indeed to overlook the extraordinary material advances contributed by experimental science. Its application through technology has increased our life span and through medical and agricultural discoveries pestilence and famine have been partially arrested.

A nagging question remains. How is it that medicine's spectacular success with the body displays no comparable success with the mind? Can it be that there is something in human nature that eludes scientific measure? Can it be that something in human nature eludes any measure whatsoever except what in the language of sageliness is called Original or the Buddha nature? Since the Buddha nature is the really real it is neither an event nor an experience. There are no field trips to reality. Experimental science cannot objectify it and so cannot measure it.

Secular liberation for all its power to liberate us from aspects of material bondage cannot liberate me from my mis-relation to myself since the self is neither objectifiable nor cognizable. It is only intuitable and once that mis-relation or self-misunderstanding sets in I cannot be liberated from it by adopting a discipline, a ways and means program that projects for itself an imaginary future liberation from my own self-misunderstanding. One is never stronger than oneself therefore one cannot begin on the basis of self-misunderstanding to overcome it. This is what is meant by the expression, 'the illusion of agency,' that one is the author and finisher of one's deeds. This is clear from the plain fact that whereas one can plan for the future one cannot plan for the present. The present as the future of even a moment ago never conforms in all respects to the future I had planned for it. Further, upon the very instant of apprehending the depth of my self-contradiction I am already subject to the momentum of routine habit and deeply ingrained self-misunderstandings that I count on but never bring to consciousness. Nonetheless, the misunderstandings form the basis for my preference, choice and decision.

In the Christian tradition in the seventh chapter of his letter to the Romans [7:19], we see how St. Paul puts this condition precisely. On rendering the Greek into colloquial English it reads: "The good I want to do I don't do and the evil I don't want to do I end up doing." He then resolves this self-contradiction by distinguishing between two tendencies, one springing from what he calls the inward man and the other the outward. The inward man which delights in the good does not triumph through any egoic self-assertion but is energized by spirit. For St. Paul, even the inward man has no egoic permanence. In his letter to the Galatians [2:20] he brings spirit so radically into the foreground that identification with his personality is dropped. "I am crucified with Christ: nevertheless I live; yet not I but Christ liveth in me." This is not just an identification with Christ in place of an identification with his own personality. Here there are not two identifications or two identities limiting each other. True, the apostle lives in the flesh, but no longer does he live his life; rather, spirit, Christ, lives him. He has dropped his self-bondage, his persona and its body-image. I find here a close resonance with the

Buddhist spirituality of Dōgen and his teaching of the dropping of body and mind.

We are now at the standpoint of ultimate liberation which is in no way conformed to any projecting of an imaginary future let alone befuddled with the notion of essential progress for humanity. Even Goethe's more sober view that humankind has only an ethical chance is not radical enough in its rejection of essential progress which imagines that we are inevitably on our way toward some omega point beyond all ills that flesh is heir to.

One of the hindrances that makes it so difficult for western thought to entertain radically the standpoint of ultimate liberation is its bondage to a fatal twist on the doctrine of free will inherited from the fourth century Church Father, St. Augustine. He asserted that all of nature had become so corrupt from Adam's original sin that human beings cannot be relied upon to be self-governing. All suffering is here attributed to moral guilt. For him, pain, suffering and death are unnatural. Moral choice and not nature is the cause of our afflictions.

This need to find reason or reasons for suffering is a common human tendency. Elaine Pagels comments on this brilliantly as follows: "Had Augustine's theory not met such a need—were it not that people often would rather feel guilty than helpless—I suspect that the idea of original sin would not have survived the fifth century, much less become the basis of Christian doctrine for 1600 years." Here she speaks of guilt only where it is irrational and inappropriate.[2]

According to Augustine free will enables us "either to consent to wrong doing, or to refrain from it." This reflects St. Paul's dilemma in Romans 7 but it does not illuminate his liberation from it which is beyond all moralism. He finds this in his relation to Christ.

The Buddha's teaching that "all becoming is suffering" also reaches infinitely deeper than any moralism can suggest. The Buddha does not presume to find a purely calculative reason for all sufferings

---

[2] Elaine Pagels, *Adam, Eve, and the Serpent*, p. 146.

but teaches a way of ultimate liberation from fundamental suffering, the universal suffering which is non-personal. This fundamental suffering, the hallmark of *samsāra*, is the cycle or round of birth and death and particularly one's unawakened view of it.

Here a linguistic note on the Sanskrit word *samsāra* can significantly appeal to the modern mind. The usual translation birth-death cycle is imprecise. *Sāra* means flowing, wandering. *Sam*, prefixed to it means the interconnected whole. *Samsāra* is the interconnected wandering about of the karma bearer through all different kinds and shapes of embodiment.[3] In short it is a career of futility. The sentiment of futility deeply afflicts the modern western temper. For all its collapse into an imaginary future liberation, its self-misunderstanding bars it from a soul-nourishing present. The span, as it believes, of one lifetime only is insufficient to bring the inward consummation it so devoutly wishes. From this standpoint, hindsight cannot but agree with the French proverb that the more it changes the more it remains the same and, anciently, the book of Ecclesiastes observes deeply: "The thing that hath been is that which shall be; and that which is done is that which shall be done; and there is no new thing under the sun." [Eccl. 1:9]

Ultimate liberation in no way rejects *samsāra*. Rather, it massively affirms it but in a way that goes beyond the logical opposites of affirmation and denial. Two short poems will illustrate this. Reflecting the standpoint of the non-ultimate, the secular, is Charles Kingsley's well known poem, *Young and Old*:

---

[3] Betty Heimann, *The Significance of Prefixes in Sanskrit Philosophical Terminology*, pp. 14, 47.

> *Young and Old*[4]
> When all the world is young, lad,
> And all the trees are green;
> And every goose a swan lad,
> And every lass a queen;
> Then hey for boot and horse, lad,
> And round the world away;
> Young blood must have its course, lad,
> And every dog his day.
> When all the world is old, lad,
> And all the trees are brown;
> And all the sport is stale, lad,
> And all the wheels run down;
> Creep home, and take your place there,
> The spent and maimed among;
> God grant you find one face there,
> You loved when all was young.

The standpoint of ultimacy appears in Gasan Jōseki's four lines left behind him at his death:

> It is ninety-one years
> Since my skin and bones were put together;
> This midnight, as always,
> I lay myself down in the Yellow Springs.[5]

The key line here, "This midnight, as always," seems to bring together two opposites: on the one hand, time with "This midnight," and timelessness with "as always." Superficially they seem to collide on the same plane. Actually "This midnight" and "as always" do not collide at all. Nor are they sublated into some higher synthesis. They are just as they are. Contemplated from the standpoint of absolute selfhood the alternation of life and death is not a species of change.

---

[4] Charles Kingsley, The Water-Babies: A Fairy Tale for a Land-Baby, p. 79-80.
[5] Quoted from Keiji Nishitani's *Religion and Nothingness*, p. 75.

Gasan Jōseki ecstatically intuited that awareness obtains between one instant and the next as well as beyond them and so "this midnight" and "as always" remain thoroughly temporal. They are in no way apart from the Buddha nature. Sri Nisargadatta Maharaj states this standpoint of absolute selfhood as "Nothing was divided and there is nothing to unite."[6]

Ultimate liberation is awaking to this absolute non-duality. How exactly, beautifully, does Ananda K. Coomaraswamy put this: "For as there are two in him who is both Love and Death, so there are, as all tradition affirms unanimously, two in us; although not two of him or two of us, nor even one of him and one of us, but only one of both."[7]

It will perhaps not be unfitting within these Buddhist temple grounds to breathe the prayer that we all, each and everyone, be a light unto ourselves.

---

[6] Sri Nisargadatta Maharaj, *I Am That*, p. 143 (one vol. edition).
[7] Ananda K. Coomarasawamy, *Hinduism and Buddhism*, p. 15.

On Non-Attachment: Some Aspects of Asian Thought
A Lecture-Sermon[1]

It is an honor to be invited to present you with a lecture-sermon on the topic, non-attachment. There is natural affinity between this virtue non-attachment, and the rhetorical form called the lecture-sermon. The lecture- sermon resembles a lecture in that it is weighted more toward information than exhortation; yet it reflects the sermon also, in that it must lose nothing of edification in attempting to clarify concepts that cross confessional lines. Here, one must somehow find the middle way between analysis and persuasion, between what is merely interesting and what is essential. According to his temperament one finds himself often attached to one or other of these alternatives. And what could be more comical than an attached speaker speaking on, of all things, non-attachment?

English possesses at least two common synonyms for non-attachment. They are 'detachment' and 'disinterestedness.' If however, we wished to include a reference to the spiritual as well as the moral our intention would be better conveyed through the concept, non-attachment. This cardinal distinction requires further reflection. Our English prefix non- expresses negation more neutrally than we commonly think and this is markedly the case in our concept, non-attachment. We might concern ourselves then in the importance of this distinction for the spiritual life; and we ought so to concern ourselves in what it points to if we claim to have any intellectual care for our growth it spirit.

---

[1] A Lecture-Sermon delivered to the Unitarian Fellowship of San Dieguito, California, May 5, 1968.

Since the decline of the Middle Ages—with the notable exception of the 18th century—our culture has not distinguished itself by its care for this virtue. In fact we might say that our culture has notoriously caricatured itself by its neglect of it, and this despite our Scriptures' commands that we achieve non-attachment. What other virtue would the Christ have had more prominently in mind when he commanded us to "take therefore no thought for the morrow: for the morrow shall take thought for the things of itself. Sufficient unto the day is the evil thereof"? [Mt 6:34]

Perhaps this unfortunate, if not perverse, neglect might account for our curious notion that we must rather recur to the great non-Christian traditions for essential light on this virtue. Nothing could be farther from the truth. Yet so difficult is this notion to dislodge and so urgent is our need to strive for this virtue that we should lose no time in devoting ourselves to it wherever we find scriptural illumination upon it. And if reverently we contemplate it through non-Christian sources of revelation, not the least of our gains will be a discovery of the light that they bring upon the ways our own Bible counsels us toward this beautiful virtue.

Were it not for "the slings and arrows of outrageous fortune" we should not require to practice the virtue of non-attachment. And yet, when we have said that, we have not yet said enough. Afflictions and tribulations could not of themselves incline us to practice distance upon the whole flux of coming-to-be and passing-away. Nor is it sufficient merely to know we are suffering. Some non-human animals seem to share with us this simple awareness. It is rather that we know it twice-over. We are able to reflect upon the fact that we know we are suffering; and this reflection becomes more urgent when we suffer acutely and personally. Precisely at this point we might or might not make a philosophical and theological discovery, and if we make this self-discovery we shall no longer experience the world as we did before.

It comes to a question of power—the power we think peculiar to knowledge. Commonly we distinguish between two types of knowledge: 'knowing-how' and 'knowing-that.' Knowing that one is in difficulties can be coincident with knowing how to get out of them. It can also be coincident with not knowing how to escape the difficulties or how to overcome them. About the latter situation we say in English, "I just have to put up with it," and we resign ourselves to last through it all as best we can, or at least until we can find some remedy for it. But what if it should turn out to be the case that there is some form of suffering for which there is no remedy whatsoever—no, not to all eternity? We should than have discovered we *know that* such a suffering exists in ourselves but also that we do not *know how* to eliminate it. Clearly, the resigning of ourselves to this suffered discovery in no way distinguishes our relation to it from our accustomed relation to the crowd of inconveniences which we put up with from day to day. Yet, this discovery introduces us to the heart of the human condition.

It is essential to the human condition that we should have intimations of immortality while remaining in and of ourselves quite powerless to achieve it as such; that we find ourselves compelled to choose, for good or ill, our ways of life while powerless to annihilate one step within the courses we have run. We might extend indefinitely this description of our impotence. It is enough for now to observe that our double self-reflection will lead us inevitably to the heart of the human dilemma: free we are, but only finitely; we sense within us the infinite and eternal, yet we cannot make the work of our hands prevail beyond a season.

Clearly, as with every dilemma, we find the middle the place of pain; for we are prone to the illusion that one alternative or the other will resolve the issue. Were we able to resolve it so simply despite however painfully, we should not have faced a life-dilemma at all but a matter for simple option—calling at most for prudence. But a life-dilemma presents us always with two equally unsatisfactory and unfavorable alternatives; and no amount of clever gabble or excursions into the distractions of pure feeling will alter the case in the slightest degree.

If, up to this point, our thinking has not led us astray, we should have rightly concluded that it seems we must next try to find whether our position in the middle of the dilemma has within it some hint of a favorable possibility which neither of the alternatives provides. A sober review of the history of religions and secular thought and practice should warn us against the evils inherent in two alternatives, namely, damning the world in the interest of other-worldliness or, on the other hand, whitewashing a merely secular life with the amiable notion that the warm puppy of happiness still waits for us around some sunny corner—it's just a matter of time and skill in our getting there. There is no need to rehearse the woeful train of failures in spirituality which these alternatives have come to represent in the history of religions, both of East and West.

Let us for a few minutes try to contemplate ourselves as creatures-of-the-middle. In so doing we shall have recurred to one of the most ancient religious and philosophical doctrines—a doctrine stressed equally in all the basic Scriptures of the great traditions. One among these Scriptures is the Chinese classic, the *Book of Changes* which is both an oracle and a book of wisdom. As an oracle it counsels us to right action, and as a book of wisdom assists us also to right vision. In the hierarchy of being it conceives man as a creature stanced between the primal powers called heaven and earth—participating in their virtues if he will, but always subject to their transcendence. On that account it makes much of the virtue of modesty, and quoting from the Wilhelm-Baynes translation teaches that "Modesty creates success, for it is the way of heaven to shed its influence downward and to create light and radiance. It is the way of the earth to be lowly and to go upward. It is the way of heaven to make empty what is full and to give increase to what is modest. It is the way of earth to change the full and to augment the modest."[2] This Scripture does not counsel modesty as an opportunistic means to success. It is rather that by acting modestly one grasps good character and makes it his own. In order to do this though, one must consent and submit himself to the creative will of heaven as devotedly a compliantly as

---

[2] Wilhelm/Baynes tr., *The I Ching*, Hexagram 15 (Judgment), p. 462.

the receptive earth takes heaven into itself and follows heaven's way; for one invites good or evil influences according to his conduct.

This sublime three-fold conception of the world and man's place in it is reflected in the Japanese art of flower arrangement—a beautiful and edifying practice which fortunately is becoming more familiar to the American home. Let us examine briefly how this visionary concept stances man, since it has cogent implications for the virtue of non-attachment.

The *Book of Changes* observes that there are three kinds of shock: that of heaven, of fate and of the heart.[3] The shock of heaven predisposes man for his spiritual birth—what in religious language we call 'rebirth,' or being born again. And thunder is its natural analogue. This form of shock reminds man how ephemeral is his passage and promotes in him that fear and trembling which duly chastens him and marks the limits of his little sovereignty. Such is shown by the natural, political and social cataclysms of history or by great personal afflictions—proverbial in the case of Job. During such times—and recent events is in our own nation recall us to review them—one must not be so attached to his own cause that he loses his hold on a deep and inner seriousness, nor so withdrawn from any cause—so *un*-attached as distinguished from *non*-attached—that he is lost to all duty and command. For non-attachment is not a floating free in some Olympian balloon from which one peers down upon a world he counts well lost. It is being not possessed by the world while yet concretely immersed within it, so that the sacrifice peculiar to his unique person which every man must come to face—will be carried out uninterrupted and made complete.

The shock of fate prepares a man for self-reflection on his relation to the practical order. It should induce movement within his mind and awaken resolution in him to take arms against a sea of troubles. He must act with presence of mind resolutely discerning and grasping all opportunities for action or he will not survive the external blows of fate's mindless course. And yet this is precisely

---

[3] Ibid., p. 199.

where we are most likely to indulge ourselves in a false renunciation, preferring to deceive ourselves that we do not want that which we need. Such self-martyrdom is not non-attachment but a craven weakness. There is a lovely, small poem repeated in the *Analects* of Confucius which reads in the Waley translation:

> The flowery branch of the wild cherry
> How swiftly it flies back!
> It is not that I do not love you;
> But your house is far away.[4]

On this, the Master said, he did not really love her. Had he done so, he would not have worried about the distance. The translator notes, "Men fail to attain goodness because they do not care for it sufficiently, not because Goodness 'is far away.'"

Then thirdly there is the shock of the heart when one is robbed of all reflection and clarity of vision. Presence of mind is not immediately available and resolution is without an object. We experience such an occasion upon receiving the first blow of calamity or some affliction. We reel like one drunk, bereft of inner bearings. All around us others are agitated either on our account, or their own or both. Unless we withdraw from the situation in time we shall surely blunder. Yet this is when our acquaintances and friends urge upon us that we must *do* something about it *now*, and without delay. Without having achieved non-attachment we cannot summon the strength of will to ignore them in order to withdraw from the affair in time despite their displeasure in us.

In our culture this is one of the most difficult of situations in which to find oneself and to overcome. Activists we are, and vainly imagine that if enough put their shoulders to the wheel we shall somehow move beyond the difficulty. Notoriously we later discover that no one had found time to check in what direction the wheel had begun to move. It is the time that calls most plaintively for the

---

[4] Confucius, *The Analects*, Bk IX.30.

correlative virtue to non-attachment; namely, patience, which calls for remaining behind the stampede until we are restored to clarity and composure.

Indian spirituality is no less explicit in its counsels toward non-attachment. One of the most celebrated verses in the *Bhagavad Gītā* expresses the essential principle of non-attachment. The Radhakrishnan translation reads: "To action alone hast thou a right and never at all to its fruits; let not the fruits of action be thy motive; neither let there be in thee any attachment to inaction." [ch 2 v 47] A sound and successful meditation on this luminous verse should lead us to discern that the fruit of any action is not necessarily its proper consummation but merely its consequence. All depends on how we relate to the consequence of action; for action and result are mere elements in the everlasting flux of coming-to-be and passing-away. Neither action nor inaction, nor their consequences are of themselves able to determine our proper destiny. They are just perishable seed and perishable fruit. But what is not perishable is the causal order which governs their passage. Now it does not follow from this that a man must reap only from such seed as he himself once sowed; but assuredly, and let us make no mistake about it, at least what he sows he must also reap.

Since in our own strength we cannot alter in the least the consistency of this causal order and since at best our foresight is so weak there is nothing for it but to offer up our actions to the Lord while nonetheless devoting ourselves humbly to right action. And in the story of the *Gītā* this is exactly what the Lord Kriṣna advises the prince. It is this very *resolve* to offer up our actions to the Lord that is the basis of the yoga of this Scripture. Any other basis, no matter how disciplined it might be, will lead only to further bondage. Nothing but this firm resolve and its devout execution saves us from losing ourselves and eternity in our dark concern for the fruits of our actions. Such is the gravity of our need for non-attachment.

One of the greatest treasures of all verses of all Scriptures is found in the *Great Forest Upaniṣad* called in Sanskrit the *Bṛhadarāṇyaka*. I shall try to paraphrase it without corrupting its meaning. "Yonder, the transcendent, the invisible Source is full; here, the same Source as immanent and visible among us is also full. The full comes out of the full. Even in taking fullness out of the full, nonetheless the full itself remains."[5] Without imagining that we have adequately brought this over into our manner of speaking we should say this means, at very least, that God's integrity is not diminished or shaken by the birth and course of His creation; that He remains ever constant among us, nearer than hands and feet.

If one could truly believe this would he not more easily achieve, maintain and express the lovely virtue of non-attachment? Yet non-attachment will not abide a moment without her sister patience. Ought we not then to pray that patience and non-attachment should share their perfect work presenting us whole, preserving our integrity that we might be found wanting in nothing. And that to this end may God help us all.

---

[5] Swami Krishnananda, *Bṛhadāraṇyaka Upaniṣad*, Invocatory Prayer.

What is Sacred?
Opening remarks to a dialogue gathering, Ojai, 1993.

In 1993, a dialogue weekend "What is Sacred?: God, Religion, and Belief" hosted by the Krishnamurti Foundation of America was opened with a short talk by Prof. Anderson. Two videotapes from the eighteen-part dialogues that Krishnamurti had with Prof. Anderson in 1974 were shown as part of the dialogue weekend. This was Prof. Anderson's first visit to Ojai. The following is excerpted from the transcription of the talk published in a KFA newsletter the following year.[1]

"... I was looking over the valley and saying to myself what an extraordinary thing to find myself among friends, and also cradled and nestled in these hills. Driving up here from La Jolla, I thought about the statement in the tenth book of the *Rig Veda* which points out that the goddess of speech, Vac, never appears except among friends. And in the little packet we received that described for us the weekend to come there was a stress on friendship, and in the modern world friendship, compared with what it was in the ancient world, is something that has fallen to a diminished state. We talk about connections now, not very much about friends. I am very thankful to be among friends.

"The responsibility of making the opening remarks that would be germane and cogent for what lies ahead of us in the days to come, I take very seriously. It has been some twenty years now since Krishnamurti and I undertook those conversations together that you

---

[1] Newsletter of the Krishnamurti Foundation of America, Volume 8 Number 1, 1994.

are so familiar with; and during those conversations Mary Zimbalist was present and I wish to thank her. I was a virtual total stranger and she made me feel welcome and at home. The culmination of my thanks is to Krishnamurti and his memory. Not a day passed after the conclusion of those tapes… though I never saw him in person again… without his spiritual presence remaining, as I am sure you must feel it yourself. Even now his spirit abides 'nearer than hands and feet.'[2]

"Our topic: 'What is sacred?' There is an inexhaustible pathos implied in the content of that enduring question. It is a question that properly belongs among those questions that we call enduring. The character of that pathos encourages us to be very serious about our approach to the question. I hope to develop in the few minutes allowed us what the character of that seriousness is and why the seriousness is at such a level. We get very uneasy when seriousness is brought forward, particularly in such a matter as the question 'What is sacred?' We protest and say, 'Oh for heaven's sake, what is all this fuss about seriousness?' If we were living sacredly, then where would the question arise? We should be ourselves the sacred. The question would not arise let alone endure. It is an amiable hypothesis but dangerously naïve, deceptive and superficial because it overlooks a permanent feature of human nature. And it's precisely that feature that requires on our part a further question which we should be asking every time a question arises for us no matter what it is, namely, what is the question's real province? Where does it belong? Further, am I quietly hearing the question before I am already galloping toward an answer? The difficulty with abiding a question has to do with what it is to be human. To abide means to stay, to stand, not to bolt, not to budge.

"Our question, 'What is sacred?' must find its place. Its place is not in the discipline of theology. Theology begins with the notion that it knows. It knows God, so discourse begins with that. It doesn't belong in the province of philosophy's theories of language. It doesn't

---

[2] From Alfred Lord Tennyson's poem *The Higher Pantheism*.

belong in depth psychology's concerns and meandering among the eruptions from the unconscious. All those disciplines require focus on something that is outside the one who is doing the study.

"This uneasiness, this fear within our question, attends self-inquiry. And self-inquiry is a meditative act. Meditation is little understood let alone practiced well. Our question, 'What is sacred?' cannot realize an answer outside of its sphere, which is self-inquiry. But even when we say that, we have not yet located its home ground. Its home ground rests in a certain permanent feature of our nature. It is one we do not like to think about. It is our capacity for self-betrayal. We can betray not only someone else but also our own selves. Our capacity for violating our own nature is human. If wild creatures in the forest lived that way they would make too many mistakes and not survive. They don't get away with more than one or two, perhaps three, and live. We have buffered ourselves through technology against that raw relation to nature, but it has not in any way improved our relations to ourselves. Unlike the wild creature whose eye is clear, our species has a confused eye. Have you ever wondered when you saw the eye of an eagle how you were going to look at yourself in the mirror the next time? I have many times, and I've had long, long thoughts about it.

"Our capacity for self-betrayal is something that we must note. I want to note it in relation to our question, 'What is sacred?' What does it mean to betray oneself'? If we can determine that in just a couple of minutes, then we can begin to look out on the vista of our question, and we shall be asking our question of ourselves, of one's own self, yes, one's own self. Upon every instant by reason of our nature we are faced with a problem of attitude, but almost always we think we are faced with only a problem of choice, preference, decision. We fail to note that they follow as night the day from our attitude. That fact is rarely brought forward.

"We have for centuries given ourselves airs that we somehow are privileged to have free will. We are free for attitude, but given our attitude, freedom stops there. Our preferences, our choices, our decisions follow upon attitude as night the day. That has the most far reaching meaning for our understanding of ourselves, and we face that upon every instant. Upon this instant, my attitude will determine everything else that follows from my will, intellect, and feeling. More radically, more crucially (though this is another topic) my access to the primal root of intuition will be furthered or hindered by my attitude.

"The role of intelligence in this is critical. Please consider, for a second, the etymology of the word. Intelligence is made etymologically upon *inter*, which means 'between', and *legere* which means 'to gather.' Something is being gathered, in between. Between what? Between the timeless and time. Which is to say, it is not the timeless that is crucial and it's not time that is crucial, but rather what is timely. And by timely I do not mean what that word has become in its vulgar sense in western civilization… a time when we have opportunistically something to grab. I do not mean that at all. What is timely upon every instant is what attends and follows precisely from a correct attitude: A meditational attitude. And when Krishnamurti pleaded over and over again that our behavior is so enmeshed, imprisoned in one thing after another so that there is no quietude, no standing still, no abiding, he was pointing to the phenomenon that we are always jumping ahead of ourselves. That is an attitudinal issue. We want something that we imagine is out there. We are unwilling to have what we need specified for us within the in-between. What is sacred then? Could it be that it is that gathering in-between, within the timely, so that our lives are lived between the timeless and time… and what I am about to say now may sound frightening… *so that our lives are lived inevitably*? If our lives are inevitable, what occasion is there for anxious worry?

"Suddenly that Biblical phrase comes alive: 'The peace that passeth all understanding.' [Phil 4:7] Krishnamurti's concern for what is whole is apropos of what we are talking about here. Is it possible, he asked, to live so that the part is included in the whole? So it isn't a question of something being pathologically wrong with thought, since in meditation thought necessarily operates. But how are we supposed to include it in the whole, in meditation?

"In his *Notebook* there is this remarkable statement on page 101, 'There is a "thinking" born out of the total emptiness of the mind.' He calls it thinking, but of course it is in quotation marks lest we confuse it with what we usually call thought. 'There is a "thinking" born out of the total emptiness of the mind; that emptiness has no center and so is capable of infinite movement. Creation is born out of this emptiness but it is not the creation of man putting things together. That creation of emptiness is love and death.' Every instant is an instant of creation and also of destruction. Yet we will not abide the destruction. And when we sense that the creation is also the destruction we won't abide that either.

"We talk about process. The creation that is pointed to here is not a process. It is instantaneous and opens us to the deep question: Is it possible to live so that the part is included in the whole?

"Now I am going to bring up something that is a problem for us all. Krishnamurti is now no longer here in the flesh, so we can't listen to his words. We have now the legacy of his words in writing. How are we going to read that writing? You must have asked yourself that question since his written words are of the past. Is it possible to read them so that the part, the past, is included in the whole? Because if we are not going to read his works meditatively, which is to say with the part included in the whole, then we should be violating not only his work, but also violating our own nature. I wrote out a question that relates precisely to this issue and I'll read it to you, 'Is it possible to read so attentively that the word, which is of the past, is included in the unprecedented present instant, the eternal now?' If it is not possible to read that way we are lost. And the question, 'What is sacred?' cannot be asked. Likewise if we were collapsed into the eternal we should have no occasion for asking the question either. So is it possible to read so attentively that the word which is of the past is included in the unprecedented present instant, the eternal now?

"I hope in our dialogues ahead this weekend we might explore that. Since the seventeenth century this line of questioning and thinking has virtually departed from western civilization. It was present in the middle ages and in the ancient world. But centuries have passed since the seventeenth, and we were brought up with no knowledge of this. In academic practice, with rare exceptions, it's never discussed. What does that say? It says that one could live out the term of his natural life and never hear essentially about what is sacred.

"Some of you perhaps will remember the poet Keats' lines from *Endymion* which are quite unintelligible unless one is capable of thinking meditatively. Since he points to what it is that is sacred in these lines he says, 'A thing of beauty is a joy forever.' How are you going to make that intelligible? Things come to be and pass away. But here's a thing that's a joy forever! Am I here forever? Don't I also come to be and pass away? You see the difficulties.

"And as though that is not enough he goes on to say,

> Its loveliness increases; it will never
> Pass into nothingness; but still will keep
> A bower quiet for us, and a sleep
> Full of sweet dreams, and health, and quiet breathing.
> Therefore on every morrow, are we wreathing,
> A flowery band to bind us to the earth...

"Not to yank us up to heaven, to bind us to the earth,

> Spite of despondence, of the inhuman dearth
> Of noble natures, of the gloomy days,
> Of all the unhealthy and o'er-darkened ways
> Made for our searching: yes, in spite of all,
> Some shape of beauty moves away the pall
> From our dark spirits. Such the sun, the moon,
> Trees old, and young, sprouting a shady boon
> For simple sheep;...
> And such too is the grandeur of the dooms
> We have imagined for the mighty dead;
> All lovely tales that we have heard or read:
> An endless fountain of immortal drink,
> Pouring unto us from the heaven's brink.

"When Mark Lee invited me to make these opening remarks I was hard pressed because I said to myself: if I bring something forward that is a disclosure from my own self-inquiry over many decades, will it be intelligible? And I said to myself, you can hardly do anything else because Krishnamurti has already prohibited anybody interpreting what he said or wrote. And I thoroughly agree and wholeheartedly endorse that prohibition. So I was left, wasn't I, with gratitude to Mark Lee, but standing before the task with fear and trembling. Not fear as catatonic fright but an extreme respect for what it is to make unprecedented self-disclosure even among friends.

"In the Upanishads there is a most marvelous statement. It reads, and I'll translate it: 'This that is here is full. That which is yonder is full. The full outflows from fullness. Even on taking away the full from fullness, fullness itself remains.' To stand within the full instant and not bolt, to stand where timeliness is gathered, not isolated by oneself but in the beauty of what is sacred, is, then, an end to anxious worry. And it's the beginning, instant by instant, of a new creation and the total destruction of the preceding instant.

"So, I decided that I would hazard saying these things, and I hope in our dialogues in the days ahead we can explore this question of this permanent feature of human nature which specifies our nature as human. We have the possibility of self-betrayal, yet we also have the possibility of timeliness which is the practical equivalent of a thinking 'born out of the total emptiness of the mind' and infinitely more cogent and apropos of our present situation than any idealization that we could imagine.

"And it is that practical element that I wish to end my remarks on. Is it possible to live so that the part is included in the whole? Is it possible to read so attentively that the word which is of the past is read upon this present instant in all its richness and glory within the eternal now? I can't ask that question for anyone else but myself. I cannot answer it for anyone else but myself. But we are friends and we can speak to one another. Those who think they are speaking but who are not friends are, when the goddess of speech is absent, babbling. No matter how erudite and brilliant the babble, it is still babble. But we are privileged to come together as friends. And in our discussions with each other in the hours to come, each one of us, in what Krishnamurti calls aloneness, can within that present instant discover timeliness and inevitability... and on that account what it is that is sacred."

Preface to *Under the Pepper Tree*[1]

Krishnamurti's legacy has left his students and followers two enigmas:
1. The nature of his affliction which he called the "process";
2. His final pronouncement on his death-bed that no one had understood him.

In making a few preludial remarks on these extraordinary events, in no sense do I mean to imply that I have understood him or the "process" which he so patiently and bravely bore. However, it is timely and fitting, in the context of Mark Lee's *Under the Pepper Tree*, to begin to examine what these phenomena might suggest for two features of human nature, namely, spiritual growth, and the human self's being an issue for itself.

The ordering of Krishnamurti's developmental progress as a whole person in *Under the Pepper Tree* brings forward in due order many direct quotations in his own words that can stand as corrections to popular misunderstandings and misreading of Krishnamurti's textual legacy. This legacy at the sheerly verbal level is sometimes difficult to clarify. Even when persuasively clarified, one may not be in a state of readiness to receive it adequately, if yet at all. The imperative to patience and perseverance remains a constant. Self-study is not a seasonal affair. Since the self is an abiding issue for itself, being and becoming aware of its self-misunderstandings persists as a changeless obligation to itself.

---

[1] Written for *Under the Pepper Tree*, a memoir by Mark Lee on his life with Krishnamurti. Manuscript to be published.

To have only an intellectual, notional grasp of these things is not enough since intellect by itself moves nothing. Self-inquiry must be *lived* through or self-awakening eludes one. "You are neither hot nor cold, you are lukewarm, indifferent. You have intellectualized your life and have lost the capacity to live and hence your intellect and your theories have become your destroyers... Because you play with life, you think that there are innumerable facets to truth...."[2]

Cultural acquired conditioning and the collective mind perpetuate the illusion that the great spiritual teachers somehow enter the world mature and fully armed (much as did Athena from the head of Zeus). They are disinclined to address the permanent features of spiritual growth such as development and suffering. They prefer to overlook the caution of D.T. Suzuki (the renowned scholar of Zen) that growth is always attended by pain.

Krishnamurti was keenly aware of this coupling of spiritual growth and suffering. His psycho-physical affliction, so far undiagnosable by physical medicine or medical psychology, kept the issue alive for him most of the term of his natural life.

While devoted to the indivisibility of the relation between spirit and matter, he was not dismayed by the fact of phenomena, teaching that it is "Through experience alone that you can grow—experience in the phenomenal world. Without phenomena, life cannot exist... to understand it you must grow through the objective, with the understanding of what is the subjective."[3]

An inspiring example of Krishnamurti's practice in spiritual growth appears in his answer to a practical question:

> Q: How can two publications of such contradictory titles as the following: *The Path* and *Pathless Reality*, by the same author, be issued simultaneously?
>
> K: The answer is very simple. One was written six or seven years ago, the other but lately. *The Path* was written by me

---
[2] Ibid., p. 130.
[3] Ibid., p. 115.

when I still divided life in that world of delusion. Now to me there is no such thing as division of life: it is all, because truth lies in everything… To that truth there is no path, because it lies in each mind and each heart. That truth does not require a path…When I realized that fully *Pathless Reality* came into being. So it is quite possible to write something at one period and to contradict it later. It is by assertion and contradiction that one arrives at truth. In you must be all contradiction and assertion because life contains all…[4]

Krishnamurti's statement that truth lies in everything is followed by "In every blade of grass, in every stone, in every leaf, in every human heart and mind." Human perception of truth distinguishes between two orders of truth, truth and falsity of statement and truth and falsity of existence. The latter entails existing in what one has understood and there, only being what one is, is true. It is in the sphere of the truth of existence or being that we as human beings share in one or more respects resonance with all beings from stone to star.

A tender reflection of Krishnamurti's sensitivity to this permanent feature of existence and his vibratory response to it, Friedrich Grohe records in his handsome book, *The Beauty of the Mountain* (under the picture of the Nandi sculpture) "The Nandi, a traditional Indian sculpture of a kneeling cow, near the Pepper Tree at Pine Cottage. I saw it with flowers on its head and asked Mary Zimbalist if Indians had been visiting. She said that Krishnamurti had told her to put flowers on it sometimes, so that it feels at home."[5]

A dry academic response to Krishnamurti's heartfelt sentiment might be, "That's just an instance of the pathetic fallacy." Perhaps a fair response to that might be Shakespeare's "There are more things in heaven and earth, Horatio, than are dreamt of in your philosophy." (Hamlet I, 5, 166)

---

[4] Ibid., p. 126.
[5] Friedrich Grohe, *The Beauty of the Mountain*, p. 60.

The last two paragraphs of *Under the Pepper Tree* present and record Krishnamurti's startling statement that no one had understood him. Mary Cadogan asks the question through Mary Zimbalist who puts it directly to him nine days before he died. "When Krishnaji dies what really happens to that extraordinary focus of understanding and energy that is Krishnamurti?" His immediate answer was, "It is gone. If someone goes wholly into the teachings perhaps they might touch that, but one cannot try to touch it... If you all only knew what you have missed—that vast emptiness." Further, "There is no consciousness left behind of that consciousness, of that state. They'll all pretend or try to imagine they can get into touch with that. Perhaps they will somewhat if they live the teachings. But nobody has done it. Nobody. And so that's that."[6]

This could not be more categorical. At first glance it sends one into a depressive despair—even while projecting the happy possibility of living the teachings, the dreadful question remains, how does one practice what one hasn't understood?

So much for the denial. Is there any positive suggestion in this categorical negation? I think so, but I offer it on the strict provision that no reader imagine or infer that in making this suggestion I am implying, in any sense whatsoever, that it stands in for an understanding of Krishnamurti.

In Krishnamurti's absolute negation there are fortunately, sternly forbidding barriers against any authoritative interpretations of his legacy. This unquestionably blocks any "apostolic succession" or any academic claims to a mastery of his works. It would be pretentious to attempt a definitive, standard interpretation of Krishnamurti's teachings. Krishnamurti's negation warns any biographer against attempting to interpret him through the back door of his life story. This leaves open only the sheerest journalistic record of his passage. If one doesn't understand the subject of the biography what else is left for the writer?

---

[6] Lee, op. cit. p. 170-171.

The positive suggestion in Krishnamurti's absolute negation is that it throws the student utterly upon him or herself in the utmost sincerity, seriousness and "vast emptiness" of self-inquiry. Only in the emptiness and openness of self-inquiry can spirit spread its wings freely, liberated from moralism, sanctimony, impatience, ambition, and self-servingness. Thus freed, it finds the ultimate in the immediate and the truth that does not require a path.[7]

During the height of the Blitz over London in the Second World War King George VI made a radio address to the nation. And the King said: "Go out into the darkness and put your hand into the Hand of God. That shall be to you better than light and safer than a known way."[8]

La Jolla, CA
2005

---

[7] Ibid., p. 126.
[8] From Minnie Louise Haskins' poem *God Knows*.

Part II
Conference Papers

Papers Presented to International Conferences at the University of Guadalajara, Mexico:

1994   Second International Conference on the New Paradigms of Science

1995   Third International Conference on the New Paradigms of Science

1996   The International Foundations for New Human Paradigms

1997   The International Foundation for New Human Paradigms

Human Transformation Independent of Knowledge and Time
November 16, 1994

Some twenty years ago I was privileged to be invited by the world renowned spiritual teacher, Jiddu Krishnamurti, to undertake with him a series of video-taped dialogues. Their object was to bring forward the kernel of his teaching. In essence he taught that each human being is responsible for his or her own transformation, which is not dependent on knowledge or time. In another context he wrote in his own hand that: "The core of Krishnamurti's teaching is contained in the statement he made in 1929 when he said 'Truth is a pathless land.'"[1]

These two statements, namely, that one's own transformation is independent of knowledge and time and that truth is a pathless land are most intimately related. Though on first glance they seem markedly distinct, nonetheless these statements are inseparable. On perceiving the reciprocal union of these two principle affirmations, one glimpses the undivided nature of genuine spirituality.

Spirituality and wholeness are also inseparable but the splendid word, wholeness, has in recent decades fallen on miserable times. It is used by many now to express the goal of growth techniques and methods by one or another party with a program to sell. This misuse of the word has provincialized the concept and turned it into a catchword that divides rather than heals. But this fine word can be rectified and restored to its proper usage if it is reunited to spirit instead of being left naked to the agendas of traditional and

---

[1] Krishnamurti, *Total Freedom*, p. 1.

popular psychologies. This hard remark provokes the question of the meaning of each word, spirituality and wholeness. I hope the progress of this paper will begin to disclose their meaning until at the conclusion of this essay I shall attempt a formulation that perhaps will help restore the words to their home ground.

The topic of this paper does not lend itself to the usual academic approach of research that leads to erudition. On the contrary, it does not move by adding one thing to another whether by information or analysis. It moves not by addition but by subtraction; it seeks not more but less. It moves in the mode of meditation. This is because it labors in the field of self-inquiry. Authentic self-inquiry has received little attention throughout the long stretch of recorded human history. This is because genuine self-inquiry is independent of both outward and inward authority—the outward being the imposition of political and economic constraints and the inward being the tyranny of ideas and the stream of consciousness that flows from them and feeds them.

Outward authority is easily recognized, the police state is its crudest form. Inward authority is much more subtle. It is a psychological self-bondage. To make matters worse, it harbors an ambivalence. It lets itself be dominated by scientific, philosophical and religious ideas which it receives at second and third hand yet at the same time it intellectually and emotionally drugs itself into a virtual substance dependency on these ideas and ideals. A principal mark of psychological self-bondage is that these ideas and ideals while in their fancied modes of truth, goodness and beauty are contemplated in abstraction only. Embodying them in real life is shunned like the plague. Moral and spiritual cowardice are endemic to our species whereas physical courage is demonstrated in one form or another every day. As for moral courage, who among us is ready to stand alone against a majority of our fellows? As for spiritual courage, who among is ready upon the instant to die the psychological death to our very imagined self-identity without which death there can be no self-liberation?

These questions cannot be answered collectively by common consent nor by meanderings among the denizens of the so called collective unconscious. They can be answered only by the individual, by oneself alone and unaccompanied. Genuine self-inquiry realizes this groundless ground which is virgin, uncharted, pathless and unimagined. One's persona disappears into this unthought and nameless emptiness for this emptiness is reality and reality is neither an event nor an experience.

These words are unintelligible so long as the persona is mistaken for the self. Self-inquiry reveals the persona as an ephemeral phenomenon of the self. To put the matter loosely, while the me is mistaken for the I the words in the previous paragraph will remain enigmatic and for some, plain gibberish. This is why pure self-inquiry has received little attention throughout the long stretch of recorded human history. That level of human transformation which is independent of knowledge and time is not realized outside of self-inquiry and for that reason it remains a rarity.

At this point in our discussion it is necessary to point up that fatal misconception which holds that self-inquiry and introspection are one and the same. This misunderstanding arises out of a failure to discern that the inward world of motives, moods, feelings and wishes is equally external to the ego as is the outer world we see, hear, touch, smell and taste. On grasping the centrality of the ego and its standpoint one is in a position to give both the outer and inner worlds their due. It is from this base and standpoint that most of the higher products of culture in the arts and sciences spring in all their ideality and beauty. Their ideality stretches indefinitely into the past while in the present artistic and scientific ideality anticipate the novel future. Unfortunately, the egoic standpoint does not overcome the illusion that the ego is an independent substance in being. This inveterate illusion generates the force of the twin concepts, personality and experience. These two concepts, personality and experience, undergird the theoretical structures of theology, philosophy and depth psychology. Even the transpersonal psychologist concerned to study the common root of personality is still faced with the question ultimately of what and who is I as agent who interprets the clinical data awaiting diagnosis? These questions prepare one to begin self-inquiry. One moves intemporally from there to the intuition that even one's sense of self-presence cannot be equated with ego. Without this distance on the normal function of ego, self-inquiry cannot flower.

Only intelligence is required for self-inquiry and not any of the games of egoic intellect which impose rules of dogma, doctrine, ways and means, method and scope. Housed as these are within conventional interpretations and social structures they are rarely studied for their power both to hide and to disclose their roots. Such roots reach down into the subsoil of primordial wisdom. Historically, those few who touched this wisdom have most often paid dearly for it. Witness in the western tradition the executions of Jesus and Socrates.

If not in league with the egoic standpoint, what is the character of that intelligence which attracts supports and illuminates pure self-inquiry? This question and the question of the self are inseparable for when they are studied with a pure act of attention these questions reveal that the ego so far from being at the center of the self is as external to it as the world of the five senses and the internal world of thought, will and feelings. These external and internal worlds are those of body and soul and the self cannot be reduced to either or both of them.

The latter half of our twentieth century has seen a growing enthusiasm for the religious thought of the South Asian and Far Eastern traditions. It is almost as though the far-ranging western missionary movements of the nineteenth century are being answered this century from the east. The dialogue that this phenomenon engenders stimulates us to investigate what there is of authentic spirituality in our own western tradition.

It will not offend Krishnamurti's spirit if in this mediation I refer to scriptural passages from our own western tradition and from others. In our eighteen video-taped conversations I quoted a number of scriptural references from various cultures. He never once objected to this practice. Rather, he objected to the misuses of sacred texts. Unless one risks the living out of whatever there is of truth in such texts, they remain part of a meaningless clutter we call knowledge, a heap which is coffined in the past and in no sense an occasion for present self-awakening. Knowledge at this level is the fund of experiences, memories, ideas which we use to measure the present. Such a standard cannot embrace the unprecedented in every present instant. Practical know-how without which we could not survive, is knowledge of a different order. Self-inquiry distinguishes these two orders intellectually but is concerned to live out the distinction rather than to hold it only abstractly. This entails an abiding vigilance and sensitivity to our tendency to collapse ourselves into the past.

Plato's virtual transcription of Socrates' *Apology* remains one of the clearest invitations to self-inquiry in our western tradition. Just before his judges render the verdict that will execute him Socrates says, "An unexamined life is not worth living." In the text he includes his own life in this. In saying that an unexamined life is not worth living he necessarily invites the question: who is the examiner and the examinee? If it is my life that I am examining, where do I, the examiner leave off and my life as object begin? Or, looked at from the standpoint of my life, the examined, where does my life leave off and I, the examiner begin? Furthermore, where does my life leave off and the lives of others begin? I am not raising these questions for the sake of mystification or as a shrewd rhetorical device by which to benumb a critical focus. On the contrary, if one sits with them quietly they open out upon a crucial distinction between two orders of attention. One we give to physical and technical matters which require a change in temporal or spatial objects. The other attention we give to attitudes which we have taken for granted in our relatively unconscious lust for security and a settled life. It is this latter attention which properly obtains while one is examining one's life.

Only such a non-utilitarian attention can reveal how it is the case that human transformation is independent of knowledge and time.

Let us examine the possibility of such a transformation through contemplating the relation of knowledge to time, of understanding to timelessness and of not-misunderstanding to timing. As we look into these, the meaning of the topic of this mediation might come clearer.

Knowledge and Time

The English word, 'knowledge,' is etymologically somewhat obscure. However, what seems fairly certain is that it derives from Middle English where it meant 'to admit,' 'confess.' The element of confession gives the word a certain religious aura which confers upon it a high seriousness. An anterior etymology relates 'knowledge' to 'note' whose main source is Latin '*nota,*' a brand, a mark by which one recognizes what is at hand. These two etymological roots lend the word 'knowledge' a high respect and an air of permanency.

Both these characteristics of the word point to the ease with which the concept 'knowledge' has uncritically attained to its eminence.

The word's relation to time is clearly on the side of the past since what bears a mark has already been branded. The bearer of the brand is easily reduced in the mind to a tool for carrying the mark as the mark is all important for identification; yet it remains an abstraction. As an abstraction it has the power to last well beyond the existence of its bearers. This seemingly magical property so enhances its dignity that it is easily forgotten that the mark, as such, is of the past and to fix the mind upon it imagining it an authentic creature of the present is to misunderstand the mark and oneself also.

These remarks do not apply to the practical order where the uses of memory are absolutely necessary. One could not drive a car, wash dishes, get to work or operate sophisticated instruments without the uses of memory, let alone undertake prodigious reckonings in the calculative order.

On the contrary, I refer here to the matter of attitude, i.e., whether the measure of my present living is a mark from the past to which I am attached or whether my attention is one of listening and watching free from attachment. One of the keys to how knowledge can and almost certainly does govern attitude is furnished by our word 'recognition.' To re-cognize is to know again. We cannot recognize what we have not known before. This is crucial for our emotional relation to symbol, dogma and ritual since all three relate so intimately to our belief structures. These structures we impose upon the present by whatever means we feel necessary and appropriate to make the present in every particular continuous with the past. Any break in this dreary chain we interpret as a threat to where and how we are in the world. This species of fear is one of the principal causes of continuing religious and political violence the world over, to say nothing of neighborhood and domestic conflicts. These are only some of the symptoms of human disease. To probe this phenomenon more deeply would require a keen examination of the abuse of imagination in which fantasy is mistaken for fact. It is enough for this paper seriously to note psychological reactionism for the deadly disease that it is.

The seminal Spanish philosopher, José Ortega y Gasset, has put this succinctly in his *Meditations on Quixote*. He wrote this paradoxical formula, "The death of what is dead is life. There is only one way to dominate the past, the realm of things that have perished: to open our veins and inject some of our blood into the empty veins of the dead. This is what the reactionary cannot do: treat the past as a form of life. He pulls it out of the sphere of vitality, and, thoroughly dead as it is, he places it on its throne so that it may rule over our souls."[2] Even though Ortega is here describing what he took to be a cultural tendency of Spain to set up what he called an oppressive "oligarchy of the dead" his image is exact for our own personal misuse of memory. Our inveterate habit of superimposing upon the present an image from the past is devastating to interpersonal relationships since it disables us from meeting the other with a fresh and innocent eye. Before we are aware of it, the experience of our first encounter with the other converts to a belief and from then on

---

[2] Ortega y Gasset, *Meditations on Quixote*, p. 49.

each new experience with the other is reduced in our mind to that belief. Such an attitude and conviction are lethal to understanding and leave us perennial prisoners of time, cemented in the past.

There is a distinction between knowledge as static and knowing as dynamic which points a way out of this bondage. Knowing is a movement free from slavery to its source. Within knowing we can distinguish three orders: knowing which serves the practical order; knowing which is accumulative, additive and increases the store of static knowledge; and thirdly, there is knowing which is non-cumulative, non-additive which moves through each present instant taking in the unprecedented, disclosed without beginning or end. Here the mind contemplates its object without imposing upon it any agenda whatsoever.

There is a remarkable text in St. John's Gospel [17:3] which, when translated strictly from the Greek, discloses this untrammeled way of knowing: "This is eternal life, that they should keep on knowing thee the only true God..." I am not concerned in the implicit theology of this text. It is the phrase, "that they should keep on knowing..." which arrests attention in the context of this meditation. Here, the verb 'to know' is in the present active subjunctive. The subjunctive is a mood expressing potentiality; the present tense indicates an ongoingness.

The term, eternal life, joins two words that seem mutually exclusive. Classically, eternity has meant timeless existence, *i.e.*, existence without change. This is not the same as infinite time or endless duration. Eternity is the ever abiding now without respect to any then or when, any past or future. However, life, as we ordinarily understand it, is subject to time. For the individual or the collective life comes to be and passes away. The life of a thing has a beginning, a middle and an end, a life cycle. Finite existence which is existence subject to change endures a temporal career. Then what can eternal life possibly mean for a mortal existence? Our text, if contemplated deeply, will generate this question.

The unprecedented in every instant is the home of the eternal. The unprecedented has no antecedent. It is the absolute new as distinguished from what is novel. The great Danish thinker, Kierkegaard, defined the instant as an "atom of eternity." This implies that it cannot be one moment among others in the temporal chain of cause and effect. The Buddha, noting the circularity of cause and effect, observed that if there is only cause and effect then there cannot be the liberation of self-awakening. Self-awakening is an instantaneous leap out of causalism into a sphere unmodified by the uses of time.

We are now in a position to contemplate the seemingly contradictory term, eternal life. Even though the sphere into which self-awakening leaps is not contaminated by time it nonetheless irradiates and redeems it. This being so, eternal life is realizable now, upon this present instant of self-awakening. Eternal life is not limited to a beginning after death but as eternal it is ever present and as life it is now. Self-awakening is not a gradual illumination as though one were lifting a shade within a darkened room. Self-awakening suddenly, instantaneously sees the intrinsic light of one's own being where before there was only darkness caused by the blindness of self-misunderstanding.

When Jesus prays to his Father in heaven, saying "This is eternal life, that they should keep on knowing thee...." [Jn 17:3] he points up that nothing of *this* knowing can be reduced to the known. This knowing is ever afresh, unprecedented, free from the duality of the knower and the known, experiencer and experienced, controller and controlled. One keeps on awakening to it that there is no intrinsic separation and division since, in the words of Sri Nisargadatta Maharaj, "Nothing was divided and there is nothing to unite."[3] Knowledge which is in bondage to time no longer hinders knowing which keeps on leaping into the sphere of the abiding, the ever present now.

Understanding and Timelessness

Every language contains certain words which are particularly strong in their power and compass to disclose what they express.

---
[3] Sri Nisargadatta Maharaj, *I Am That*, p. 143 (one vol. edition).

The English word, 'understand,' is one of these. Its clear distinction from the word knowledge is sharply brought forward in the words of an old African wise woman who remarked: "the white man knows a very great deal but doesn't understand anything." She put her finger on the heart of the word. The English word 'understand' denotes not only a work of intellect. It includes also a response from the heart. It embraces a dual meaning. On the one hand, to understand is to comprehend, to discern. On the other, it includes empathy, sympathy, the resonating of one heart to another precisely as the other's uniqueness is intuitively embraced. These features of understanding are open to intelligence but closed to calculative reason. Whatever intellect can abstract from these affections cannot stand in for their concrete expressions; so, one can say to another, "yes, it is the case that you know all about me but what really matters is that you understand me." At that point, unless I am mistaken in the other, a gentle peace suffuses our mutual presence and, as we say, we understand one another.

The duality in unity in the word, 'understand' lies deeper than the distinction within it between a matter of the head and the heart. Quite simply, the word means to stand under. To stand under comprises the counter-motion of a simultaneous movement both upward and downward. 'Stand' has for its root the Indo-European *sta*, to hold oneself upright. The human person and the tree have in common that each stands at 90° to the earth that supports it. This geometrical relation, through no fault of its own, contributes to the human psychological illusion that each of us is the center and pivot of his or her natural world. But even freedom from this egoic self-deception cannot change our human necessity, namely, that we are counter-directed between the movement upward by which we stand and the movement downward that roots our posture to its base. Further, the borderline between these counter-tendencies is not geometrical. It exists vibratively, waveringly and, to an obstinate perspective, even waywardly.

As this is so for the body, how much more so it is for the psyche. The soul is stretched between its desire to exist more loftily and that lowly equanimity which does not try to go beyond where it cannot yet begin. The foolish illusion that one is the center of the universe can be dropped but not this counter-tension which is a permanent feature of our human nature. Unlike the spirit which has no agenda, the soul must awaken to the counterplay between exaltation and humility. These are almost universally misconceived, exaltation as prestige and humility as humiliation.

Even when exaltation and humility are understood in their correct relation in which humility is the exaltation, the soul's counterpoise still obtains since the health of the spirit is always critical, always at risk, instant by instant. "The reason the sage is not sick is because he is sick of being sick; this is the secret of health" says Lao Tzu [ch 71].

Since this structure of our nature abides without change, it is a matter of bearing it well or ill in the now. To bear oneself well is to stand under the obligation to be true to one's own nature. It is a question of authenticity, whether or no I will hold to my own way of being what and who I am which existence has required of me from the moment I came into the world. Existence has always the first move and specifies in advance not only my way of being but also the way of every being throughout the term of its natural career. The truth of any being's existence hangs in fidelity to its unique way of being, even at the cost of its individual existence. There is not only cognitive or logical truth but also existential truth, the truth that lies outside of thought. Erich Frank defines existential truth as "To be that which one is, is true."[4] This authentic way of being cannot be expressed self-consciously. One cannot, in the strict sense, copy oneself. Yet, self-betrayal is a fact and an all too frequent occurrence. It happens when thought obtrudes upon one's intuitive response to what is at hand. Timely action is lost. Almost inevitably at such times we say, "I have let myself down."

From this it follows that living true to myself, bearing myself well, is not a matter of developing from a worse state to a better as

---

[4] Erich Frank, *Philosophical Understanding and Religious Truth*, p. 114.

though one could progress from self-betrayal to self-authenticity. Rather, it is a matter of not falling out of one's natural state to begin with. In the natural state there is no identifying with my idea of myself or even with my felt self-presence. Every world-class athlete understands this at the level of physical action. Not all such athletes realize that principle in living out their lives as a whole. The attitude that frees them for superlative physical feats is the same attitude that frees us all from self-betrayal when that attitude governs the actual character and quality of our total living. This attitude of full openness to the unprecedented present instant cannot be one attitude among others but must inform my every action if wholeness is to obtain.

What is the stance that underlies my bearing myself well? It is patience. This answer might surprise given the low esteem to which this concept has fallen in this century. Contemporary Standard English translations of the Greek New Testament in numerous instances replace the translation, 'patience,' with the word 'endurance.' These words, when contemplated in depth disclose how dramatically they differ in spirit. Patience transcends time, endurance is time bound; it looks for release.

The beautiful Greek word for patience, ὑπομονή (*hypomonē*) means literally, 'remaining under' or 'staying behind.' The kinship between patience and understanding reveals itself on noting that they are free from any projection upon the future. Unlike endurance whose strain longs for relief to come, patience neither tries nor expects, as understanding neither withers nor blows its own trumpet. Knowledge can parade itself theatrically. If understanding became self-conscious it would perish. Patience and understanding though operating with time are not the children of time. They are above time while bearing up activities within time. Patience consists in suspending the will to completion, in leaving it empty of design, detached and open to the unprecedented in every present instant. In like spirit, understanding stands abidingly under a thing's way, supporting it, resonating to it regardless of the thing's style or fortunes for good or ill. Understanding as a work of love abides timelessly.

Not to Misunderstand and Timing

To misunderstand is to misinterpret in one or more respects something or someone already known. We cannot misinterpret what is not in some degree already intelligible. This holds true even for meeting the strange. Unless the strange exhibited at least one feature we recognized, we should be unable to apprehend it at all. This is so obvious that it is apt to escape notice. However, the philosopher studies the obvious to discern those qualities that lie below its surface. Since time out of mind the paramount question for thinkers has been what of all there is, is the fundamental reality; or, what is the case beyond all doubt? In the main, western thought has held, with the exception of religious thought, two different answers to this question. They are the realist and idealist theses. Realism, the first and older of these two, holds that the world of things is all there is to reality and that I, in the midst of them, am one of those things too. Idealism rejects this and claims rather, that the sole reality is the subject who thinks the world. Instead of taking the world as it is, as does the realist, the idealist makes the world to be what it is, a creature of thought. The radical difficulty for each position can be put quite simply. For the realist there can be no absolute certainty that what exists there in front of him continues to exist after he has left it. For the idealist there can be no absolute independence of thought since the thinker never finds himself other than coexisting with something else in front of him, facing and opposing the very self he takes to be himself.

In the last three chapters of his *Some Lessons in Metaphysics*, Ortega offers a deep and brilliant critique of both realism and idealism, demonstrating the inadequacy of both. He then offers his own alternative thesis to both at the end of the critique: "Absolute reality, as life, is at once immanent and transcendent.... but that immanence does not mean that it is converted into subjectivity, into I myself. *I am not my life. This, which is reality, is composed of myself and of things. The things are not I, nor am I the things. We are mutually transcendent, but we are both immanent in that absolute co-existence which is life*.... My life is not mine, but I belong to it. This is the broad, immense reality of my coexistence with things."[5]

This last statement, "my life is not mine, but I belong to it" brings us full circle back to Socrates who neither collapsed himself into the world nor the world into himself. In proclaiming that an unexamined life is not worth living he saw his life as not his own while nonetheless he yet belonged to it. Life's transcendence of the world and of oneself calls for our correct relation to it. What one belongs to has the right of disposal so that a thing's inadequate relation to life sometimes results in life's withdrawing from it absolutely.

Life is lived out between the timeless and time. Situated as it is in the middle it does not enjoy the absolute security of the timeless nor is it reducible to the sheer accidents of time. It both hints of timelessness and threatens dissolution. Life then is problematic for us and calls for the keenest attention if we are to live well. It is not the case that life lives itself out mechanically in us; rather, it is in our quality of living that we lay hold on life.

Life lived well is not a matter of timelessness or of time but of timing. By the timely, I do not mean something opportunistically grabbed. What is timely upon every instant is what attends and follows from a meditational attitude. A meditational attitude is receptive to the voice of Socratic intuition or what I call primal intuition. This is the voice that Socrates said never told him what to do but what not to do. This requires an astonishing degree of faith to obey it since reason has no part in it, indeed cannot have a part in it since primal intuition opens out upon the incalculable, the unprecedented in every present instant.

Before we bolt from this, let us note that intelligence is not embarrassed by it. The root meaning of the word intelligence means something gathered in between. Between what? Between the timeless and time, which is the timely.

Intelligence, which is never restless, waits quietly, unattachedly within the in-between. It waits upon what is specified for us

---

[5] Ortega y Gasset, *Some Lessons in Metaphysics*, p. 158.

in advance, what we can have no knowledge of ahead of time. Intelligence obeys the negative summons of primal intuition and rejoices in the unheralded that comes to pass.

Primal intuition calls upon that creative inhibition that halts before what at the time ought not to be known or acted upon and might never be known or acted upon since it would land us in self-misunderstanding.

Not to misunderstand, then, in this context, means not to misunderstand oneself by disobeying the warning from primal intuition against a particular present action. Obedience to it places oneself precisely within the timely. Timeliness is the practical equivalent of what Krishnamurti calls in his *Notebook* "a 'thinking' born out of the total emptiness of the mind; that emptiness has no center and so is capable of infinite movement. Creation is born out of this emptiness but is not the creation of man putting things together. That creation of emptiness is love and death."[6]

The creation pointed to here is not a process. It is instantaneous. Human transformation, if genuine, is instantaneous since it is a creation. As a creation, not a making or re-making, it necessarily is independent of knowledge and time since the transcendence of creation is also the total destruction of what preceded it.

Perhaps we are now in a position to attempt a descriptive definition of both spirituality and wholeness. In the first I shall employ some of Krishnamurti's words to describe spirituality: "It is to see the false in the false and to see the truth in the false, and it is the truth that denies the false. You see what is false and the very seeing of what is false is the truth."[7] Spirituality consists in denying what is false without knowing in advance what is truth. Spirituality is the instantaneous obeying of primal intuition's negative summons without knowing why its warning should be heeded. Wholeness is the intact condition of our original nature. It is realized, awakened to, instantaneously. It is not reached through a process nor is it an integration of aggregated parts.

---

[6] Krishnamurti, *Krishnamurti's Notebook*, p. 101.
[7] Krishnamurti, *Total Freedom*, p. 271.

These definitions will seem radical. They are meant to be since human transformation is not a matter of knowledge or time. It is the instantaneous awakening to the freedom of being a light unto oneself, the destruction of the bondage of causalism, for the former things are truly passed away.

Inner Transformation and Bearing
November-December 1995

Last November, 1994, at the Second International Conference on the New Paradigms of Science, I read a paper with the improbable title, "Human Transformation Independent of Knowledge and Time." The subject matter was drawn from the eighteen dialogues Krishnamurti invited me to undertake with him with a view to presenting the essence of his teaching. Though last year's paper was not a summary of those dialogues nor an interpretation of Krishnamurti's teaching, it was, I hoped, an independent inquiry consonant with his spirit.

Your kind and enthusiastic reception of that paper a year ago encouraged me to make this present attempt to deepen it. I divided that paper into three sections: one on knowledge with a subsection on knowing; another on understanding and the third on not misunderstanding. I tried to show that not to misunderstand is not the same as to understand. With this last section on not misunderstanding I hoped to offer a new point of departure from the measures we call conscience and insight. I invited us to return to Socratic or what I call primal intuition, what Socrates called the voice and spirit within him that always told him what not to do, never what to do. This principle of inward negation is exceedingly far reaching for understanding human nature. It is also a corrective for the dogmatic and authoritarian postures that have wounded human thought and practice down through the centuries. This present paper will extend further the topic of primal intuition with a view to helping us, through the practice of self-inquiry, to live well rather than ill.

Inner Transformation and Bearing, the title of this paper, is no less improbable than the title of last year's paper. With the exception of certain Scriptural texts the course of western intellectual history has paid little attention to the subject and category of bearing. Raising it to the eminence and dignity of the concepts Being and Becoming seems strangely extravagant—perhaps even impertinent. Yet, genuine self-inquiry apprehends bearing as not only one of the permanent features of existence but sees it in the foreground of concern for self-knowledge.

The term inner transformation means transition from deafness to heedfulness, from blindness to wakefulness, from apathy to earnestness, from self-bondage to self-liberation.

Abstractly conceived, who would not favor such a transition? Concretely, though, the matter so easily escapes us that it rarely becomes an issue. This is because what is at issue is the self which of all things is the most hidden. The five senses, the internal world of thought, will and feeling, the ego, even the psyche are relatively easy of display. Witness the vast literatures on them. By comparison, with the exception of the scriptures of world religions and some profound commentaries, the self regarded as spirit enjoys no comparable parade.

The pathos in disregarding and even losing self Kierkegaard points up with irony. In his spiritual classic, *The Sickness Unto Death*, he notes that anyone can get along fairly well living the ordinary life in the ordinary way "and it may not be detected that in a deeper sense he lacks a self. Such things do not create much of a stir in the world, for a self is the last thing the world cares about and the most dangerous thing of all for a person to show signs of having. The greatest hazard of all, losing the self, can occur very quietly in the world, as if it were nothing at all. No other loss can occur so quietly;

any other loss—an arm, a leg, five dollars, a wife, etc.—is sure to be noticed."[1]

It will not serve the purpose of this meditation to go into an extended analysis of the word self. Self does not mean ego nor my idea of myself nor even my felt self-presence. Its two primary features of hiddenness and manifestation upon the same instant rest first of all upon its being unqualified, which accounts for its hiddenness, and secondly its objectifying itself as the persona. Abstractly, there is always the persona but concretely the persona is multiple and transient, being ever subject to change. This duality in unity sets up a tension between self as unqualified and self as persona, a tension which finite consciousness must bear. Finite consciousness cannot avoid bearing the tension within this duality of the self. Neither intellect nor will can make the slightest difference to this structure and the bearing that it entails. Unflattering for us, it is the case that in the finite order of our nature, intellect and will are only expressions of a much deeper priority, the priority of intuition, instinct and natural automatisms. We prefer to think that intellect and will can combine to impose themselves directly upon intuition and instinct but this is a pitiful illusion. If they can overpower that deeper priority, how shall we explain to ourselves that we have made no moral progress in getting along with one another since the ancient Greeks?

The grand illusion of the power of our hands-on agency to save ourselves calls for a different approach from the modern one which looks naïvely to the experimental sciences to reveal the core of our nature as well as the way to heal us. This meditation invites us to return to the study and contemplation of our original nature, our original innocence, since if we cannot recover our originary stance we have no hope of finding our bearings.

A material aid toward correcting the self-misunderstanding of our nature can be rediscovered in the study and contemplation of certain texts in ancient Scriptures. For instance, the Chinese *I Ching*, the first of the Confucian classics, offers an image of human

---

[1] S. Kierkegaard, *The Sickness Unto Death*, Tr., Hong and Hong, p. 32-33.

nature graphically portrayed in the hexagram. The hexagram is an image composed of six lines. It is easy to draw. The lines beginning with the first are spaced one on top of the other somewhat like a ladder. The first or lower three lines represent Earth. The remaining or upper three lines represent Heaven. We now have a figure for the cosmos. We as human are represented by the two middle lines of the sixfold structure.[2] As such, human nature is composed of the lowest line of Heaven and the uppermost line of Earth. Human nature, then, has no intrinsic independence of where and how it is in the world. In this figure we are shown to be derived, borrowed if you will, from the primal energies of Heaven and Earth.

This ancient view of human nature is not only Chinese. In principle it occurs also in ancient Hebraic vision. The second chapter of Genesis describes the human soul or being as comprised of two primordial energies, the breath of the Creator and the dust of the earth in which the divine breath is embodied. The career of this composite is, strictly speaking, not its own. It comes to be and passes away precisely as the One who made it disposes. Ancient creation myths of other cultures agree in principle with this vision of human nature's intrinsic dependence on a primordial initiative other than human.

This mythic view of the dual relation between Creator and creature is still current among theologians, religious philosophers, priests, ministers and rabbis and the pious whom they instruct and influence. Alternatively, the secular view of our nature credits us with an autonomy that has no need of the Creator/creature perspective which it regards as superstitious. Our 20th century has seen a spread of the secular view beyond the imagination of former centuries. In the operations of experimental science, which is independent of religion, we have split the atom, broken the genetic code, and visited bodies in outer space. Also, we have killed more human beings this century than at any other period of human history. Neither this century's religious perspective nor the secular one prevented this

---

[2] Wilhelm/Baynes, tr., *The I Ching*, p. 7 footnote.

atrocity. If neither conventional religion nor applied secularity have been able to save us from ourselves is there another way?

Since time out of mind the sages of our species have taught another way, the way of self-inquiry. Broadly speaking, it has had almost no appeal. The bulk of humankind does not engage it. There are two principal reasons for this. In the first place self-inquiry is not one way among other ways. It is the one way that must inform all our ways but this requires the utmost earnestness, vigilance and an abiding pure act of attention. Now since there is no worldly reward for this activity most of us will regard it as superfluous. The second reason is that self-inquiry is not publicly verifiable. Since it enjoys no social acclaim, it being wholly private, there can be no society, church, club or organization to direct it.

How, then, shall we account for self-inquiry's abiding career throughout the ages? What we call classical, whether as practice or product, is kept alive and preserved only by the passionate few. Yet, even the unheeding populace will recognize the names of the greatest sages such as for instance Buddha, Jesus and Socrates. There is in every human heart a vague sense of an unfulfilled promise and while for most it does not issue in personal crisis it continues to prick one for the term of his natural life. It is a goad which, as with our nature, is given to us in advance on our coming into the world. It is something we must *bear*. It is impervious, indifferent to any influence from our will or intellect. It is an objective condition beyond appeal.

Bearing and Understanding

We have been taught since the beginning of western classical metaphysics that *what is* is to be understood in terms of itself or as a substance, a constant; its cause is a constant also, whether we term it "God" or "Being" (with a capital B). This reduction of things to their virtual atomic, constant identity was given enormous emphasis in the Middle Ages when the salvation of the individual human soul was the overriding obsession. In our own time this religious perspective has largely given way to an impersonal focus on what we call the phenomenon whether it be observed in language or experimental science. But this change in perspective has not altered our inveterate habit of seeing things as fixed ontological units, limited to and by their own essence.

We pay a severe price for this view of things. We lose the freedom of what Krishnamurti calls "the choiceless awareness of our daily existence and activity."[3] We cannot realize and enjoy that freedom while we are busy worrying over how to protect and maintain our fixed identity from colliding with other fixed identities in a world of essential oppositions and estrangement. The psychological ramifications from this self-misunderstanding are not confined to western civilization. The *Bhagavad Gītā*, perhaps the most influential Hindu Scripture, describes the Lord Krishna's appeal to Prince Arjuna to drop this very same self-misunderstanding. That fully eighteen chapters are required to complete this Scripture indicates how grave and all encompassing this self-misunderstanding is.

The prince is willing to listen to the instruction that, if followed, will release him from self-bondage, but he cannot know beforehand all the spaces he must encounter. Each of these spaces if not met openheartedly will become roadblocks to his enlightenment. Each space, chapter by chapter, opens up a new abyss. The prince must walk up to each one without flinching and hold patiently until he grasps the attitude and movement that will carry him safely through one crisis to the next. Each new space affords the prince another context within which to face up to the awful question: what and who are you. Are you constantly, concretely your self-image, your idea of yourself? How can that be since it is always changing?

Krishna brings Prince Arjuna around again and again to face the same question because of all questions it is the most difficult to stay with and to hold to courageously, patiently, soberly and quietly. Perhaps, impatiently, we will explode with: "Oh, for heaven's sake, this is ridiculous. If I didn't know who I was I'd be an amnesiac!" But this won't do either, since no one is willing to be reduced to

---

[3] Krishnamurti, *Total Freedom*, p. 257.

one's name, form and activity. As with Arjuna, so with us. We either stay with the question until breakthrough or we bolt from it hoping that, in our rush to rejoin the crowd, the question will not follow us.

Existence, which has always the first move, lays this question upon us at a very early age. Not that the question is intellectually formulated at that age. Indeed, it might never be so formulated for the term of one's natural life. However, the normal child between the ages of two and five *feels* itself subjectively as subject. This felt self-identity is often called "ego-consciousness," a rather unhappy term since it appears to collapse subjectivity into the function of ego. This verbal collapse is indulged in a great number of writings on spirituality which advise that the destruction of the ego is the means to release from self-bondage. This is a misleading notion since it is not the fault of the ego that self-misunderstanding occurs. Without the function of ego, we should lose personal pronouns whose grammatical uses are spiritually neutral. Self-misunderstanding belongs to the self, not to the ego.

Let us return to our Chinese model in the *I Ching*. The six lined hexagram is composed of the two trigrams for Heaven and Earth. Human nature is displayed by the two middle lines, the topmost line of the lower trigram for Earth and the lowermost line of the upper trigram for Heaven. As we noted earlier on, these two lines, while representing human nature are not intrinsically our possession. On taking seriously this image, it invites us to step back from the classical western view of ourselves as individual selves, as substances, separate from the *interplay* of Heaven and Earth, which are respectively primal energy and its embodiment. On accepting the invitation to step back, what comes into view is human nature as pattern, an embodiment of primal energy. As such we are but players in the interplay of the primal powers of Heaven and Earth and subject to their suasion. They are the playwrights of our ways in the play of the one cosmic dance.

Here, there is no ontological estrangement between self and other. Instead of a cosmic arrangement of fixed substances here is a panorama of integral movement bound only by the Unconditioned.

Each of us is a *way* of primal energy patterning itself as the cosmic drama unfolds. The career of this boundless movement is not imposed from without. Rather its activity is intrinsic to itself; it is satisfied by its own exercise. Lao Tzu describes the intrinsic, non-authoritarian hierarchy of this cosmic movement this way:

> Man patterns himself on Earth,
> Earth upon Heaven,
> Heaven upon Tao (the Way of ways)
> And Tao accords with itself.[4]

Elsewhere he says: "Tao (the Way) does nothing, yet leaves nothing undone."[5] This marvelous vision of the Groundless Ground, this intuition of Tao, the Way of ways overcomes the dualism of the One and the many. It is the One *as* the many and draws us back to the originary and absolute present. Lao Tzu says that the movement of the Way, the Tao, is a turning back. It is a turning back from the multiplicity of beings to Being and from Being to Non-being from which Being comes. It is precisely this turning back that discloses the role of bearing at its depth.

Before opening out the character of bearing let us note how self-misunderstanding arises. It is much less complex than we might flatter ourselves is the case. It must not be confused with clinical neurosis with its attendant visceral symptoms, anxieties and phobias. As Kierkegaard noted, "losing the self can occur very quietly in the world, as if it were nothing at all."[6] On the other hand when self-misunderstanding collides with the self's readiness to become healed from it and accepts the course of healing, symptoms very like those of neurosis often obtain. They are the result of withdrawal from habitual misperceptions of the way things really are. However, one does not become dysfunctional in the ordinary affairs of living during that withdrawal.

---

[4] Lao Tzu, *Tao Te Ching*, ch. 25.
[5] Ibid., ch. 37.
[6] Kierkegaard, *The Sickness unto Death*, tr. Hong and Hong, p. 32.

The beginning of self-misunderstanding occurs upon the instant reflection seizes upon a memory of the self's behavior whether of action or reaction. Imagination then fixates that image. When the self identifies with that image or representation it has misunderstood itself. It has reduced itself to a belief in a disembodied consciousness which remains constant. The self invests this fiction with a name and properties. True, it is tinkered with and edited over the years under the duress of changes in body and opinion but the belief in its permanence is held indefinitely. It is now the self's final arbiter and judge of any and every thing.

What is it that draws us toward and into self-inquiry? It is the abiding pressure of bearing. Western culture, with its inveterate alienation from nature, tolerates thinking that bearing as suffering belongs primarily to our human species. It is argued that since animals do not have verbal language with which to communicate thoughts and feelings that animals do not think and feel. The seventeenth-century philosopher Descartes believed animals to be nothing but automata, machines.

In a remarkable and scholarly book by J. M. Masson and S. McCarthy, *When Elephants Weep: The Emotional Lives of Animals*, the authors quote an unknown contemporary of Descartes:

> The [Cartesian] scientists administered beatings to dogs with perfect indifference and made fun of those who pitied the creatures as if they felt pain. They said the animals were clocks; that the cries they emitted when struck were only the noise of a little spring that had been touched, but that the whole body was without feeling. They nailed the poor animals up on boards by their four paws to vivisect them to see the circulation of the blood which was a great subject of controversy.[7]

---

[7] Jeffrey Moussaieff Masson and Susan McCarthy, *When Elephants Weep: The Emotional Lives of Animals*, p. 18.

Not all thinkers were persuaded by Descartes. Voltaire, Newton and Locke took the side of the animals. Lest we think that our alienation from nature affects only species other than our own we should remind ourselves of the atrocities we have wreaked upon our own kind since time out of mind, the Inquisition and the Holocaust are but two instances of our depravity. Human nature continues to display unimaginable extremes from sacrificial love to intense, heartless cruelty toward all forms of life. It is not difficult to agree with the prophet Jeremiah who cried out that the human heart is desperately wicked and deceitful above all things and who can know it? [Jer 17:9]

Our usual human response to this spectacle is to avert our gaze from it, as long as we can, since to dwell on it leads only to despair and perhaps even to clinical depression. But this attitude does not take bearing seriously. It seeks only to escape from it. To take bearing seriously entails a shift of perspective, a shift from seeing bearing in personal terms only to contemplating it for what it really is, namely, a permanent and irreducible feature of all existence. This shift is not easily made. It requires a deep empathy with the lot of any and all creatures that share life with oneself. Linda Hogan, the Native American poet, essayist and novelist has said, "A change is required of us, a healing of the betrayed trust between humans and earth. Caretaking is the utmost spiritual and physical responsibility of our time...."[8] She offers a beautiful example of this reciprocity on nothing "how water and earth love each other the way they do, meeting at night, at the shore, being friends together, dissolving in each other, in the give and take that is where grace comes from."[9]

Let us note now how we as human first encounter bearing. Whether there was or was not a preexistence for us, it is certain that upon the moment of conception we are housed as the sheltered promise of our birth. Earth which is housed in space houses our mother who in the deepest recesses of her person houses the promise of our birth, our arrival into the world, itself a house,

---

[8] Linda Hogan, Dwellings: *A Spiritual History of The Living World*, p. 115.
[9] Linda Hogan, op. cit., p. 46.

a dwelling awaiting us and given to us in advance. This is how Existence conditions us and mothers us into being. Our life career is an embodied one from the start. This principle of embodiment the language of myth calls Earth. The spirit that is embodied is called Heaven. The *I Ching* calls Heaven the Creative and Earth the Receptive. They are the Father and the Mother of all lives and as primal energies they specify our natures in advance. But the *Classic* teaches us also that unconditioned spirit is unfathomable, unbound by any determinants and utterly beyond explanation. This is Tao, the Way. As conditioned spirits we must revere it in silence yet it is our true origin and ultimate nature. The relation between it and our conditioned existence provides a way to contemplate and ponder the mystery of bearing.

As human we enter the world unable to stand. For many months we lie most of the time parallel to Earth. As adults we can hardly, if ever, recall how arduous it was for us to raise ourselves from our horizontal posture to the vertical one of standing upright and unaided. On standing upright, on our own, we make our first formal gesture of independence; but it is a conditioned independence. What conditions us lies much deeper than our need for continued parental care and social affirmation.

The depth of our conditionality discloses itself if we suspend our calculative point of view and adopt for the time being the mythical or intuitive perspective. This is the meditative one within which our potential sageliness can flower and poetry sings. For example, it is only within meditative thinking that faith, hope and love truly reveal themselves. They consistently elude rational explanation but we do not on that account regard them as illusory.

How does our human standing upright condition us in depth below the psychological and social spheres of our needs and desires? Mythically speaking, by standing upright, we mediate what is above us to what is below and what is below to what is above. We are the face of that midpoint between Heaven and Earth, the Creative and the Receptive, Spirit and Embodiment; but we do not stand as effortlessly as we recline. Standing tires us, so we sit or lie down where and when we can to compensate for that fatigue. In fact, at least one third of our lives is spent in reclining for the sake of restoring our energy through sleep and rest. It is in standing that we *bear* our humanness.

This point of view discloses that the moment of the infant child's first standing unaided is, humanly, the first decisive moment of its life's passage. In standing alone it declares its individuality and all the inwardness which that entails. Yet, ironically, this very statement of individuality provides our principal occasion for self-misunderstanding. This crucial point will be developed in the next and last section. In standing alone, Existence has called the child to the universal human vocation which the child must bear and carry through in its own way. Human nature's vocation is to mediate, to bear spirit to body and body to spirit. The intersection of these powers tradition has called the soul which is an unstable equilibrium. It is an unstable equilibrium since every instant is fraught with the unexpected, the unprecedented, whether observed or not. The soul is the intermediary of endless beginnings and it is only through memory and imagination that it can fancy itself to be otherwise. Try as it might the soul cannot in fact, in actuality be elsewhere than upon the threshold of every present instant.

This link between spirit and body which, from the individual standpoint, tradition calls soul is from the cosmic standpoint the intersection between being and becoming, the axis of value and process. Yet, beyond these, there is a deeper intersection, one which today we hear almost nothing about. It is the point between what Plato called the Good and the whole interplay of Being and Becoming. Here, the Good is beyond the correlation good/evil. Plato tells us in the dialogue, the *Republic*, that the Good is beyond being, surpassing it in dignity and power. Precisely as one is enabled to pass between being and becoming, one comes upon this deepest of all intersections, that between the Good and the whole manifest world of coming to be and passing away.

Bearing does not disclose itself in its radical character until the intersection between the Unconditioned and conditioned existence is intuited. Since the Good is beyond Being it is beyond conceptualization. Plato's calling it the Form of forms does not reduce it to a concept except negatively just as the name Non-being is a negative concept which is simply to say it is beyond what can be conceived. The Good, the Ultimate is not this and not that.

If we can for a moment disengage from our collapse into abstract, disembodied consciousness and ask seriously what is the condition for relating viscerally to Non-being, we should have to say it is bearing, which is to say, plainly, suffering. Precisely here some non-dualists will object by asserting that with self-awakening suffering disappears. But this is a hasty notion. Rather, it is *suffering over suffering* that disappears and not suffering itself. If suffering as such disappeared with enlightenment, how is it that some sages have died so painfully from cancer? To say that they did not suffer their pain is a trifling, semantic quibble. On the contrary, their bearing and their sacrifice provide us a profound lesson. Existence is not meant always to be docile to our arts and sciences, five year plans and manipulative cleverness.

The intersection of Ultimate Spirit with the flux of existence occasions detachment in us. The occasion for detachment does not actualize it. It only invites our consent to it. Yet without detachment bearing, as suffering, puts us in bad faith with existence. Another mistaken notion is that adversity produces fine character. On the contrary, without detachment adversity alienates and embitters us. However, detachment rescues us from self-pity and returns us to origin, to our natural state in which we do not act for an object but from timeliness, the detached response to necessity.

In the detached response of timeliness we lose the illusion of agency and so act without contrivance. Complete detachment within the intersection of Ultimate Spirit and the world turns over our view of things 180° and what appeared above is now below and what was below is now above. This is beautifully portrayed in the eleventh hexagram of the *I Ching* in which Heaven is placed beneath Earth rather than above her. The hexagram is called Peace. Peace is not the cessation of hostilities. Peace is dwelling in our natural state, our original innocence. Masculine and feminine energies once estranged are now nearer than near.

Our natural state reflects the point of which Ultimate Spirit meets whatever body it energizes and informs. This point of our original innocence has no lust to possess an end in view and no nostalgia for a beginning once enjoyed. Our natural state abides in the time *between* times which is the timely, the ever present and unprecedented now, obedient to the suasions of Heaven in which is perfect freedom—the freedom from having to choose. Visionary matters are notoriously difficult to communicate and prose is not the happiest medium to convey them. So I shall try a poem and call it: Between.

Between
Who can wander for a lifetime
In the valley, on the hill,
And not see the face of heaven
On the swift and in the still

On the swift and shining waters
In the smooth wet-molded stone
Wide, wide heaven beds among them
Lies where all the leaves are blown

And the wafted leaf in autumn
Comes, like us, to find its ground
Falling where the hand of heaven
Cups the seeker and the found.

If one is not vigilant, the perspective of these lines can encourage a false comfort. It is infinitely more pleasant to imagine the ideal embrace of Heaven and Earth and how they cradle us than it is to remain alert to the inevitable contradictions and collisions of our embodied existence. Abstract contradiction we take easily in stride. It is when contradiction touches our being that we are devastated since it overturns all we have taken for granted. The real tests me through contradiction in being. Without existential contradiction we have no occasion for learning detachment and distance on our surround.[10] Only in detachment is the spirit free to discern the false in the false and the true in the false. Spirit is released to its vocation when soul lets spirit be its eyes and ears. Unfortunately, the soul usually prefers to outward eyes and ears of the body and rarely discovers the inward eye and the inward ear. Unless the soul makes the transposition from the outer to the inner it remains turbulent indefinitely, unable to rise above the storms and stress of material flux.

In one of the uncanonical gospels, the *Acts of Phillip*, Jesus is recorded as saying, "Unless you change your 'down' to 'up' (and 'up' to 'down' and 'right' to 'left' and 'left' to 'right') you shall not enter my Kingdom (of heaven)."[11] Clearly, this oracular admonition requires us to transpose our levels of being, the horizontal (right, left) and the vertical (up, down). Our transfiguration depends upon it. Naturally, if these relative qualities are exchanged on the same plane, they cannot effect an inner transformation. The depth and character of their transposition appears in St. Matthew's gospel. This text is usually given a tiresomely moralistic interpretation. But Jesus was not a moralizer (had he been one he might never have

---

[10] We can distinguish two levels of existential contradiction: The first occurs as a result of my attachment. Even in non-attachment, however, existential contradiction in *being* remains because I am existentially ordered to the possibility of reaching a higher level of being—and I'm never finished off; abiding consummation is my birthright. I am where I am in relation to my perfectibility and I am never coincident with my perfectibility. This is the exact location which Jesus referred to as the offense [Mt 11:6, Lk 7:23]: I take offense when I refuse to accept that there is something expected of me in the face of this existential contradiction. And yet, if I think it depends on my will, I am caught in the contradiction that I don't leave room for grace. Grace isn't going to force me to accept being raised. There is no formula for adequately performing what is expected of me while not offending Divine Will.

[11] *Acts of Phillip*, ch. IX, v. 140.

been executed). In this text bearing becomes acutely aware of itself. The following is a standard translation of the text [Matt. 7:13-14].

> Enter by the narrow gate, for the gate is wide and the way is easy that leads to destruction, and those who enter by it are many. For the gate is narrow and the way is hard, that leads to life, and those who find it are few.

The word 'hard' that describes the way or road that leads to life is not, in the Greek text, a simple adjective opposed to the word easy which describes the way leading to destruction. The Greek word translated 'hard' is *tethlimménē* which is a form of the verb, *thlibō* meaning to press together, to compress, to contract. What is hard about the way that leads to life is its pressure, its compression. The word *tethlimménē* beckons us to look at it still more deeply. This form of the verb 'compress,' means literally 'in the state that results from the act of compressing.' Now our text reads more amply and precisely. It tells us not that the way itself is hard but that the way is a result of something else that is hard, namely, a compressing which metaphorically means an oppression, distress, affliction.

Strictly speaking, the one thing said of the way is that it is a result and this result leads to life. Further, the only thing said of the act of compressing is that it has a result. Neither the act of compressing is the way nor is the way called an oppression, an affliction. This distinction is far reaching and a check against hasty conclusions about the spiritual life. Some see the spiritual life as an agony undergone for the sake of a later, a heavenly reward. Others see living spiritually as a blissful deliverance from bearing, from suffering. The text supports neither of these viewpoints. Rather, it implies that bearing as suffering is a necessary but not sufficient condition for realizing life and that the way to life is a state that results from that condition.

Etymologically, result derives from Latin *salire*, to leap. Result, then means to leap back; to reverberate, to echo. As a leap it is a transition from one level to another, as a reverberation, an echo. Just as an echo is not a repetition of the material conditions that produced it, so the way that leads to life operates in a higher sphere above our personal sufferings; yet, these sufferings abide as that out of which the way is realized. To put the matter simply we can say that while we are bearing our trials in good faith, we are upon the same instant leaping into the only life worth living, the life of peace that passes understanding. This leap is intuitive. It has no causal antecedent nor can it be anticipated as something waited *for*. It can only be waited *on*; it will come or not come in its own good time. In the meantime bearing remains. It abides impervious to our manipulations. It does not change.

Since bearing does not change it is given to us in advance. We cannot choose it. Like language, bearing, given to us in advance, is fraught with mystery. We speak of understanding language but we do not understand its origin. We speak of understanding bearing as a personal response to adversity and we think we understand what it is but we do not understand that it remains abidingly the case with every existent from stone to star.

Since these things are so, our understanding does not transcend its primitive meaning in English which is to stand under. Ultimately, what is it that we stand under? It is the obligation to be true to one's nature, one's own way of being who and what one is which existence has required from the moment of birth. This requires patience and an undistracted listening to the voice of primal intuition.

Not to Misunderstand and Bearing

Once in a dialogue with Krishnamurti during which we explored the relationship between inward hearing and seeing, he made the remarkable statement that hearing is not letting anything interfere with seeing. This statement arrests attention because it reverses an emphasis on seeing that has characterized western culture for well over two thousand years ever since Aristotle described sight as the noblest of our senses. Krishnamurti's statement seems to imply that hearing is the guardian of seeing, that hearing protects seeing from whatever would disorder it or prevent it from apprehending its object. What can it mean that hearing is the guardian of seeing? Let us briefly contemplate how the ear and the eye dispose themselves toward their surround and the matter might come clearer. The eye is open to the world intermittently; first of all in the sleeping/waking cycle and also during waking the normal eye opens and shuts rapidly in what we call blinking. This means that the eye apprehends its object sequentially. This intermittence is from the side of the eye, not from the side of the object. The eye measures continuity of vision by discrete units of vision as they appear in sequence. This gives the eye a decided bias toward quantity which is measured by the least unit as, for instance, so many centimeters make a meter. It is the opposite with quality which uses the greater to measure the smaller as, for instance, the best is always the measure of the worst.

Now, the normal ear is never closed and receives its surround from its own side uninterruptedly. Any discontinuity in presence must come from the side of the object. As the eye favors the quantitative, so does the ear the qualitative. The *I Ching* describes the eye as clinging to outside things and the ear as a hollowed cavity. In other words the eye stops at the surface whereas the ear penetrates to interiority. The difference between ear and eye is much more complex both factually and symbolically than these notices indicate. However, they help us to face the issue.

These contrasted characteristics give us a hint toward noting how it is that hearing guards seeing. They signify that the whole measures and embraces the parts and synthesis is the proper object of analysis. As St. Thomas Aquinas observed, we distinguish in order to unite. When the relation between quality and quantity is misperceived as it became more radically so after the 17th century in western civilization, a spiritual displacement occurs and the inclination and power to listen grows weaker until we arrive where we are today when genuine dialogue is rare. Most often today, instead of dialogue we hear two monologues which seem afraid or unable to meet.

So we ask what is it to listen with the inward, the spiritual ear? What is the relation between deep listening and bearing? These two questions are related to what Krishnamurti calls in his *Notebook*, "A 'thinking' born out of the total emptiness of the mind; that emptiness has no center and so is capable of infinite movement. Creation is born out of this emptiness but is not the creation of man putting things together. That creation of emptiness is love and death."[12] This thinking is a thinking that hears. It hears within the emptiness what Lao Tzu calls Non-being out of which Being arises. This emptiness is the home of Silence. Out of Silence, speech arises; speech as distinguished from chatter. Chatter is a form of noise whereas speech is careful of its words since in every word there is something silent. Silence in the word renders it an omen of the unexpected. This is the source of how the word arrests attention since the word is more than what it merely signifies. Unless one genuinely listens, which is to say listens with the *inward* ear, the pregnant silence in each word escapes the hearer and this failure to listen generates the loneliness and estrangement from the impending that so marks our present century.

The inward or spiritual ear is the organ of primal intuition which as Socrates described it, is a voice of divine spirit which never told him what to do but what not to do. Primal intuition opens out upon the incalculable, the unprecedented in every present instant. This negative summons requires an absolute trust to obey it since reason cannot have a part in it. Primal intuition presents only silence and the word of warning that arises from it. This word of warning is not an explanation. It has no content. It simply says, no. Yet it is this creative prohibition answered by the listener's receptive inhibition that preserves one against danger and, sometimes, disaster. We share this primal intuition with the animals. It has been called instinct but this quite misunderstands it since instinct is propulsive whereas primal intuition is creatively inhibitive. There is no content here to understand but only a negation, something *not to misunderstand*. Obedience to this negative summons shelters us from having to bear more than we can stand to bear or warns us against attempting to escape from what we must bear.

---

[12] J. Krishnamurti, *Krishnamurti's Notebook*, p. 101.

The second question of the relation between deep listening and bearing finds an answer in a biblical paradigm. The writer to the Hebrews [5:8] says of Christ that he learned obedience through the things which he suffered. This does not point to the conquest of actual disobedience but to the negation of potential disobedience. This negation is his Father's will which in Christ's bearing leads him forward toward what he must bear: the cross, his execution. The Greek text indicates grammatically that there is no time interval between the suffering and the obedience. In both Greek and Latin the words for obedience derive from the verb 'to hear.' Since bearing, as such, persists and never changes bringing with it the unexpected, the unprecedented it calls for an abiding listening and for this the ear is perfectly adapted since it never closes.

This implies that the relation between deep listening and bearing is an intemporal one. Their juncture is exact. Their dwelling is one of love. Since love is the source of creation and creation, as distinguished from making, never creates the same thing twice, listening with the inner ear abides in the never and the always.

In the fourth of his one hundred love sonnets to his wife, Pablo Neruda embraces not only his Matilda but, though unintended, his last stanza also embraces the subject of this meditation. Here is Stephen Tapscott's translation:

> That time was like never, and like always.
> So we go there, where nothing is waiting;
> we find everything waiting there.
>
> Y aquella vez fue como nunca y siempre.
> Vamos allí donde no espera nada
> y hallamos todo lo que está esperando.[13]

---

[13] Pablo Neruda, *100 Love Sonnets: Cien Sonetos de Amor*, tr. Stephen Tapscott.

Awareness, Consciousness and Bearing
December 7, 1996

Many of us were present during the last two International Conferences on the New Paradigms of Science. In 1994 I presented a paper with the title, Human Transformation Independent of Knowledge and Time; and in 1995 another paper on the topic Inner Transformation and Bearing. It was my hope that the second paper would deepen the first. Likewise, I hope this present meditation will deepen the two papers that preceded it.

These papers are concerned in that rarest of human activities, genuine self-inquiry. Genuine self-inquiry is independent of outward and inward authority. It cannot be coerced by political and economic constraints nor does self-inquiry obey the tyranny of ideas nor the mind-set of the times. Genuine self-inquiry enjoys an unlonely aloneness which is secured by the most earnest vigilance against self-misunderstanding.

Though self-misunderstanding includes a host of confusions and an ongoing anxiety over the prospect of the next day, its basic character is simple: I misunderstand myself precisely as I take myself to be this or that, i.e., when I identify myself with my particulars.

Genuine self-inquiry awakens to it that one's real self is the Unconditioned which is not an idea, an event nor an experience since the really real is devoid of plurality. Indeed, as one long-time self-inquirer observed, "I may come to any view about myself, because all are equally wrong.[1]

---

[1] George Grimm, *The Doctrine of the Buddha*, 157n.

Awareness

When speaking and writing English formally, the words awareness and consciousness are easily and often confused. Nonetheless, their meanings are as sharply distinguishable as the words 'know' and 'understand' which in usage are also often confused. However, the confusion between awareness and consciousness is the more serious confusion.

Let us take an example from English usage that will point up a difference between the words 'aware' and 'conscious.' One might say to a friend, "Are you aware that John left town a couple of days ago?" That represents a normal usage. To have asked, "Are you conscious that John left town a couple of days ago?" sounds rather strange—almost as though one was doubting the mental state of the friend. Further, the use of the word 'conscious' in that question need not imply one or more things to be alert to. It is quite otherwise with the word 'aware.' It puts one on notice that here is an event which needs attention; indeed, it might imply something dangerous as though one were standing at the edge of a precipice. It is this sense of the word 'aware' that has the most far reaching significance for the practice of self-inquiry. Self-inquiry recognizes two aspects of awareness; the first has to do with practice and the second with the natural state of human nature as distinguished from its dysfunctions. Unfortunately, it is human nature's dysfunctions which, for the minds of many, appear to be the fundamental character of human nature itself.

On pondering awareness from the side of practice it is helpful to consider the etymology of the word 'aware.' The root of the word means to guard, protect, preserve, pay heed to, give watchful attention to. Here we have moved afield from an emphasis on knowing which the word 'conscious' expresses.

On the field of practice, then, to be aware is to guard, watch over, to heed what needs protecting, preserving through watchfully attending it. This recalls the words of Lao Tzu: "Know the masculine, guard the feminine."[2]   The name of his book, *Tao Te Ching*, is variously translated, *The Way and Its Power* or *The Way of Life* among others. What is cogent here for the practice of self-inquiry is the Chinese word '*tê*' which is usually translated 'virtue' but whose primitive meaning is 'knack.' Accordingly, we may translate the name of the work as "*The Book of the Knack of the Way*."

Knack has something magical about it. It goes beyond skill and strength. Strength without skill misses the mark and skill without strength cannot reach it. Neither skill nor strength nor their combination is equal to the unexpected. Only knack is equal to that contingency. Knack is purely intuitive. When someone brings off an action seemingly impossible to execute, we say "Oh, well, she has a way with her" or "He has a way with him." This is a fair description but explains nothing.

Knack is an immediate response to primal intuition, that negative summons from within, that Socrates said always told him what *not* to do, never what *to* do. Obedience to that inward negative command requires absolute trust since there is no further instruction on what will happen if primal intuition's warning is disobeyed. Yet, miraculously, it is precisely the unexpected that is met harmlessly, creatively when the warning is obeyed. The effects of knack are easily discerned from athletics to state-craft. Unlike strength, knack cannot be trained and unlike skill, it cannot be learned. We call knack a gift, a grace, since we do not know the source of it nor can we control it.

Knackful performance at its most exact is not expected of everyone. We tend to feel an unhappy admiration for those superlatively gifted with knack. This painful admiration is the better side of envy since admiration arises innocently from wonder and astonishment. Yet the unhappiness stems from a grudging sense that something is going on here that is not quite fair. If knack cannot be earned since it is a sheer gift, why has it not been apportioned to

---

[2] Lao Tzu, *Tao Te Ching*, ch 28.

each and all equally? Speculations on this question are various and some far reaching yet remain empirically inconclusive.

Ironically this unhappy admiration hides within it a hint of its real basis. It is only human knack that we envy. Superlatively knackful performances in other creatures we regard as incomparable to our own. We do not envy the strength of the lion or the grace of the gazelle. We envy human knack precisely because we sense that there is something genuinely comparable between my deficiency of knack and the other human person's sheer display of it. The adjective sheer points up a radical feature of knack since it derives from an Old English word meaning clear, bright; hence pure, sole; hence transparent, perpendicular.[3]

Knack enjoys the absolute quality of being without admixture of any kind. It is free from process, increase or decrease whether of intensity, as with light, or of duration as with time. This characteristic situates it upon the vertical axis of instantaneity, the moment, the instant which Kierkegaard called "an atom of eternity."

At this point one might be asking what on earth has knack to do with awareness. It has everything to do with it precisely because unlike its special embodiment in psycho-physical performance which is particular to gifted individuals, genuine self-inquiry energizes the gift of primal intuition which is no respecter of persons. All have it equally. It might be objected that not everyone is in a state of readiness to listen to it. The objection is beside the point since the matter at hand is one of nature, availability and not use. Likewise, we do not hold that a human baby is by nature less human for not yet being an adult. Primal intuition is available to all, though not all may be ready to receive it. That inability is a privation and perhaps in some cases a deprivation. But it is not an essential feature of human nature. On the contrary, primal intuition is an essential feature of human nature.

Now we come to the heart of the matter. Response to primal intuition's warning *not* to act is *instantaneous* whether that response

---

[3] Eric Partridge, *Origins: A Short Etymological Dictionary of Modern English*.

is in accord or dis-accord with it. Calculative reason can have no part in it since there is no known objective or goal to envision and plan toward. To heed primal intuition's warning *not* to act is precisely the knack of obedience to the necessary in oneself. This necessity is not a private possession. This obedience secures one's freedom. True freedom is not having to choose.

Awareness of primal intuition is a matter of attitude, not of will. It is not from will but from attitude that preference, choice and decision follow automatically as night the day. Attitude is our sole responsibility. When one is attitudinally attuned to primal intuition, identifying with one's idea of oneself, even one's felt self presence, vanishes completely. It is the quality of attitude that distinguishes the sage from the unsagely. When this is realized the Neo-Confucian description of the sage comes clear, namely, that the sage is in accord with his nature and acts with ease.[4]

Obedience to the necessary in oneself is not conformity to representational definitions of human nature such as man is the symbol using animal or the tool maker. Clearly, one's nature is the necessary in oneself but it is never revealed in abstraction. It is always becoming discovered in the moment, instant by instant as one obediently accords with one's nature through the most attentive listening to one's inner voice of primal intuition.

Now we may return full circle to the root of the word 'aware' which means to be on guard, watch over, to heed what needs protecting, preserving through watchfully attending it. We now ask, what is it that needs guarding?

Between the experiencer (subject) and the experienced (object) lies the possibility of self-misunderstanding. The experiencer, the subject, can identify with the object experienced and also identify with his or her own self-conception. As either or both of these self-misunderstandings obtain, the pure acts of listening and witnessing are corrupted. This condition is described biblically in the well known statement, having eyes to see and seeing not, having ears to

---

[4] Chu Hsi, *Reflections on Things at Hand: The Neo-Confucian Anthology*, trans. Wing-Tsit Chan, p. 8.

hear and hearing not. [Ez 12:2; Mt 13:13-14; Mk 4:12; Lk 8:10] Yet, the possibility of self-misunderstanding is the indispensable condition for self-awakening. Endemic to our human species is the actualization of this possibility for self misunderstanding so that if self-awakening is to occur this spiritual pathology must be negated.

Any pure act of attention is immune from the possibility or actuality of self-misunderstanding since one cannot be both self-consciously and at the same time single mindedly attending to whatever is at hand. A pure act of attention annihilates distraction whether through identifying with oneself as the experiencer or through an emotional collapse into the object experienced. Krishnamurti puts this exactly in his phrase "observing without the observer."

How is it that on hearing these words and grasping their meaning theoretically one so easily fails to embody them in conduct? It is because this negation must obtain upon every instant since every instant brings with it the unexpected. Clearly, one cannot attend to instants, instant by instant, in succession. Only attitude can relieve one of such a burden, an attitude of vigilance against throwing oneself away to the distraction of the moment or recklessly attacking it with the ambition to control it. Either movement makes matters worse.

We are now in a position to answer our question: what is it that needs guarding? It is our natural state, our original innocence whose voice is primal intuition.

The field of action, the home-ground of practice, is where the unity of striving and consequence plays itself out both grossly and subtly. Gross action is a matter of displacement, the movement of body, a transposition. Subtle action pertains to attitude, not to external movement. Essential action is a change of heart. With a change of heart the quality of one's being changes and that attracts a different level of life. The eye that sees externals only cannot perceive a change of heart. On seeing no gross displacement, no transposition or transportation, it thinks itself in the presence of inaction only. On that account the *Bhagavad Gītā* [4:18] states that the wise one sees action in inaction and inaction in action. The essence of action is the leap from self-misunderstanding to self-awareness.

This leap does not fall under the illusion of agency by which one imagines oneself the *doer* of the action. On the contrary, the mark of self-awareness is the awakening to it that one is not the doer of the action. The illusion of agency is the result of attachment to egoic activity. This attachment imagines itself the doer and controller of action through superimposing its self-misunderstanding upon the unconditioned self. Since the unconditioned self is not another existent but being itself, it cannot be an object. It is the unconditioned subject of all objects and objectifications beyond any split between subject and object.

Awareness is of the very nature of the unconditioned self, changeless, primordial, groundless, undivided and uncaused. It is the *light* in which the duality of subject and object play out their scenarios in the whole drama of coming to be and passing away. It is in this sense that incorruptible awareness abides between the experiencer and the experienced as the pure witness of our roles in the flux of existence.[5] Awareness also transcends its residence between experiencer and experienced. It is aware of the universal field of consciousness but consciousness cannot be conscious of awareness. Only through a supra-relational intuition is awareness apprehended—never comprehended. Awareness remains entirely independent of our apprehensions of it.

Awareness and Consciousness

The inherent duality in consciousness declares itself unmistakably in the etymology of the word 'consciousness,' as con+sciousness, L. *con*, together, and *scisere*, to seek to know; thus, to seek to know together, a shared knowing. The seeking to know betrays the affective, the emotional element within consciousness. The ever seeking to know bespeaks a felt need that seeks its satisfaction. It implies that consciousness is not its own goal. But how could it be since consciousness is in time? If

---

[5] Sri Nisargadatta Maharaj, *I Am That*, tr. Maurice Frydman, p. 14.

consciousness seeks its fulfillment within itself, time will rob it of its object for time entails process and process has beginning, middle and end. Temporal process cannot provide the end, the goal that consciousness desires, which is to be self-luminous. For that it would need to be independent of time. Consciousness cannot be independent of time since it is tied to change. Its luminosity is borrowed from awareness. Consciousness shares its reflected light with its object. Its object being subject to change within the flux of existence, consciousness can find no abiding ground within its partner. Since consciousness is within time, it cannot find an abiding ground within its own nature either. It remains totally dependent on awareness for whatever light it enjoys. To make matters even more humbling for it, it cannot be conscious of awareness though awareness is ever aware of consciousness.[6] On that account timeless awareness appears to time-bound consciousness as unconscious.

I am aware that this view of consciousness differs from that of modern philosophy and psychology both of which often have tended toward absolutizing consciousness by regarding it as wholly other than its object. But consciousness is not independent of being any more than its object is incapable of being known. Consciousness and its object oppose one another dialectically not absolutely. Neither consciousness nor being is an ultimate principle. They presuppose a third principle whose ultimacy makes consciousness or knowledge able to know and being able to be known.[7] This ultimacy is awareness. Awareness is of the very nature of Reality. In the sixth book of the *Republic*, Plato calls this ultimate principle the Good which, he says, is beyond being surpassing it in dignity and power. [*Republic* 6.509C]

The way to this great intuition is not found through argument or publicly verifiable experiment. Plato found it in the life and teaching of his master Socrates who said, "I know that I do not know." Some would say that the statement is contradictory since to know that one does not know is still a knowing. This superficial misapprehension

---

[6] Ibid., 263.
[7] Erich Frank, *Philosophical Understanding and Religious Truth*, 115n.

of the sentence is typical of the modern mind whose attitude and mode of analysis is without a sense of wonder. The medieval and ancient approach to the sentence would trust the last half of the statement, "I do not know," as indeed the case. That being so, the word 'know,' in the first half of the statement would be understood differently. The spirit of this Socratic statement comes clearer if we render it "I am aware that I do not know."

This rendering not only suits the Socratic attitude but implies the function of awareness on both its near and far sides. On the near side it illuminates the dialectical tension *between* experiencer and experienced, knowledge and its object. It guards against their confusion and conflation and their imagined independence from each other. On the far side, awareness in its beyondness is the effulgent source making consciousness possible as the illuminated object of awareness itself.

This perspective on the *borderline* between awareness and consciousness brings into clearer relief how it is that the possibility of self-misunderstanding is the indispensable pre-requisite for self-awakening. Consciousness both bears and obstructs the light of awareness. Insofar as it obstructs the light through misunderstanding its derivative nature and role it nonetheless remains potentiated to realize its natural state as transparent to awareness. Yet insofar as it is open to the irradiation of awareness it cannot abide in this illumination without constant earnestness, vigilance, and testing in action so as to distinguish between reality and fantasia. Sri Nisargadatta Maharaj explains the need for testing: "How do you know you have realized unless you watch your thoughts and feelings, words and actions and wonder at the changes occurring in you without your knowing why or how? It is exactly because they are so surprising that you know that they are real. The foreseen and expected is rarely true."[8] Genuine self-inquiry says amen to that.

Awareness does not coerce self-awakening. One can remain in self-misunderstanding indefinitely. Equally, realization is not a

---

[8] Sri Nisargadatta Maharaj, op. cit., p. 400.

static state but as noted above requires constant testing. However, it is not action that removes self-misunderstanding since action is not opposed to it. Whether unrealized or realized the possibility of self-misunderstanding obtains and is therefore to be negated instant by instant through sound attitude. The dependency of consciousness upon abiding awareness is a permanent feature of its nature. Its strength is in its ability to become changed; its weakness is that it is not self-correcting.

Bearing

The two previous sections have laid a preliminary groundwork toward further inquiry into bearing which was introduced in last year's paper on Inner Transformation and Bearing.

To bear is to hold up from a position beneath; therefore the English word, uphold. It means also to carry, especially to carry from below as in the word support. The word offer is another in the family of bearing. The Latin *ob* + *ferre* means to bring before, i.e., to present a gift, to sacrifice. Here we are in a different mode of reciprocity from giving and taking. Giving and taking can be quite mechanical. Offering and receiving presuppose an emotional link between the one who offers and the one who receives. Essentially, to offer is to present freely; to receive is to accept gratefully.

In earlier times when existence was approached with religious awe and philosophical wonder it was possible to share a meditation on offering and receiving while fully confident that the sentiment for them was abidingly alive and intact. Unfortunately, this is no longer the case. Our attitude toward technology has changed all that. It is an attitude that has deadened our sensitivity toward the unprecedented and unexpected which are the hallmarks of Reality. Today we boast easily that we are captains of our souls and masters of our fate. Haven't we gone to the moon and back, the moon which was once ignorantly thought to be a goddess? Now we know it is only a ball of stone and dust. It is just a matter of time before our technical skill will emancipate us from all the ills that flesh is heir to.

Such an attitude is rife among the so called developed countries—technologically developed, that is—and hardens with each oncoming generation. A very large number of those who cry out for environmental reform call only for a saner use of technology. But who has ever persuaded insanity to become sane? No doubt Mother Nature will have the last word, yet her word will not be persuasive but punitive.

Is it any wonder then that the category of bearing is so hard to communicate in our time? Bearing has two faces. On the near side, on the side of becoming, bearing has to do with behavior, how one carries oneself, disposition and its embodiment in gesture and conduct. On the far side, the side of being, bearing is a permanent feature of existence itself. As such, bearing does not change. This face of bearing reveals that all things bear from stone to star. Within the flux of existence, the stream of coming to be and passing away generates and wears away every individual being according to the term of its natural career. No matter how tenaciously any individual holds to its natural form, that embodiment of its identity bears the steady dissolution of its flowering. It must bear the tension between its unfolding and its fall.

Many nondualists are fond of declaring that this phenomenon is of no matter since it is all illusory. The only thing that matters is to awaken to it that one is not one's body but the unconditioned self. Curiously, they overlook it that one needs the body with all its frailties, let alone charms, to find that out. Losing their footing on the ground, they ascend like a helium balloon into the sky of pure abstraction. This paralyzes earnestness, perseverance, resolution and courage which function within the fissure between awareness and consciousness where the drama of bearing is played out. Only on the integrity of this drama is consciousness guarded against an unstable career and raised to an ever higher level of quality and power.

To speak of the fissure between awareness and consciousness where the drama of bearing is played out is not to contradict the great aphorism that "nothing was divided and there is nothing to unite." On the contrary, it is to hold in mind at the same time another Asian Indian sage's admonition: "Keep the truth of non-duality ever at heart: never should you translate non-duality into action."[9]

The cleft, the abyss, the narrow pass between the nonduality of awareness and the duality of consciousness is one of function not of substance. Without that chasm there can be no flow of manifested being where phenomena arise and fall according to their appointed destinies. There can be no such thing as action without duality. Once a great baseball player advised hilariously and with ironic wit: "When you come to a fork in the road, take it!"[10]

Self-awakening entails the clear realization that while action is not the realization, it is action that validates it. One awakens to the unconditioned self within a supra-relational intuition. However, earnestness, perseverance, resolution and courage do not drop away. Wisdom and love are required for testing on the field of action the difference between reality and fantasy. Since the essence of action is attitudinal, the tester, the tested and the matrix of testing are within. The drama abides immune from the illusion that one is the doer of the action. One no longer takes the world personally.

A nineteenth century English poet, Algernon Charles Swinburne wrote some remarkable lines in his play *Atalanta in Calydon*. Though highly renowned in his time, our own century has not shown him the same degree of respect. I shall quote a stanza from his play which I find bears the mark of seership though Swinburne was not a sage. Perhaps the lines exhibit those flashes of intuition that come unbidden to poets in the course of their more typical works. Here are the lines:

> Before the beginning of years
> There came to the making of man
> Time, with a gift of tears;
> Grief, with a glass that ran;

---

[9] Sri Ramana Maharshi, Supplement to 40 Verses on Existence, #39. *Ramana Maharshi and His Philosophy of Existence* by T.M.P. Mahadevan, p. 137.
[10] Yogi Berra, *When You Come to a Fork in the Road, Take It!*

> Pleasure, with pain for leaven;
> Summer, with flowers that fell;
> Remembrance fallen from heaven,
> And madness risen from hell;
> Strength without hands to smite
> Love that endures for a breath
> Night, the shadow of light,
> And life, the shadow of death.[11]

One of our 20th century's most celebrated poets, T.S. Eliot, had only this to say of this passage: 'That it is effective because it appears to be a tremendous statement, like the statements made in our dreams; when we wake up we find that "the glass that ran" would do better for time than for grief, and that the "gift of tears" would be as appropriately bestowed by grief as by time.'[12] Clearly, on reading these lines, the intuition of the functional cleft between the infinite and the finite, the eternal and the temporal, the necessary and the free quite escaped him.

These lines empathically disclose Swinburne's sensitivity to the category of bearing. Time, he says, comes with its gift of tears *before* the beginning of years. Time's dwelling then is somehow within the timeless, so that out of this timeless dwelling arises a gift of tears. Our tears are offered to us from a source infinitely deeper than a mood whether of joy or sorrow. It is grief, not our tears, that time sets a limit upon. The hour glass runs out. The last verse of the stanza, "And life the shadow of death" seems rather mad and opposed to common sense. Yet, it is not so on recalling that consciousness, in its own power, cannot be conscious of awareness even though awareness is aware of consciousness. Awareness must appear to consciousness as a nothing or death, unless awareness irradiates it.

---

[11] Swinburne, *Atalanta in Calydon; and Lyrical Poems*, selected by William Sharp, p. 45.
[12] Quoted by Henry Treese, *A Selection of Poems by Algernon Charles Swinburne*, ed. H. Treese, p. 15

The drama of bearing's career is played out between the primordial changelessness of awareness and the shifting character of consciousness. Precisely as consciousness bears opening itself to awareness by letting go of its self-identified attachments, it discovers the beatitude of the non-measuring mind.

Primal Intuition and Bearing
November 27, 1997

This is the fourth in a series of meditative papers that I have presented to our Conferences concerned in the search for new paradigms.

The change of name from "paradigms of science" to "new human paradigms" implies for me a sharper focus upon the question of human nature. It is abundantly clear that if human behavior does not undergo a profound transformation we will either extinguish ourselves or reduce ourselves to a level of barbarity unknown to history. How could it be otherwise when we have it in our power technologically to destroy ourselves and our home, the planet Earth?

Shifts in paradigms, when subscribed to by a mass population, do in fact alter human behavior but there is a gulf between alteration and transformation. Alteration manifests a change *in* will whereas transformation requires a change *of* will. John Dewey makes this distinction in his essay, *A Common Faith*. I wish to adopt it here. Shifts in styles of behavior span the whole spectrum from fashion to variations in custom and tradition from one era to another. It would be downright foolish to infer from such alterations that what we call "a change of heart" is required for the alterations to occur. Shifts in group and mass behavior have gone on since time out of mind and will no doubt continue to prevail as modifications of the collective will.

On the other hand a deep change of heart in the individual person does effect a change *of* will but such a transformation invariably exacts a social price. Mass behavior is a behavior of conformity and has little tolerance for exceptions to it. Some individuals who have undergone a deep change of heart persevere in their new way of life despite the sometimes severe ostracism which their social group imposes.

Many years ago a university student of mine underwent a profound change of heart that put him at odds with what his family had planned for him socially and career wise. He decided he wanted to build his life from within out rather than simply reflect a way of life his parents and close friends kept persuading him to adopt.

One day he came to my office and announced: "I've decided to go away clear across the country and build a new life for myself. I want to furnish my new apartment with things that touch my heart rather than with what is the fashion now. And I want to study how to come to know myself. But my mother especially and my close friends think I'm ready for the little man in the white coat. But I'm not really crazy. What do you think?"

I said, "If you are truly serious about making this one hundred and eighty degree turn about you will do it anyway and whatever I might think or say is quite beside the point. But to answer your question, I'm 100% on your side. You will never regret being true to yourself. So go to it."

It wasn't long before a very angry mother came to see me, her jaw tightly set. "What have you done to my James, encouraging him in this madness?" And she went on at length lecturing me on my obligation to teach young people social responsibility instead of subverting all her son had been brought up to respect. When finally she stopped to draw a long breath I asked her, "Do you want James to become authentically himself or just a carbon copy of what others want him to become?" "Well of course I want the best for my son" she said. "He has an older brother who also went away. He lives in Hawaii now and is a very successful practicing dentist. Why can't James be like his brother?" She was a bright woman and in a few seconds she saw the contradiction in her question. Then she brought the conversation to an end with "Oh well, perhaps you're right, I'll just have to let James do what he wants. But why did such a dreadful thing have to happen to me??"

I have recounted this real life incident to distinguish between a change *of* will from a change *in* will. James underwent a change *of* will by obeying his inner voice which did not tell him what to do but rather what not to do. It simply warned him against trying to become something other than what he was by nature. It warned him against self-betrayal. His mother, however, underwent only a change *in* will. She superficially resigned herself to her son's wishes without understanding them or even wanting to. Unlike her son she underwent no genuine transformation but only an alteration of behavior from an outwardly and inwardly hostile mother to only an inwardly disapproving one. This change *in* will cannot bring her closer to James nor James to herself. In this matter they will remain life-time strangers unless and until James' mother undergoes a change *of* will which is the natural expression of awaking from self-misunderstanding.

The story illustrates the role and meaning of what I call primal intuition which is a warning from one's inner voice against self-betrayal. This inner voice from primal intuition is most apt to go unheeded when the social price for obedience to it seems too high to pay. But that calculation remains ignorant of what Pascal taught us, namely, that the heart has its reasons which the head can never know. Later, when hindsight proves we should have obeyed we most often complain, "If only I had listened to myself!" Later on in this meditation I shall further develop the concept of primal intuition and its relation to change *of* will.

Change *of* will is never a mass phenomenon. Two world scriptures, the Gospel and the *Bhagavad Gītā* make this very point. In the Gospel, Jesus is recorded as saying that the way that leads to life is one which only few find.[Mt 7:14] In the Hindu scripture, the *Bhagavad Gītā*, the Lord Krishna says that among thousands perhaps one strives for perfection and, among those, perhaps one knows Him in very truth. [7:3]

Down through the centuries both these scriptures have deeply affected social behavior within their respective religious traditions. Christians and Hindus have undergone uncounted changes *in* will especially within the form of movements that have dominated collective behavior from time to time. At peak moments in the career of such movements, the collective will is so unified that followers will claim that a glorious new era has dawned and, now that people are of one mind, social, political, economic and religious conflicts are becoming a thing of the past. During such so-called "good times" the emotional collapse into these external conditions can produce a mindlessness that is impervious to any invitation to a change *of* will; it is now believed that the new condition proves that a change *of* will has indeed taken place so that to bring the subject up is redundant. But, since all things pass and nothing stays, new wars break out and the cycle begins again. One thinks of the French proverb: The more it changes the more it remains the same.

About 200 years ago an idea exploded within western civilization that has had the most far reaching consequences for not only the west; since then it has spread worldwide. It was the idea of progress for humanity as a whole, a progress promising a secular liberation for all human beings.

Earlier centuries thought of progress as largely an individual matter depending on one's gifts and luck. Given normal intelligence, one was expected to advance from naïve childhood to the wisdom of old age. It was thought that the human condition had historically changed for the worse. The Golden Age was in the far reaches of the past and not expected in the future. If the human condition were to be liberated from its wretched state it would have to be by divine supervention one that would bring the worldly world to a cataclysmic end.

Modern western societies no longer hold that view. Now it is expected that our children's future will be better than our present and made possible through collective ingenuity, i.e., through socially organized scientific inquiry. We now operate under the notion that the advances in experimental science are the technical shoulders upon which our children can stand and their children after them. In short, this attitude within socially organized scientific inquiry promises an unlimited progress from one material glory to another. As for emotional and religious sensibilities, these too are believed equally subject to experimental science and control. This conviction has produced one of the greatest collective changes *in* will known to history.

Under the spell of this linear and utopian projection who pauses to consider the fatal flaw within it? It remains incorrigibly the case that every newborn must travel the road to wisdom on the strength of self-inquiry alone independent of inherited knowledge. The grim fact is that knowledge does not and cannot teach one how to handle it.

It is precisely the enigma of the handling of knowledge that is the Achilles' heel of depth psychology's dream to become counted as one among the experimental sciences. Experimental science depends for its validation upon publicly verifiable measure. Depth psychology is vulnerable to the simple fact that the will cannot be measured.

Certainly psychiatrists and clinicians can persuade their patients and clients to a change *in* will but not to a change *of* will. This is because a change *of* will entails a psychological death to one's ideas of oneself and self-presence. Zen has a useful phrase for this: the dropping of body and mind. The Psalmist prays, "Create in me a clean heart..."[Ps 51:10] The Hebrew word for create here is a verb used for the agency of God only—as different from making, forming, fashioning which are within human power.

We are the inheritors of one of the most extensive changes *in* will that history displays. I refer to the 18th century movement called the Enlightenment. The Enlightenment attempted to substitute rationality for the irrational sentiments that supported and promoted traditional social, political and religious ideas. Its theological movement was Deism which denied any supernatural interference with the laws of the universe. The Enlightenment gave credence to what then and since has been called natural religion.

The clockwork universe cannot accommodate true prayer, miracles nor any divine interference in its mechanical career.

The enormous impetus which the Enlightenment gave to socially organized scientific inquiry has realized itself in that principle of knowledge called rational empiricism, the backbone of experimental science to which we owe so much for our material and technological progress.

The mistake of the Enlightenment was to set off against each other the rational and irrational without allowing for a third principle, the non-rational. I refer the non-rational to phenomena which do not depend for their expression on the rational nor are they frustrated by the irrational. The highest expression of the non-rational is the awaking from self-bondage to freedom from all experience. This is the true enlightenment which, as such, is not an experience at all.

A contemporary movement, another expression of a change *in* will, identifies itself as *New Age*. Within its rhetoric one hears and reads again and again the phrase "enlightenment experience." This phrase also recurs in relatively current interpretations of Buddhist and Hindu non-dualist thought and practice. The phrase is repeated often in D. T. Suzuki's works, that master pioneer in the introduction of Zen to the west. I was relieved to hear from a fellow faculty member, himself a Buddhist, that toward the close of his life Suzuki retracted the words.

The Buddha's name translates literally to Awakened. There is no implication in it or reference to experience. The concept, experience, implies the division between experiencer and experienced and genuine enlightenment is free from bondage to duality. However, this freedom from bondage is not the opposite of bondage, an opposite colliding with it on the same plane. Enlightenment transcends the world while still operating in the world or, as the Taoists say, while still within the dragon's pool and the tiger's lair. Since Reality or (as it is sometimes called) the really real is neither an event nor an experience, how can there be an experiencer of what is not other or an event?

Enlightenment is awaking to the light of original nature and original innocence which are not private possessions. Unenlightenment is the misunderstanding that I am the sole possessor independently and privately of my own nature and I project this upon all others. Enlightenment is liberation from that misunderstanding. It is observing without the observer, listening without the listener, scenting without the scenter, tasting without the taster, touching without the toucher, thinking without the thinker, realizing without the realizer.

Now those words are apt to be misunderstood. I am not saying that the personality plays no authentic role, that the personal is a figment of imagination, an inference made by many professed non-dualists. The inference, though sincere is hasty. Because a thing comes to be and passes away does not make it unreal. It is real as long as it lasts. To observe without the observer is not to discount the personality as unreal. It is, rather, to drop one's imaginary standpoint from which one's own self is believed to be an irreducible unit of being over against all others. In this artificial light the others of whatever kind are inferred to be equally isolated from oneself and each other. It is not difficult to understand how Freud built a whole psychology on the fantasy of the essential alienation of human nature. He can hardly be blamed for making such an inference on looking at human behavior at large. Estrangement is indeed one of the principal marks of the human condition. Yet this standpoint has a fatal flaw. It cannot answer the question of how, despite the alienation, things somehow continue to hold together.

The subject of enlightenment is not any such isolated unit of being. It is abiding original nature itself, the substrate of all beings and it is not a private possession. On that account there can be no such entity as a self who comes to be and passes away who is enlightened. The Buddha, the Enlightened One is called Buddha not because he, a person who lived and died gained something, as though the historical man, Siddhartha Gautama, captured the most elusive quarry in the world. On the contrary Siddhartha lost something, namely, his self-misunderstanding that he was by nature this irreducibly alienated unit of being situated among others likewise estranged.

There is no rational route to enlightenment. Indeed, one can reason one's way to apprehending the limits of reason but enlightenment is not at the end of a line, it is not a terminus but a consummation. There is a rational preparation for enlightenment but to prepare for a thing is not sufficient to bring it about. The advent of enlightenment is neither rational nor irrational. It is non-rational.

The second example of the non-rational is primal intuition itself. Its voice arises from the level of original nature which is not a private possession. It is the inner warning against action that is untimely. Estimated by that measure most of human action is untimely. We are most often either too early or too late. I am not referring here to clock time but to the passage of destiny. Destiny as the ideal measure for one's passage from birth to and through death can be failed. Realizing one's destiny adequately is a matter not of mechanical but of living time, the time for advance or withdrawal within any life situation.

Timing in this sense is not difficult to understand in the light of such common statements as "I don't know why, but I felt it was not time to go forward, so I waited against, as it seemed, all reason." This is an example of what Socrates meant when he claimed that he had a daimon, a spirit, a voice that always told him what not to do—never what *to* do. Hindsight invariably bears out the wisdom of such timely action but to intuit what not to do at the time as a case of primal intuition carries with it no explanation why one should obey this negative summons. This is its embarrassment to calculative reason and why it seems unreasonable to our acquired conditioning.

It is always within the context of acquired conditioning that one hears the voice of primal intuition and obedience to it enables transcending the world while yet in it. Acceptance of this reversal of standpoint from self-misunderstanding to total trust in life's benevolent power to live my life rather than my trying to live it out of a "head-trip" constitutes a change *of* will.

So far, I have suggested two ways of our seeing ourselves in the world. One establishes itself upon the standpoint of self-estrangement which grasps the environment as essentially hostile toward my efforts at self-determination. On the whole, tradition and so called conventional wisdom are less friend than enemy and I envision freedom as an escape from the dead hand of custom and the inherited acquired conditioning over the centuries. This places the full burden of decision taking upon the isolated individual and the finite mind which can never take the full scope of existence in view let alone in hand. This handicap promotes a full scale conflict of motives.

On the other hand, the standpoint of primal intuition rests upon original nature and original innocence which are not problematic as our contrivances and projections necessarily are. In the practical order primal intuition's challenge for me is obedience to it. Under its counsel I have no need to try to take the whole in view nor to attempt a titanic control of things. It is enough to hear what not to do within the flow of instants each one of which carries always with it the unexpected and unpredictable. Now the true vocation of intellect can be enjoyed which is to discern relations and their character. Obedience to primal intuition is a matter of intelligence which we share with all beings. The confusion between intellect and intelligence is still one of the hallmarks of our human species. This confusion promotes what we sadly call the human condition.

In the practical order the chief mark of intelligence is timing within one's lived space—whether to advance or withdraw to say nothing of holding one's ground before the abyss of groundlessness—a subject for another time. Wild animals appear to have perfect access to primal intuition, a phenomenon which we carelessly attribute to instinct. Instinct is propulsive. Primal intuition is creatively inhibitive. An example of obedience to primal intuition is well portrayed in Carlos Castaneda's novels on the teachings of the Yaqui Indian sage, don Juan. One day his apprentice remarked that if the old sage were walking down the road and someone hidden from view aiming at him through a telescopic could indeed kill him. The old man instantly agreed but added that the difference was he would not show up.[1] It is not the sorcerer's magic powers that protect him from certain death but unquestioning obedience to primal intuition. He does not need to know why at that time he should not go down that road. It is enough to obey the warning against it. An intelligent response. Here it is timing, not cerebration, that decides the saving outcome. Clearly, as a commentary on the Confucian Classic of Change, the *I Ching* says: "The only thing that matters is that things should happen at the right time."[2] Obedience to timing, not cerebrating, decides the fullness of life.

Obedience of this order is the foundation of bearing since it is humanly difficult to bear obeying a directive for which no reason is offered in advance. Hindsight might supply it but hindsight cannot illumine the present. This is a human suffering deeper than the universal suffering that all flesh is heir to. Such obedience requires absolute trust, confidence and love. None of these is self-serving. I mean by suffering the bearing, the undergoing of a natural tension. Insofar as this tension is natural it is not a dysfunction. Still, it entails continuing attuning, vigilance, alertness, courage, resolution, compassion and patience. One is not forced to embody these in conduct. However, when attunement is neglected it exacts a heavy price: an abiding restlessness, anxious worry and a sense of futility.

This occurs precisely when the misrelation between personality and impersonal original nature befalls the individual. To be healed from this misrelation is not a matter of discarding personality in favor of original nature. Personality is a natural expression of original nature. The misrelation occurs when the individual human being takes the world personally. This dysfunction occurs when the individual measures his or her own existence through the medium of his or her own personality. It is a simple error of perspective and a slackening of attention.

---

[1] Carlos Castaneda, *A Separate Reality, Further Conversations with Don Juan*, p. 220f. (As to whether Don Juan is fictional or real is of no significance here.)
[2] Wilhelm/Baynes, *The I Ching*, p. 591.

From the time we are born into this human world our development, training and education are an acquired conditioning from which there is no escape. Social efforts to escape it in the form of attempted utopias, revolutions, separatist communities never succeed in leaving it all behind. The problem with any vacation is that I must take myself along, too.

Since acquired conditioning is inescapable, self-examination must take place within it. How? By undertaking a reversal. Instead of measuring things by my idea of myself plus whatever others think of me, instead of seeing things and attending them through my bundle of moods and motives I can let the time for action or inaction announce itself rather than my calculatively contriving it and attempting to force the future. Primal intuition naturally heeds the time and unfailingly announces when not to advance or not to withdraw. This shift of responsibility from my attempted cleverness and manipulative contrivance takes not only the world off my shoulders but even more liberatingly relieves me of my idea of myself and all the fantasies that it entails.

It is the irony of the history of religions and the wisdom traditions of all cultures that every one of them has phrases that point to and describe this reversal yet the number of individuals who attempt this reversal is exceedingly small.

I have preferred in this paper to leave extra time and space for questions, answers and mutual explorations. In short, to leave a time for sharing the unlonely aloneness of standing upon the threshold of that reversal which each must tread alone.

Part III
University Lectures

These are combined transcriptions of notes two students made of a course Dr. Anderson gave on Krishnamurti in 1979. The course was based on the video series 'A Wholly Different Way of Living' which records the 18 dialogues Prof. Anderson had with Krishnamurti.

In order to understand the discussions, it is important to view each video or read the transcript of the dialogue along with the class discussion. The bracketed note [Video—Title] shows when the video was watched in the class. The video titles provided in these notes were the ones used in the book compiled from the videos. However, later publication of the videos used sometimes different titles. For reference, footnotes in the following text provide titles under which the videos are currently published.

While it is possible that students made errors during transcription, two different transcriptions were compared carefully and all discrepancies were resolved. Any errors are the editor's.

Knowledge and the Transformation of Man
January 30, 1979

In 1974 I made 18 video tapes in conversation with Krishnamurti. We'll have the advantage of seeing the living character of his message. The series was made toward the end of his being given an opportunity on this medium to state what it was in the round. The producer (a devotee) scheduled 20 sessions. When we got to 18, Krishnamurti asked whether I thought we needed to go on. I said it wasn't for me to say. He said, "I want to know from *you*." He is always anxious for the other to say what is on his mind. I could hardly ignore his insistence. It did seem to me that there was nothing more to touch on, though much more to expand upon. So we stopped at 18.

[Video—Dialogue I: Knowledge and the Transformation of Man[1]]

When he said, "I met you yesterday" he was recounting an historical fact. It was the first time I'd met him. He is disinclined to undertake small talk. When introduced, he looked steadily at me and asked, "What is truth?" I looked at him, it was clear he expected a reply. I made an attempt after two or three seconds (it's amazing how *long* two or three seconds can be): "Truth is what is the case." It pleased him, fortunately. I added, "the case" because the word 'is' [by itself] seems to embarrass rather than help. We got on famously after that. Why do you think that pleased him? It's important. 'Is' refers to actuality, and I think we might say a distinguishing mark of

---

[1] Video published by the KFA under the title "Knowledge and Transformation".

his concern is to be always sharply aware of the actual now, not what is likely to be, etc., but what is actually the case now. It has a great deal to do with knowledge and its role. Our relation to knowledge is diseased and it prevents us from knowing what is actual, now.

My primary function throughout is essentially to do two things: 1) to give him an opportunity to say precisely what is on his mind; and 2) to listen to the quality of his language measured by the academy. For example, many academicians write him off as unintelligible. Others, disenchanted, welcome him as an alternative to the way they have been brought up. On the one hand there are those with no interest in him, and on the other, those who identify with him and cut themselves off at the root from their social and educational background. I think he'd regard both positions as lunatic.

The secondary function I felt required to perform when it seemed fruitful was to attempt a translation into language more accessible to those with academic training. This was *not* the purpose of the program however. For example, the formula, "I am the world and the world is me" patently, if one examines it with care, it is not quite as simple as it sounds. Why? On the one hand, he has stated clearly that unless the individual person changes, nothing changes in the world. It seems also to be clear that if one attempts to change the world, one isn't going to get anywhere by applying to the world. So there is a problem with the formula that puts academicians off. Recognizing that it requires clarification is *not* sufficient reason to pay no attention to it. We ought to understand what he's trying to say else we're letting words get in the way of actuality.

In your class work, try to discern intellectually what he's saying, and if some of his constructions seem annoyingly imprecise, you must not allow that to get in the way of what he's saying. Undertake a work of justice with respect to what he brings forward. We should equally avoid collapsing into him. I believe he is saying something of immense significance. I could wish he'd said it more acceptably to the academic mind, but given that misfortune it is not sufficient for any academic to write him off. Find the middle between the devotee and the supercilious critic.

Student: What does Krishnamurti mean by his statement, if I change the world, I'd have to be changed?

A change in you is not effected by your changing the world. It works the other way. While I am undergoing transformation, the world also as I impinge is undergoing change. He seems concerned to express that if I go out and do revolution, it is a sign I haven't changed at all.

Student: I get the impression he uses things like, "I am the world," as a rhetorical device. Is he deliberately trying to overstate the case?

It would be helpful to ask him that. I have the feeling that particular statement is not used merely rhetorically. "The description is not the described," yet "I am the world and the world is me." These statements refer to different orders of being. Some say he is a crypto Buddhist where he says "be a light unto oneself" which recalls the last few words of Buddha: "Ananda, be a lamp unto yourself." Clearly there is a close relation if not a parallel between that aspect of Buddhism and what he wishes to say. It would be unfortunate to attempt that sort of academic classification. It would outrage him, and won't lead us to understand what he's saying. You'll see in future video tapes that he'll say, "I don't know." He doesn't mean he doesn't know anything. He means what Socrates said; he had an advantage because he knew he didn't know. That must be some sort of knowledge, but not an ordinary sort. In part the difficulty is verbal. I must understand that I don't know what in its nature cannot be known, rather than give myself airs I know a little or will be able to creep up on it. It is rare to understand you don't know what can never be known by the finite mind. You can't arrive at that understanding through inference.

I want to lay for you a philosophical basis for the possibility of such dialogue so the course can properly be one in religious studies, not a course in the phenomenology of religion. I'm *not* inviting you to a guided tour of the zoo of religious thought. Try to understand *what* is being said in the interest of a deepening of my understanding of my relation to myself.[2] Involve yourself in what's going on when he's speaking. Ask the questions he's asking of yourself, else you haven't a prayer of understanding, you will not accomplish anything.

In the film when he said, "I've been doing this for 50 years" it was an historical statement in relation to his concern. When he said the same thing at the end of one of the talks with a shrug, he meant something different. There he's saying the actual effect of my teaching is appallingly slight.

Student: Does he teach because he wants to?

Contemplate the character of his vocation. Is it what one *wants* to do? Is it deeper than that?

Your assignment: 1) Keep a journal; 2) read *Flight of the Eagle,* Ch. 1 and Ch. 10; 3) read *Awakening of Intelligence,* "Inner Revolution" chapter.

He uses two words, 'seeing' and 'listening' and I hope you will try to grasp what he's up to. This assignment will give you the opportunity to reflect on the matter he brought to our hearing in this conversation.

Go at your own pace through *Krishnamurti's Notebook*: commune with it joyously. Start your own notebook in relation to your own passage.

Notice the impression he gives when he talks about change of the individual person. Of course any transition is dramatic—it is what we fear most. When we feel ourself specified by anything he has said or drawn to attempt the change he speaks about—put it in the notebook, fast! Some thoughts one can think in one's lifetime only once. This implies there are thoughts worth thinking. If I don't materialize them, I am insofar without remedy because I may never meet them again. Be diligent. Put it on your cuff if you have to (a good test: is it worth a shirt?).

---

[2] Dr. Anderson often switches to the first person as a rhetorical device to encourage the student to question him or herself.—Ed.

The last point might put Krishnamurti off. I don't mean to offend him! There is an ontological aspect: whenever we are confronted with change, there is always something present in it which is unintelligible. Transition is unintelligible. That it can be observed does not imply it is intelligible. I can describe it, but it is of such a character that I cannot grasp it intelligibly—it is a limitation on our being as human. I cannot comprehend transition, though I can apprehend it. Yet unless we are related to it correctly, we endanger ourselves enormously. Think carefully in relation to Krishnamurti's invitation to change: if it is the case that transition is unintelligible, though apprehensible, then we're being asked to do something in the order of the unknown—it must for each be unprecedented.

1. Don't confuse knowledge with understanding.
2. If one is to undergo self change, he must be correct when he says change is independent of knowledge and time if transition is incomprehensible though apprehensible. Nothing frightens us so much as the unknown. Ask yourself if he's not right on target when he says we're always trying to fill it up with the known, with what in no way can take the place of the filler. Yet we're always trying to do it, to fill the yawning chasm that frightens us.

Despite the fact he's not a trained philosopher, he says "we must go into this deeply" and we must. Notice he said knowledge has a place. We must find out what that is so we don't put it where it doesn't belong. Maybe he's saying something we ought to learn, but we won't be able to work it out by cerebration, but only by an increasingly sensitive relation to oneself.

Consider:

1. What is my relation to myself?
2. How am I in relation to myself?
3. What am I doing with the gap between the I and the me?
4. What am I doing with the gap between I and thou?
5. What am I doing with the gap between I and the world?

It comes back to the word "to be." How do I am?

Would it be intelligible to say, "Let's am"? Proceed in that fashion. With some practice in self-examination you will make a start in understanding him, else not. Not because of the relative imprecision of the language, but more importantly because I don't ask the questions seriously of myself. The only questions I ask are about me and what's over there. If there is something I want or don't want, I say I like it and I want it, etc. In recognizing my desire I think I understand my relation to myself. Not so. That's *not* what he's talking about. To come into relation with oneself is not only rare, but on first confrontation, is profoundly frightening. If I don't come into self-relation, nothing will change.

Notice he's not impressed with progress. You heard what he said about evolution: a species of proliferation, which doesn't get to the heart of the matter. Begin to become as sensitive as you can about the relation of oneself to oneself. Statistically it will be quite a phenomenon if you bring it off. So with a shrug, he says, "50 years." See how full of dread it is?

You must do your best in your notebook to distinguish between the heart of it and the babble. What flows out has life in it but it's helpful to rewrite it in a more precise way. This will give insight into Krishnamurti: you can understand him only on a practical level, through act. Of course we don't want it that way. If we have an idea about it, he'll say you're off the subject. What do you think you're doing writing what hasn't been understood?

Make sure, since knowledge has a place, you don't show contempt for a Ph.D.—but since you can't make it on the basis of knowledge and time, don't get confused. It will take some work, we haven't been taught that distinction. So this will be an upper division course in kindergarten.

Knowledge and Conflict in Human Relationships
February 6, 1979

The reason I've asked you to keep a journal is that it is difficult to hold up an authentic mirror to oneself. Our notions of introspection are shallow; practice is difficult but must be undertaken if not with enthusiasm, at least with energy. As a society we are other-directed. Whatever we've had of individualism is being lost. The religious fervor with which we practice leveling is an example of it. We begin our notions of introspection from the point where we say, "I'm in relation to the other." I'm not even aware of being in relation to myself yet. Suppose in doing your assignment you ask yourself: what degree of receptivity am I bringing to myself? To become truly receptive to myself is a rare achievement. I have in my history much that I take for granted. I rarely scrutinize it, or if I do, I use other things taken for granted to do it. To get to the point where one is quite ready to undertake the self-examination is to reach a point which is rarely reached. I mustn't confuse readiness with canvassing my feelings. That is not the point where I begin. There is a radical distinction between registering one thing when I ought to be in a state of readiness to do something different.

Krishnamurti is not easy to travel with because of the razor he uses. He is saying you must use that razor yourself because you *are* the razor. You don't go get one. This is the point of departure for working within his prescription—everything else is useless.

For him there is no in between, there is no way to creep up on what he's asking. My preparation for beginning to do it is not preparation in the ordinary sense but rather a movement from my accustomed position to a new point of departure. This isn't a dialogue in the ordinary sense. You can have a conversation with him, but not in public. He's there to make a statement, not to discuss. I hope you will see the character of my point of departure is one that excludes creeping up on it.

[Video—Dialogue II: Knowledge and Conflict in Human Relationships[1]]

What emerged as his most urgent concern in this dialogue? I think it was the absence of automatic or organic passage from fragmentation to wholeness. There is no evolving from fragmentation to wholeness. On page 60 of *Awakening of Intelligence*, he says "Unless one goes into this matter very seriously, really taking trouble, with deep interest, with passion, I am afraid one will not be able to go very far; far in the sense not of time or space, but very deeply within oneself." i.e. taking pains not to lie to oneself—that's where the pain comes in.

On page 71 of the same book, he says, "Sir, look, this is not an argument, there is nothing to develop." Our culture has a love affair with development; therefore it is increasingly difficult to take a different posture before what is the case. He's asking us to go against our cultural bent. I don't know if we can.

Student: Is it fair to ask?

Yes if it introduces us to wholeness.

Student: If we ask, maybe we are holding ourselves back…

I'm saying I don't know if we can because we lack the will to do so. There is some activity to be performed right *now* that has nothing to do with opening out on development in the future because that act is not bound by necessity to the past. If the past is in all respects

---

[1] Video published by KFA under the title "Knowledge and Human Relationships".

radically necessary, the future cannot change. The past is not conditioned by necessity to that degree, else how could he account for the possibility of the new and the saving act of deliverance? He says, "This isn't an argument" and he means that. He wants neither a development nor a retrogression. (He recognizes there can be no freedom from self-bondage through canvassing personal history; nor do we develop out of disorder into a state of health.) Is Krishnamurti saying that there are marvelous prospects for the future? I don't think he'd advise approaching self-transformation on the basis of the historical perspective of psychoanalysis, nor a five-year plan. He's really inviting us to the present—this instant, and let's face it—few of us have a present. We're oriented to the future. Both capitalism and communism share the view that what's really good lies ahead. He says no! And neither does it lie in the past. Note that the contemplation of a golden age in the past or future doesn't require much seriousness. Neither is involved in the sense of crisis now. Notice how comfortable he felt when I brought up the wild animal. Notice every time I refer to the products of culture he's not too fond of it. Of course I don't stop on that account. Every time I referred to nature there is a profound affirmation from his spirit. Water returning to itself—that's *now*. He wants us to be as alert as a wild animal must be in relation to the environment—that alert in relation to ourselves without dividing ourselves into the observer and observed. We have to see if it is possible. There's only one way to find out: try it! It might increase our confidence to consider that if one person has done it, we too could do it, since we all share a common nature.

There is an apparent dissonance in his writing but I don't think he's confused. Note he will not be shifted—he holds onto his subject with enormous tenacity. He always knows what he wants to say, and always says the same thing, generally in the same way. It requires a certain discipline. We must keep on attempting to make practical applications!

Let us consider the past as such in relation to coming into existence or becoming. That is *not* the same as to be. What has come into existence, become, either is an authentic coming into existence or is simply a repetition. If something really comes into existence then it has appeared, it is present. There must be something about it that has not been, or else it has always been and we are fooling ourselves when we say something is coming to pass! There is an aspect of what is going on that escapes pinning down. It comes when it will and it will pass when it will. We must take into account two observations: "there's nothing new under the sun" [Eccl 1:9]; and what I just said. There seems to be a contradiction. Now, Krishnamurti wants us to relate to the repetitive character of passage without losing our freedom in so doing. So his problem for us is one of the relation between necessity and freedom. He feels sure it admits of solution so that in the midst of necessity we can be free. We have the problem of finding out how to be free since as finite beings we are subject to change. I think that's what it comes to.

The problem is how to be free while, since finite, necessarily subject to change, a change which if it is to be intelligible must possess the same essential features as something in the past, otherwise each moment would be out of context to what went before. (There would be no sense in speaking—words would be unrelated.) He wants creation to be distinguished from novelty—he wants to understand it in relation to intelligence. When the creative act occurs, accompanying it is the awakening of intelligence which is the awareness of the true character of intelligence. What is the proper object of the intellect? Being! And all these particulars *be* and are all in passage. Isolate if possible what he is saying that can be seen intelligibly and preserve a profound commitment to what is uniquely and pristinely present, untarnished by the past. See if you can isolate that.

This past stuff: if the past is in all respects necessary, then the future cannot help but repeat it in all respects. Heraclitus said, "You can't step in the same river twice." There could be no coming into existence in the strict sense. Caesar crossed the Rubicon. It is eternally the case that he did (if in fact he did). The fact in the order of event cannot be changed. There's something in it that is passing strange. While it is eternally so that he did he cross it (if he did) that in no way prejudices how he might have done it. To have crossed it was to have seen something coming into existence which had not been before. In a different sense, one can't step into the same river twice. Precisely because the past is not absolutely qualified by necessity it is possible for there to be a future and the past. There's something going on in becoming that is unprecedented. I think he's saying that unless we are freshly and alertly present to the present, the unprecedented escapes us. If it does, we are living in a way that isn't worth living. He makes no gradations; he never talks about being almost awake. One is awake or asleep. In that respect of course his position is the same as that of the great religious traditions. Buddhists speak of being enlightened or unenlightened. Christians: saved or lost. You can't be half lost. The Hindus: liberated or in bondage. I think he's saying the same thing in principle.

Consider how ill prepared we are to entertain such a notion, let alone act! We're brought up on the notion of gradual progress, on the pious thought that if we behave well we'll be able to work on the environment in such a way that we will have to get better in the long haul. Look at the progress of technology—we're impressed with it. It in no way qualifies us for coming into relation no matter how clever we are—with that order that is always ingressing into disorder. He'll say that within disorder there is some order, though not that one is in possession of it consciously. There's always a place to start. He never says we're hopeless unless we persist in the delusion of essential progress—then we are lost because we make no effort to begin differently. We won't shift our gaze or tune our ears. What he's pointing to is always actuality. Notice how in these tapes the word 'act' will take on an increasingly important role. Soon you will hear an effort I made to understand what he meant by using the term "fall out of act." He seemed to accept that. Insofar as one is in act, one is whole. In a state of fragmentation, one is in a hostile relation to the environment. So the emphasis on act is to draw attention to existence (necessity and essence are the same). Knowledge isn't bad—we need it to operate. However if knowledge is all you have then you're in a dysfunctional state. We must become sensitive to existence, alert to what one cannot prepare for but must remain receptive to. We can't manipulate it, nor can we manipulate ourselves to bring us into a condition to receive the incalculable. We can't creep up on it, nor can we tag along after it.

Student: Are we either fragmented or whole?

Yes.

Student: Then there is no falling out of act. How can you fall out of being whole?

Logically you can't. But psychologically mysteriously, you can. I don't know how to be fragmented and I don't know how to be whole, there's no technique for either one.

Student: There is a technique: be free of fear.

That's not a technique. There is nothing to place between me, my desire, and having my goal realized. There is no instrument. If so, I could progress toward becoming whole. Nonsense. It is not the case.

Student: What about Krishnamurti's psychology?

Were it the case that the precondition for his change necessarily had to be conformity to the ideal, then in principle we would say it would be the occasion for our revolt. Krishnamurti rejected this view. He says ideals are idiotic. From the side of existence, that is sensible. Not, however, from the side of essence. Many things he says are crazy from the side of essence. Essence is the power which makes a thing be what it is. Existence only makes it be. Existence is free of the necessity by which something is specified as this thing. Existence refers to the fact that something is, it doesn't constitute what the thing is; that is, the thing's way of being.

Most of our relations are grasped on the side of essence reductively—what Krishnamurti calls reducing things to the past. What he's really saying is that we are profoundly disordered, confusing essence with existence. The reason I'm not embarrassed to quote from Scripture is because I don't think he is saying something radically new… he is saying it in his own way (but each has a way). He's correct when he says our grasp of our cultural heritage is reduced by us to essence; therefore there is no life in what we have received. Whose fault is that? Jesus remarks, "he who has ears to hear, let him hear…" [Mt 11:15] He doesn't say: let him hear and let all the others try and I'll make up the difference. What is the difference in principle between having ears to hear and Krishnamurti's discussion about listening? Another point, if what he's saying is in all respects absolutely new, it would be unintelligible. We couldn't receive it. If on the other hand what he says is true and what Scripture says is true, they *cannot* disagree. Or let's say someone has the idea Krishnamurti is adding something to what Scripture has said. Krishnamurti says, I'm not adding because I don't believe in progress. He is operating—this is why in public he doesn't have a conversation—he's making a statement which does not admit of development through the give-and-take of dialogue. This is important: when he speaks it is to declare the truth. When I speak I'm speaking only in the interest of making it as intelligible as possible. He's not inviting an inquiry. Inquiry for him means an attempt to follow what he prescribes, but not because he is an authority. Inquiry means self-inquiry, not inquiry of someone else who perhaps knows more than I do. He knows how rare the activity is, and how unlikely anyone will pursue it. Even though we have begun, we might not continue. More than likely, we won't. To emulate his seriousness would be an enormous accomplishment, an enormous shift in our cultural stance. At least the Hindus in their four stages of life don't suggest that towards the term there will be an opening out on ever widening vistas. The last stage is *moksha*, release—*my* liberation. My passage is in its beginning and ending a passage in relation to myself. We have placed ourselves in a lunatic posture from his point of view. The rigor with which he refused to be budged from this issue of one's relation to oneself is as orthodox a Hindu notion as you could find. How does that differ in principle from *any* great religious tradition? Study him with increasing effort to question most seriously our basic assumptions about our relation to ourselves and to our environment. Keep at it in your own notebook. He agreed when I suggested that if I start from the relation of the observer I'm going to be frightened because it is the proof I offer to myself on the side of essence of my own existence, therefore to engage it throws into question my own existence. That's a little unnerving. I'm trying to isolate existence, the incalculable—that mystery of order that continually revivifies, which makes possible a world in which coming into existence can happen authentically. He wants us to be in immediate relation with that phenomenon. Everything else is useless since if I'm right with that, everything else takes care of itself.

Read *Flight of the Eagle* chapter 1 again and chapter 2.

Have a long thought about passage. We are wild about it in the order of development. Any thought of anything besides development is almost impossible to engage. Have a letter to yourself about the nature of development. Secular life has a mystical relation to potentiality—we know that actuality is God-awful. We look to potentiality to bail us out. We're drunk on the notion. That's why we don't have a present. Not to have a present is a dreadful thing. In St. Paul's language it is to be dead in your sins. [Rom 6:2] Krishnamurti calls it doomed to repeat the past. Examine it with care, perseverance, and ever more in-depth—it will be shocking. In that shock is the possibility of waking up and falling in love with actuality. Without that shock, there's more of the same old boring continuing illness and violence.

What is Communication with Others?
February 13, 1979

Student: Krishnamurti seems to talk in sharp either/or terms. Where does development occur in relation to the radical change he describes?

In classical Western thought we speak of causality in terms of Aristotle's four aspects; the material, formal, efficient and final causes. Krishnamurti doesn't have anything to say about the material cause. The material cause has two aspects. First, it is the principle of continuity in change, that which undergoes change. Second, it is the potentiality or ability to become changed.

Krishnamurti raises the question of the relation between knowledge and freedom but doesn't seem to answer it. He is quite sure that they are compresent so it isn't that with freedom one suddenly leaves knowledge behind. Krishnamurti is aware of this interrelation, but he doesn't want to talk about one of the poles, the pole of knowledge. And yet, if change is to be understood intelligibly, something more must be changing: the whole person. I don't think he's addressing a disembodied mind. If that were his objective, how could he become so exercised over this social reality that the world is on fire? There's a reason why he won't address the material issue.

Student: Bohm spoke of diverse material energy as springing from a common source.

To reduce multiplicity to unity doesn't answer the question! You haven't analyzed process, and can't account for growth.

Student: I don't see Krishnamurti's work as a critique of natural process.

If he doesn't talk about it and doesn't say he won't talk about it, there is something left to be done. We have to consider what he's saying in relation to the material cause.

[Video—Dialogue III: What is Communication with Others?[1]]

What makes things difficult for us when listening to Krishnamurti is the potential for confusing the psychological and philosophical orders. By psychological I mean the order of motivation. By philosophical I refer to the effort to state as clearly as one can fundamental structural aspects of what it is one is talking about. It goes back to the old philosophical problem of the relation between structure and process. Since Krishnamurti is primarily concerned with the psychological order, he tends to regard both process and progress as fraught with so much dysfunction that he doesn't want to talk about them. There are many things he doesn't want to talk about which still cry out to be talked about.

There are two ways one can approach his teaching: one, as a person who has diligently sought salvation from the traditional structures of religion, but found those structures unproductive. The other way to approach his teachings is by listening to his refreshing iconoclasm until conceptually liberated from one's own cultural understanding.

Recall that when I suggested there might be a continuum between negation and self-denial? His reaction wasn't "that's interesting." He said most wouldn't do it. But, of course, the behavior of the majority is irrelevant. He is imposing the past on the discussion at that point. To answer as he did is to violate his own principle. Why? There is a reason in the practical order: a work of prevention. He's attempting to prevent a complication arising from the past (after all, Scripture is an historical document) that would deflect perhaps from what he

---

[1] Video published by KFA under the title "Responsibility".

wishes to say. In the practical order, understand how that could be a concern. Yet the problem remains. Either we say there is nothing about his doctrine that is in continuity with the past, and thus Krishnamurti is an absolute event—how can that occur in a finite continuum? Or, if he isn't an absolute event, he must be in continuity with the past. Are we to say his "be a light unto yourself" is different from what the Buddha said? He is pointing to the most urgent of all needs for our species, namely to undergo this transformation, even though he may not have solved the problem philosophically. So when he asks about the relation between knowledge and freedom he can supply the psychological answer, but not the philosophical one. If I don't have an adequate philosophy of change, I can't claim to understand whatever might have occurred inwardly at the level of motivation. Fortunately piety need not be understood for it to be practiced and to be efficacious. I'm not overlooking putting first things first. "These ought ye to have done, and not to leave the other undone." [Mt 23:23 and Lk 11:42]

Your assignment will be not to leave the other undone. If we persevere in not leaving the other things undone in the spirit of his exhorting us to remain fully attentive to the problem at hand and not impose upon it conclusions or solutions, we could hardly be going astray. But, on the contrary, perhaps we should be rendering some service to a very, very valuable invitation from him. We must address ourselves responsibly to the problem of change.

Now that you've been given that dreadful assignment, let's explore what it is he points us to. I think it is to the possibility of attaining to the highest order of awareness available to our species: Enlightenment. It is simply the case that no previous preparation for such a change is sufficient to produce it. That's a far cry from saying some things aren't necessary. The distinction between the necessary and sufficient is not addressed, nor does he address what it means to be changed. In order to grasp what he is saying, we must understand the aspect of change he is pointing to.

Student: If a person is transformed, then subsequently falls out, does he fall to where he was before?

Generically speaking, yes. For example, he says once I see something is poison, I don't go near it again. There are two things involved: 1) the knowledge that I have been confronted with danger and 2) that I must remain alert. The two problems remain. Even if in most respects it is the same danger, I might not be sufficiently alert. Also the danger likely isn't the same in all respects. Perhaps changes occur at the level of appearance to such a degree that the mask is altogether different and if I can't penetrate behind it I could be deceived again. I don't think the awareness we require is a species of omniscience—he never makes that claim. We have to keep on remaining alert.

He told us a story about dissolving the religious organization. He was adopted by the Theosophical Society at the age of eight or nine and he was trained to function as a world savior. So he was brought up feeling he was an answer to the seekers' prayer.

Student: What had he done to make them think that?

It was based on someone's intuition. You can get some sense of it in the biography called *Krishnamurti*. In his late 20s he asked himself seriously if the claims of world saviorhood were soundly based with respect to himself or anyone. He underwent a spiritual crisis. He decided they weren't, and dropped it all cold. He then knows what it is to change identity in terms of one given by the past and the new one. When he says "the past" it is an emotionally loaded term. Mostly we come in and maintain an identity consistent with what we were brought up with. We don't begin a totally new identity. Psychologists claim we couldn't support such a change without having a nervous breakdown. There's much to that. The past isn't an idea. We're talking about a relation to the past that is concrete and informed with pain. No wonder he regards it as unlikely that we'll understand what he says. Why? We're not prepared for bringing our identities into the light, for risking the introduction of discontinuity in our own passage. His break with the past which is compresent with what he regards as his own salvation becomes for him the necessary and sufficient condition for the transformation he speaks about. Whereas far from suggesting we assume a new identity, he is suggesting that if we make this break with the past that requires we face the present without imposing historical solutions rooted in the past, we will on the instant become transformed.

Student: I don't understand.

If we will no longer impose upon the present the conclusions we bring to it, upon the instant we are totally transformed. That's what the notion of negation consists in. I was sorry he didn't want to explore the suggestion about the double negation. The listener is left with the impression that all he has to do is negate the environment. That's not what he means. I'm talking about the relation one has to oneself. It is so dreadfully difficult to take that stance, to perform that act because it's not a step forward. That's one of the reasons for the "move back, not forward." He's not confused about what he's doing. He won't be swerved. But then whereas he might know what he's doing, I might not know what I'm doing while watching him.

Student: I see a contradiction—how is negating the past avoiding danger?

If I discount the past, I can't count on my memory. But he doesn't say memory has no function. What is the relation between knowledge and the possibility of freedom now? You don't progress to freedom. I don't progress into freedom, enlightenment, and yet knowledge has a place in the transformation which occurs independent of knowledge and time. What is its place? We must do our best to do everything to illuminate it.

Student: Does knowledge rest in the midst of freedom?

Yes. But the problem is that conceptual models are not going to answer the question. Krishnamurti is concerned with the practical relation in behavior.

Student: Krishnamurti speaks of rational and irrational knowledge. Perhaps the danger would be perceived as rational knowledge.

I doubt he'd say irrational knowledge was not dangerous also. That he wants to go beyond discursive thinking is clear, but he's not saying to lose touch with rationality. There is no possibility of order breaking through unless I perform this act in which I am serious, and unless in talking to you we are talking together seriously. If that's not the substratum on which we rest, nothing is going on. I hope you're impressed with the either/or characteristic of his pronouncements. He hardly ever says "a little bit." "Very serious" isn't a higher degree or a different activity. If I were to mention the neo-Confucian notion that seriousness is concentration on one thing, I would probably have gotten another irrelevant reply. Consider in what will develop in the tapes the possibility of there being a continuum between his teaching and the best of spiritual teaching that we have as a deposit from this dreadful thing we call the past. If so, it might be that in applying him to Scripture and vice versa that there would be reciprocal illumination.

Student: I never read his biography but it doesn't seem that at the time of this spiritual change it was the first time he questioned the role he was playing.

I didn't say he hadn't questioned it, but he hadn't yet decided. He had to bring himself to the point of being able to disengage himself from the only thing he'd known from a child. Think how much more difficult for him it was with his ethical awareness, with all the confidence placed in him. Have I the right to reject this whole business?

On the one hand, his relation to the past is stated in terms of a categorical break. He has abstracted from that to the principle that there must be in each of us, if transformed without relation to knowledge and time some comparable break. But in more recent years there are all of his schools. If one can't go back how can one go forward? How do you get teachers who represent him correctly? A tradition is developing… how can he break with the past and accept one that opens out in the future? His characterization of change, grasped in the round, is beginning to have a career independent of one of the cardinal principles of his thought which he supports. In conversation with him in the presence of some of the trustees he talked about the character of his schools and the future he hopes for them. I didn't ask how could he do this? I didn't ask it because the character of my meeting was different—but still, the question remains.

In spite of Krishnamurti's efforts to disengage himself from the teachings that we call spiritual, that the past stored for us, we should study in what respect he's in continuity with those teachings. If we did, then it might turn out to be the case that in applying him to Scripture, and Scripture to him, we might come to understand both better.

So I'm laying out some questions for your continuing inquiry with the same spirit he asked us to bring before the problems of the present. See if you can't wrestle with what seems to be going on with respect to his teaching and come to understand that teaching better. If you go about it correctly, it requires a tremendous expenditure of moral energy. We're not dealing with ideas but with the most important question for anyone serious about personal human existence. If we're not serious, we won't do much. His thought doesn't consist in putting diagrams on the board. It's eminently practical; it's concerned with the character of human behavior. We are not dealing just with ideas but with the most important question for any of us as individual persons who claim to be serious about our studies of him. He writes off most human behavior as dysfunctional. His alternatives are enlightenment or total blackout. Society, he claims, is totally immoral. However, he is also saying we can, individually, be totally moral. If one isn't totally moral, one is totally immoral. He offers a sharp either/or.

I want to understand what he's saying as much as you do. I have for years steeped myself in study because as a child there was one text, from the Jewish/Christian traditions, which seemed to be the most important counsel around: "Wisdom is the most important thing. In all thy getting get understanding." [Prov 4:7]

In Hebrew, wisdom and understanding are different words as they are in English. It's interesting that the distinction is made. Wisdom is the principal thing, and yet, if I don't get understanding, I'm wiped out. From my childhood days, I've wanted most of all to understand. I think Krishnamurti too is deadly serious about understanding. I hope insofar as you can spare time to align yourself with the spirit of that scriptural passage, you will enter into that wisdom which is the most important thing and in all thy getting get understanding. If I can approach it in that spirit I'll have an altogether bright prospect. If I'm less than serious, I would just be talking about talk—and I don't have time for it.

Read *Flight of the Eagle* chapter 6: "Motiveless Passion to Understand." Notice how he loves that word passion? You know that he does because he doesn't overuse it.

What is a Responsible Human Being?
February 20, 1979

Student: Does Krishnamurti's statement, "the observer is the observed" allow for self-transformation?

Relate this to our discussion last time about his want of discussion relating to the material cause. I don't think you will find what you're looking for in what he has written. What is being said in "the observer is the observed"? You won't find out through the usual philosophical analysis which attempts to grasp being through change.

Student: You said we too often confuse essence and existence. What do you mean by that?

The way a thing is in the world cannot be reduced to what it is. A thing's 'what' and a thing's 'that' are not collapsible. Your way of being cannot be reduced to the abstraction or "being of reason" that is called essence—else how should you change?

Ideally a thing's name is an expression of its essence. But when we say "tree" we don't account for everything about *this* tree. In the social order we reflect this fact—we have a given name and family name.

[Video—Dialogue IV: What is a Responsible Human Being?[1]]

---

[1] Video published by KFA under the title "Responsibility and Relationships".

In Aristotle's great work, the *Metaphysics*, there is a chapter which he called the "Book of Difficulties." By analogy, I think we've reached a place of difficulties—the conversation we've just seen is surely one of the most difficult in terms of the problems he raises.

There are five difficulties with this dialogue:

1. The first difficulty centers on Krishnamurti's relationship to the world's cultural deposit we call the "great literatures," what we call Scriptures. Is there any virtue in studying them at all? So much of what we call education is predicated on their availability and what we call their value. Has one lost anything essentially if one never turns to them? Was the invention of writing a mistake? One wonders what the point is in publishing his books.
2. What if there were no books at all, would the problem be the same? Of course. But is it the case that the books stand in for solving the problem or do they serve in some other way? And is that way valuable or isn't it?
3. Is there decision at all? He says that a mind that sees clearly doesn't choose. We think we are free because we can choose. Is it the case that if one sees clearly, one has no need to choose?
4. He indicates that if I am related to you and you to me, I have no image of you and you have no image of me. A freedom from the known is a freedom from the image. How can this be understood?
5. The non-violent quality of behavior is abstracted from the act of violence and then a conflict immediately ensues, and one uses the abstraction to measure the quality of one's behavior, which is the fact. He says ideals are idiotic. We must try to find out what he is saying there. You see, there's a theory of knowledge in the notion of fact and non-fact—maybe what he's trying to say is perfectly sound but the way he's saying it admits of more confusion than clarity. There's something strange about saying one abstracts the ideal from the non-ideal.

Student: If one is enlightened why should one read about it?

If one is present, one is enlightened.
Back to mind and image: it is crucial to him and must be for us as well. As soon as image is interposed, relationship has been destroyed.

Student: Does he mean that memory imposes itself on us?

He seems to be saying that if relationship is the case, there isn't any image. I think we must go into this very deeply, passionately. What he has said about the image doesn't account for *how* it gets there, without respect to *whether* it ought to be here. We have a work of negation to perform. We must negate everything that qualifies us dysfunctionally in the order of relationship. But how did we get there? There is a level at which one cannot offer a rational basis for irrational behavior, but that isn't to say there aren't contributing causes.

Student: Is the imposition of the image rooted in fear?

The real question is what enables us to be conscious of change in such a way that enables us to have these images? Clearly animals fear—he praises them—they fear correctly. It saves them. We fool around.

Student: Is it in the physiology of the brain?

Wouldn't animals have it too?
What I'm saying is that the image has a function, that it is present, and that there is no way to dispose of the image. Rather than saying there is no image in relationship, were he being careful he would say: when I behave in such a way as to destroy a relationship, my relationship to my image is dysfunctional. For me to know that I know what I'm looking at is not the same as simply to respond to what confronts me. If I'm truly self-reflective, I must know that I

know. In knowing the object I must be aware of being aware. I must therefore be aware of an ideal bearer of what it is I am looking at. So in this instance you have before you a notebook. The first thing you see is not *this* notebook but just notebook, identified by species. What we apprehend first is essence. We possess that immaterially, not materially. When I look at a chair, I have it in my head but not as wood. I have an ideal representation of that as such. I abstract from that an ideal form which in species is true for all chairs. That's not where my mistake usually is. More often than not we abstract correctly, therefore I cannot imagine how we cannot have an image. The problem isn't with our capability to abstract the essence of a thing from the operation it presents. Rather the problem is at a different level: precisely at the point where I will or will not make a correct judgment about the way what it is, exists. I could have abstracted the essence and still not behave correctly. I could have grasped what it is and still not have grasped how it is.

If I abstract the image of teacher from Krishnamurti, what's the matter with that? Isn't he a teacher? He might say he's a fellow student, but he is not so balmy as to say there's no difference in degree of understanding. Would I be betraying the present if I recognize in him someone capable of teaching me something? It would be a mistake to "lay on him" a painful or pleasurable past grounded in my relation to other teachers. That has nothing to do with my recognition that he's a teacher. Be careful to distinguish between the capacity to grasp essence and to make correct judgments about existence. A thing is disordered when it can behave dysfunctionally in relation to what it is. The distinction here is crucial—else we misunderstand what he's up to. My role in these conversations is not to correct his rhetoric but to assist him to say what he wants to say. Our chances of understanding improve if we penetrate the real character of what he's saying. Maybe there are one or two instances when he says something that may not be what is the case.

Student: Are you saying that I have an image of myself that is disordered and of you and you of yourself and you of me?

Right. That's four images often in violent contention.

Student: Krishnamurti's reaction to quotes from Scripture is negative. Does that imply he has an image?

He's concerned that his listeners don't get the idea that what I'm doing in quoting Scripture is worth doing, else *they* might start!

Student: It's hard to believe that he hasn't read anything.

I imagine he was rather intractable. But you see he's not insensitive to language.

After one of these talks when I was hanging on like a dog to a bone, not giving up these quotes—he said in a very informal manner, "Sometime I hope I can recite for you a hymn to Lakshmi." See, he wouldn't do that on TV. Yet if you only present an iconoclastic front, what you'll be doing is encouraging your listeners never to go near Lakshmi. That is equally disastrous.

If we are to be equally understanding and caring before whatever confronts us, then we must be aware that an image of a thing is perfectly proper. What we bring on the side of our affections to the encounter with that image is where the problem lies. If from the side of the affections we are diseased, then the intellect is hindered from grasping that form chastely, purely. But chastity in the order of my receiving the world happily does not require I go around destroying images. If will is correctly disposed toward whatever confronts me, I cannot but be clear, except for my irreducible stupidity.

Maybe he's not far from the Buddha when he gave his sermon in the Deer Park—he didn't say anything, he just held up a flower.

Through the history of thought there has been a tendency either to negate images completely or to celebrate the image. Neither is an end in itself. How devilishly hard to find the middle! By that I don't mean a compromise! What I'm trying to get at is that it is one thing to speak of that which grounds our active negation in the interest of function (so that in negating, intelligence breaks out). It is one thing to say we must negate in the interest of behaving functionally.

It is another to fail to account for the possibility of negating in our nature an emotional attachment to an image as if such attachment were necessitated by our nature. The first is a psychological problem, a problem of motive. The second is ontological, a problem of being. If we're going to think well we must never study motive exclusive of an awareness of being because being is that which is motivated. The being of a thing is always prior. With an incorrect grasp of image we can only flounder.

Student: Is that the same as expectation?

Yes if by that you mean an attachment. Rational expectation need not mean that we inform the present with an overload that is generated by our fear that the future won't pay off. What could be harder than to negate that? He doesn't want to say simply that that is to be negated as though we were invited to a manipulative relation to negation. (Were it, the object of the manipulating would lie outside the manipulated and that's not what he is talking about.) I think it turns out to be a double negation, but I wasn't able to get him to talk that way. It might be the result of a different disposition of mind—some things he feels are not that important to understand. They are for me. I can't get excited about the fact that they don't appeal to him. I want to really understand. I don't want a blueprint. I want to operate this negation, but I want to understand it in its operation and have a correct vision of it. I'm not persuaded I am incorrigibly illuminated from the point of seeing the light on. I don't think that's the case. Perhaps unless one has suffered brain damage one is unable to forget one has seen it—that's a far cry from remembering and embodying it in action—especially in terms of the social price one pays. How can you account for the prayer of Jesus, "Father, let this cup pass."[Mt 26:39] I'm not quite disposed to think he was a darkened mind! If he could add "… yet not my will…" he must be making a negation, praying for it to be made, recognizing his contribution and recognizing that the first impulse is to call the whole thing off. Maybe something is going on we could explore in depth.

Read *Flight of the Eagle* page 88 on the question of fear and habituation. Also read Chapter 7, look at the way Krishnamurti answers questions. Notice the relation between the content and the form of the question and that of his reply.

Order Comes From the Understanding of Our Disorder
February 27, 1979

Can the conscious mind uncover the unconscious? You'll notice that Krishnamurti gives dream analysis short shrift. In *Flight of the Eagle*, page 94, he says analysis by the conscious of the unconscious is not the way. For example, he says, one funds a store of material called dreams after-the-fact of a malady. Studying the evidence of pathology isn't the same as dealing effectively with the pathology.

Student: How can Krishnamurti know that he hasn't dreamed, that it is more restful not to, and so on?

Student: He is talking from his own experience—what's true for him.

Student: Why doesn't he say so instead of giving a prescription?

From his perspective it might be that your mind is so tired from dreaming that you have no measure by which to measure your fatigue. In his defense he does say don't copy the speaker—though he does pronounce. There are many times when he feels his audience has related to his words badly and he'll say, "The speaker has no authority." If you were paying attention to the speaker as a role model it must mean you weren't paying attention. So when he says, "pay attention," it must mean to yourself, to your own conscious activity—then you'll be paying attention to me.

Student: If one is paying attention to dreams, couldn't it be a pure act of attention?

I would've thought so. I think the point is well taken vis-à-vis dreams. By his own principle, it would seem that any dream is fair game.

[Video—Dialogue V: Order Comes from the Understanding of Our Disorder[1]]

Student: I tried Krishnamurti's method of changing a habit—it didn't work. I noticed that if one has a behavior pattern then resistance makes it continue.

Perhaps you have answered your own question. You're making an object of your behavior pattern then assigning both it and your idea of yourself a value. It would be better simply to observe your habit. There is a distinction between being aware and being aware of. If aware of, then the mind has an object of measure. Thought is operating when I am aware in such a way as to represent the other to itself conceptually. I give the object of my thought a value and I give myself as the perceiver a value. I think the effort to distinguish the two values leads to intelligibility, but it is measured by the measuring process. A measure that is descriptive is not harmful to my integrity. To use it descriptively won't bring me into disorder—descriptive measure then is the only measure I should perform. What I must undertake unceasing attention to is any comparison I undertake which is invidious. Comparison that is descriptive plays a healthy role. Comparison that is invidious is corrupting.

Student: Is there a correlation with "Be still and know that I am God"?[2]

There could be but not necessarily. The text says, "Be still *and* know..." The kind of measure he is opposed to will interpret texts

---

[1] Video published by KFA under the title "Order".
[2] Ps 46:10

like that by replacing the conjunctive with "in order to." The same mistake happens with "But seek ye first the kingdom of God, and his righteousness; and all these things shall be added unto you."[Mt 6:33] In this sentence, the Greek for 'and' is not *ina* (in order that) but *kai*; that is, *while* I am seeking the kingdom, all these things are being added. "Seek ye first the kingdom of heaven" is generally subject to an if/then exegesis. It isn't an if/then at all!

The reason I said it "might be" in relation to an awareness of God is that wonder might be present but not necessarily awe. Unless it is deeper than an aesthetic experience, I haven't been shaken to the roots. I came to ecstasy not enstacy. I am moved to feel as though standing outside of myself I can have a peak experience but that is not enough to bring me to radical intuition of Ultimacy which introduces me to the peace that passeth understanding—something I could, were I correctly disposed, abide in continually, and not be subject to an episodic career of peak experiences. Unfortunately that which so much of the literature called "mystical" introduces us to is ecstasy. Genuine mystical activity is not attained simply by reference to an intensification of one's affective state. Genuine mystical activity is the abiding intuition of the abiding overflow of being into the world. That's a very different thing from an ecstatic experience. That's why it is associated with peace and stillness and not with ecstasy as such. The test of mysticism is whether I can carry on my daily affairs while maintaining myself in peace of heart.

It is also unfortunate that most of the discussion of mystical experience is precisely what Krishnamurti is deploring—descriptions of powers absent in what is called ordinary consciousness. Genuine mysticism is not extraordinary consciousness but a rectified consciousness; a rectified consciousness which, because related to itself correctly, is self nourishing. I don't necessarily attain to that when I'm ravaged by the beautiful. I want to be sure you are not seduced by most of the current literature which is misleading. Now I'm sounding like *I'm pontificating*!

Go back to simply being aware. To be aware (not aware of) means there is no disruption in the relation between me and what confronts me in the order of act. For instance, I have a slight bit of tea. If I could focus on drinking it without going into some thought such as "I'd rather be doing something else," and so on, I'd enjoy the tea more. I would simply be aware, and the tea and I in all respects would simply get along. If I'm "with it" I'm aware, not mindlessly disposed towards it, but superlatively attentive—every fiber of my being resonating to the emanations, the energy field of the other with whom I participate resonantly in a present wider field of energy. So when I'm with it, there are always three of us attuned in act: me, the other and the field in which we move. When one attains that experience abidingly, at the highest level of awareness, then one has attained to the mystical state.

Student: Is the mystical state timeless?

I want to criticize my use of the term 'state.' I employed it in the interest of the way we ordinarily speak. The emphasis in that activity is not properly on condition or state but on the *activity*, therefore to call the highest awareness the highest state is to miss the mark.

Why am I making this distinction? I think of state in terms of something to be attained to that lies outside. I think if I am to make the movement to enlightenment, I move to a higher state. That puts it on the wrong foot. I think Krishnamurti is right—the movement from one quality of act to another is instantaneous in the order of awareness. And to say it is a timeless state is fraught with unfortunate occasions for misunderstanding. Because time is not annihilated in that state—on the contrary, it is a matter of timing that is always present within the activity when I am in the world. I'm not saying that I am the tiger etc. essentially, and thus I can make residence with it with impunity. But precisely as my consciousness of my environment is disordered, my environment will appear to me as hostile because I am hostile toward it. So I am the world insofar as the world reflects me to myself in the most precise correspondence.

Krishnamurti always is talking about the phenomenon of awareness as such. He isn't making statements about the essential order. It is difficult to grasp act because we stand in our own way.

Student: Could we have a summary?

Yes. We find someone who appears capable of higher states of consciousness and affix paraphernalia to his person. We find it does appear that his physiology differs, so we have a graph of the ordinary and the non-ordinary. We study the graphs and think we've understood. In fact we have no measure of either which is genuinely descriptive because we have no subject. We have two objects and the subject slips out. We say we're dealing with a subject matter—what is it? By definition it is not transferable since it is essentially private. Krishnamurti is at enormous pains to encourage us to attain to an intuition of being, even as everything in the environment with the exception of untrammeled nature conspires to seduce us away from it.

Student: Could we say, "I am existence, existence is me"?

The quality of my existence determines the quality of my reception of other existences because of the one-to-one relation in order of value. If I am disordered, everything else is disordered in my undergoing the act of existing. It seems to me there is no way around that. It is terribly difficult to attain to that intuition.

Student: The attainment is action?

Yes.

Student: Measurement is an illusion therefore everything is an illusion?

It is only as unreal as I am unreal. It isn't that all this is illusion. If I am illusorily related to myself, everything else is illusory. Let me get practical about essence and its distinction from existence. What is it that grounds the notion of essence? That something is observed to perform in a certain way consistently. Water is always wet. Krishnamurti fails to touch on this. There is a difficulty in saying that the intuition of order occurs through seeing disorder. It's a bad way to talk because it uses a non-nature to discern a nature. That isn't the way the mind works. Water is first of all in terms of act, wet. So if we called it wet, we'd be closer to what is going on. What is always making wet we give a name to and call it water. What is actual, what exists, is wet. I didn't say wetness. The nature or 'ness-ing' is water. Unlike Krishnamurti I don't want to lose nature or the '-ness,' of essence, but I want to stay with him. Water then is a being of reason which is inferred from wet, moist. I haven't been mistaken in that. What it is, that which is primordial is a movement we call wet or wetting—existence is what is utterly prior. It is terribly difficult to taste. We talk about fire, but it is burning and lighting from which we infer fire. It's the *act* of burning, not a process. There is something before the process—simply act. Act prior to a career is existence, it is actuality. Act with a career is process. Actuality is not a concept! That's what the mystic grasps with all the levels of his or her being—physically, psychologically, and intellectually. The mystic grasps it naturally, morally, spiritually—he grasps it! Get a sense of how rare it is. A person as sensitive as Jung says it was not until he was 40 that he grasped existence. So what was going on until then?

Student: Biblically it says "… the Word was God."

The Greek imperfect "was" is not the simple past but the pluperfect. "In the beginning was the Word…" and it is still was-ing! If I can be was-ing along with the Word…!

Student: Are "word" and "act" interchangeable?

The word primordially (not theologically) seems to me to be the outcry of my awareness of existence. We start out with this lunacy to find the origin of language by trying to get apes to talk, etc. as though that has anything to do with the word. Or we say language began in communication. We are closer when we say it began with "ouch" than when we say it was to communicate my wants. No, language is grounded in my intuition of actuality. Therefore, the word has for its locus properly always the center, the act of existence. We don't want to be in the center. We want it to be over there so we can have a look at it. If it's over there, where am I? Out of it. We cannot leave well enough alone.

Why does poetry move us? The answer to that will take us close to the origin of the word. It does because great poetry introduces us to something that if we relate to correctly, causes fear and trembling because there can be no other word than one that is used. It introduces us to necessity. A thing is necessary because it is, but it is not necessarily what it is before it comes into being. Once it arrives it is necessary. Because a thing is, it is necessary. So there is something peculiar before that thing came into the world. Once it has, nothing can be done—it's perfect. That's the meaning of a correct relationship to God—"I shall not be moved." There is no way to move me. God could, but He won't. How should He if He and I in act are in perfect union? Why would He disorder himself? That word shall not be moved because it is necessary. Before that, anything could happen.

With a great poem we are faced with the inevitable. Inevitability quite boggles the mind because we have both its inevitability and the mystery of its eruption into the world. If it were here because it is necessary, there would be no mystery. Necessity cannot have a past—it turns only on itself. We're caught in the middle. There are texts in the Bible (in translation!) which have that power to move us: "God is love and the one abiding in love is abiding in God and God in him" [1 Jn 4:16]—what word or words do you want to move around? You'd be ready for the padded cell if it occurred to you to do so. We have Keats: "a thing of beauty is a joy forever." And Wordsworth:

> She lived unknown, and few could know
> When Lucy ceased to be;
> But she is in her grave, and, oh,
> The difference to me!

There is not a smidgen of sentimentality and yet it brings one to tears. That's what catharsis is based on. When feelings are momentarily purified because for that moment we have been invaded by actuality—for that moment we are cleansed. However, we haven't on that account changed our ways.

Krishnamurti's focus is always on that overflow of being into the world. All he's doing is asking us to be aware without doing violence to the need to be aware of.

When something happens that puts us immediately into sudden shock we are invaded by actuality. We aren't "aware of" anything. We see as we've never seen. Krishnamurti is talking about being uncorruptedly related to my senses so that consciousness is given a keel. I'm not referring to a diseased lust after consciousness that receives anything and everything indiscriminately. Consciousness not grounded well in nature is rabid, a prey to anything. Krishnamurti has set his face incorrigibly against that. So he says make a pure act of attention.

Think very carefully about the difference between our nature as human and that of those we call animals. Animals remain pure whereas we go on impurely and yet we share animal functions with them. Ask yourself most seriously: What is the occasion we respond to badly that causes self-corruption, an occasion that is perhaps never present to animals? How are we suspended in being in a way that makes for the occasion for self-corruption? I am not asking what is wrong. What in our very own nature as human makes for the *possibility of* self-corruption? Human nature has in it an occasion for self-corruption; we recognize that occasion and yet we are able to respond to the occasion badly. Since it is proper to our nature, it is clearly out of the question to try to remove it. What is it?

The Nature and Total Eradication of Fear
March 6, 1979

We must come to terms with Krishnamurti's statement that perception is the action. Can that rhetorical expression be supported? If not, what is it in the statement that *can* be supported? Try to see in what sense it fails (if it does) in the order of clarity. Can it be supported if stated differently?

[Video—Dialogue VI: The Nature and Total Eradication of Fear[1]]

I think what he's really talking about would be better expressed by the word 'anxiety' rather than 'fear.' I don't know why he didn't make the distinction rhetorically. I should've asked him why he didn't use it, but I was concerned with trying to follow him.

You notice he's beginning to loosen up, to get much more spontaneous. I think he has decided that although he has the misfortune of talking to an academic, I really don't mean to put stumbling blocks in the way of communication. He gets much warmer. In the last video, as we said goodbye he put his hand on my knee and said with heartfelt emotion that I had taken the trouble to listen. He doesn't think anyone is listening.

Why does he say, "I don't know whether…" and doesn't finish his sentence? What does it mean?

Those who have had some philosophy will remember Plato's love affair with the Forms or ideals. When I had to study closely Plato's dialogues I had the extraordinary feeling that, even though

---

[1] Video published by KFA under the title "Fear".

moved to the bone by what I was reading (for example at the end of *Phaedrus*, Socrates makes a prayer to Pan, "May the outward and the inward man be one"), nobody really cared. I thought I really cared, but it's a long way from caring to getting on with the job: that is, to dwell within the ambience, the effulgence, the abiding glory of the Forms, and allow that communion to inform your attitude and discourse, not as one activity among others but as the sole activity of the being that informs all else is to appear rather strange. An abiding relationship to the Forms in that sense brings about a change in personality structure. You are likely to come over in a social situation as having something odd about you. And whenever you open your mouth in an effort to express your abiding love affair with truth, goodness and beauty, after making your statement you simply do feel like looking at the person and doing what Krishnamurti does when he leans forward and says, "I just don't know...." There is an infinite gulf between the light you follow and the interests and concerns that occupy most people most of the time. For apart from his prophetic role, what qualifies his aesthetic role also conduces to give him the notion that he's not quite making himself intelligible. That takes me to the heart of our difficulty—your assignment.

What *is* the occasion that permits the phenomenon in human conduct of self-betrayal? Though he doesn't use the expression, it is uppermost in his mind that we cut out self-betrayal. So I'm asking you, not as he does with a rhetorical question (more often than not, if I make an effort to reply he'll backtrack). I'm asking an interrogative question. The reason he is so concerned to utter rhetorical questions is because he wants to come to terms with personal existential crisis—so when he says "what is fear" he doesn't expect me to come up with a definition. That almost invariably puts him off. He wanted to be sure I never spoke as an academician. He likes it when I tell a story. Remember how closely he paid attention to that business about water? He thinks that stuff is real; for him, that's the only thing that is real. Everything else is illusory, worthless. If he hadn't thought he was touching me existentially he would not have permitted 18 of these dialogues to occur. As a matter of fact he had a conversation with a Tibetan guru that he stopped right in the middle. "We're not getting anywhere," he said.

Student: When you quoted scripture, what was his expression?

There is a certain sharp concern that the corrective he was attempting to bring would be obscured by my quotation. There is a lot to be said for his concern. Let's face it—if any of us goes to divine service and says the Lord's Prayer and recites the general confession which uses the first-person plural, he's probably not listening to a word he's saying. T*he Book of Common Prayer*, the King James, and Shakespeare are easy to get drunk on because of the beauty of the language. While he would not object to being moved by the beauty of the language, he *would* object if we let self-entrancement stand in for understanding. You get the same feeling when the priest reads the words and the congregation replies. The Episcopalians are always bobbing and weaving. It's really quite a rich dance, very beautiful. But if it is merely an aesthetical exercise, what has happened existentially to the soul? There has not been a change effected that is perseveringly related to after the service is over. That's what he is concerned about—nothing is changing. So he will ask the same jolly question 25 times. He doesn't want an answer except in the heart. So when you hear the question, take the part of one being asked a question not by Krishnamurti but by oneself. That's why it's rhetorical—we must ask it of ourselves. You must ask it of *yourself*. You must hang in there with it. For him the question is always infinitely more important than the answer. It doesn't mean that the answer should not be arrived at. It means the answer is subject to become deepened and expanded in terms of my self-understanding. Without the question, there is no possibility of that. See how different it is from an authority who asks in a catechetical way? Mostly you're not required to do any thinking. He wants me to have an existential confrontation with myself. Until it occurs and is persisted in, nothing changes.

I think it is a misfortune that he takes such a dim view of practice. It's confusing for him to say, "keep on," and not recognize that as practice. I suggest we put ourselves on notice that we should be attentive to the fundamental rhetorical thrust of his utterances. By and large his concern is with the corrective, not the principle. The reason he doesn't dilate on principle is because he doesn't want us to relate to it simply as doctrine. That's why he's able to say unphilosophically that out of an examination of disorder, order breaks through, and goes on to suggest that order is intelligible against disorder. You can make a case for that only clinically, not from the side of health. On the other hand, it is health we take for granted and he doesn't want us to take anything for granted. He doesn't want us to take our attention off the fly on our nose for an instant. While the fly is there, our attention is focused, everything else is blotted out.

Recover the relation between principle and corrective so you don't misunderstand the proper force of both orders of rhetoric.

We can learn a lesson with respect to Krishnamurti's rhetorical style. We must be careful not to allow ourselves to be confused by a one-sided aspect of his rhetoric which focuses upon the corrective to the virtual exclusion of principle. For example, if we say justice should obtain virtually everyone agrees, cerebrally. The problem arises at the point where we require to make an application, through deeds. Then a thousand reasons are made why fundamental injustice should obtain instead of justice. Thus a corrective is important to bring forward. However, there is a danger of losing one's grasp of principle in listening only to the corrective, and of doing something silly: erecting the corrective in the place of principle. There is an example in the history of the Academy: in opening the doors to all and sundry, quality declined. In the interest of applying a corrective, sobriety was lost. In applying a corrective indiscriminately, minds ill suited to the task were accommodated, standards had to be lowered and students were shortchanged for want of decent deportment and rhetoric on the part of faculty! That's always what happens when the corrective is exalted to the status of principle.

Student: Would reading Scripture provide the principle from which we could then read Krishnamurti?

It isn't the case that we need to read Scripture to get on with what he's doing. And one doesn't have to read Scripture as though it were pontificated. It is the case that since Scripture at its best agrees with most of what he's saying, how beneficial it would be to be able to recur to it when we can't listen to him!

Student: Isn't that putting authority outside?

The 13th century Christian mystic, Meister Eckhart once said, "If we could read the book of nature, we would have no need of Scripture." But we can't, therefore we need this medicine. I don't think we as a civilization can claim we can read the book of nature! An example of a culture who can read the book of nature is the American Indian. Poverty stricken as he might be (for reasons which don't honor us) he will look at his beaten up saucepan in which he is heating canned soup and that saucepan he contemplates as one of the cups of life. So the saucepan isn't some utensil that's standing between him and the soup. He is timelessly related to the cup, and to the fire under it. Things are invested with holiness the way nothing is for us—so we can't read the book of nature. We are brought up on notions like existence is meaningless, an absurd notion. Is it any comfort to make that discovery? A careful reading of Scripture will reintroduce us to the holiness of what is because everything that is, is an embodiment of divine energy. What is the quality of my being if I don't intuit that? Alienation. Everything is reduced to a means, not an end. It is all seen as something for me to get my hands on in order to satisfy my caprice, so Krishnamurti says we're totally depraved and not at home in the world.

Student: Scripture too often encourages in us an unhealthy relation to idea or notion.

There is a way of relating to Scripture that is altogether healthy.

Student: But don't we have to be healthy to relate to it that way?

All he's asking us to do is make a pure act of attention to our disease. He claims that if we persist then a change occurs from illness to health. Scripture bears that out saying that by beholding we become changed.[2]

I'll leave you with this: the occasion for self-betrayal that qualifies us as a species is the possibility of violating our own nature. We can refuse to follow our essential bent. This is really remarkable. That's why Krishnamurti used the expression, "doing your own thing," with such disgust. For him, such a sentiment has nothing to do with the fundamental orientation or bent of my nature. I might change my "thing" after all. He regards the whole posture as corrupt and illusory. He might not like talk about one's own bent, but would say, I think, insofar as I persist in looking squarely at myself, regardless of how terrified I become, that order will break out, or break in; and as I persist, the correlative breaking in of order secures that I make my passage without fragmentation. You see, that's tough. There's a perfect equivalent in, "Because strait [is] the gate, and narrow [is] the way, which leadeth unto life, and few there be that find it." [Mt 7:14] What is it but sharpness of focus, not allowing my attention to wander from the question I am putting to myself: what is fear?

Student: He seems full of hope.

The man believes we don't have to persist in self-betrayal. He's not a fool; he's obviously persuaded we're not going to pay any attention to him. But he's not going to infer we don't have the possibility for doing so.

I have to give a lecture next week on mystical experience. This is part of a distinguished series concerned in Dimensions of Consciousness. For each, there's been a reading list of learned

---

[2] "But we all with open face beholding as in a glass the glory of the Lord, are changed into the same image from glory to glory, [even] as by the Spirit of the Lord." [2 Cor. 3:18]

material. Naturally I read the books on my list. What's astonishing about this is that the books almost without exception are on the phenomenology of mysticism—which is to say they're running around watching people called mystics or the mystical experience called ecstasy, or in our vernacular, a high. It's good reading, academically perfect. But there's no sense of something called the peace that passeth understanding. [Phil 4:7] That's not a high, rather it points to an abiding integration of all one's energies. So from day to day, and night to night there is no longer any conflict of motives. Maybe for tests and measures that's not interesting. To use Huston Smith's fine word, it is a question of enstacy which Krishnamurti is trying to teach. He's not suggesting we run around having beautiful feelings about the world. That's not the measure of what he's attempting to present. Neither is there anything in the University of California's list that discusses what Krishnamurti means by the effort taken to persist in asking the right question. So the fundamental, abiding discipline of the mystic is given scant if any operational notice. That's not unusual. Krishnamurti's perspective and that of the great scriptures vis-à-vis the reading list is different. The Upanishads are clear: "it cannot be attained by the weak."[3] In another place it is described as walking the razor's edge.[4] There is an enormous risk to mental health in applying oneself to those questions which is not touched on where the measure of mystical experience is sheerly aesthetical. So if I insist on saying mystical experience can be comprehended in terms of a series of highs, I am profoundly mistaken. It is as though I go up but I can't stay there, I have to do the dishes. So I float back down and pray it will be vouchsafed to rise again as a helium balloon ecstatically surveying the cosmos.

Student: Scriptures seems to speak of these things only indirectly.

---

[3] *Mundaka Upanishad* [3.2.4], from *The Upanishads*, tr. A. Shearer and P. Russell, p. 129.
[4] *Katha Upanishad* [1.3.14], from *The Upanishads*, tr. A. Shearer and P. Russell, p. 150.

Scripture can speak as directly as Krishnamurti does if you'd just divest yourself of much you been taught about scripture. To understand it is to be involved in what he says we should do. So try to attend not only to the treasures available from his mouth but also listen to some things enunciated in the literary deposit.

Consider with care the possibility of violating our own nature, an activity we seem ready, willing and able to undertake at the slightest notice.

Does Pleasure Bring Happiness?[1]
March 20, 1979

On page 94 of *The Flight of the Eagle* it says, "Learning is always in the active present." There are some logical difficulties with this statement. Krishnamurti continues, "Knowledge is always in the past and when you act, the past is determining that acting. We are saying learning is in the very action itself." If the past is determining the acting it seems strange to put learning as an action that is always present. How can you have it both ways? The past is determining acting if knowledge has any relation to learning. You might claim knowledge and learning have no essential relation. Then you would have to show that learning is a process. A process is embodied activity. If we make a distinction between activity and process then it will be clearer. "Knowledge is always in the past..." so it's difficult to grasp how the phrase "when you act" would not also include the action he calls learning. He doesn't qualify it. That's a problem. We'll try to see how he gets into it and how it is unnecessary.

Let's consider the ontological difference between activity and process. It is difficult to think of process as infinite whereas it is no problem to think of activity as infinite. It is difficult to imagine process as infinite because of the relation process has to body and how body is concerned materially. Body is always an expression of some order of limitation.

---

[1] For the previous seminar date, "Understanding, Not Controlling, Desire," March 13, 1979, Professor Anderson was away; students watched the video for Dialogue VII (published under the title "Desire" by KFA) and discussed among themselves.

There is another problem with learning as a process that isn't related to the past. For us in our world process has discrete parts, a career. It is determinable. To say that learning is a process and not leave it as an activity places it necessarily in relation to knowledge. That makes sense—on the basis of what I know, what I'm now attending to is intelligible and I make a connection. It is difficult to see how learning is prejudiced by that. So when he says that transformation is independent of knowledge and time, what is it in the activity of transformation that *is* independent of knowledge and time? When he says it is a process that is not related to knowledge, he's asking for trouble. The ontological difficulty is crucial for understanding without being confused. To say learning is in the active present raises the question of how to understand learning as a process without relation to the past. To say it is in the active present can be sustained. There is a difficulty in failing to distinguish between the activity of learning and the process of learning, and seeing both in relation to transformation. It is possible to isolate learning—something going on in the present, and possible to relate that to the activity of self-transformation which is independent of knowledge and time. In both is it necessary to exclude learning as a process?

[Video—Dialogue VIII: Does Pleasure Bring Happiness?[2]]

Student: How can a tree on the mountain give joy if there is no non-joy from the past?

He seems to be saying that as one is attending to anything, anxiety is not present.

Student: He seems to have anxiety about the world condition.

Concern and anxiety are not the same. He doesn't strike me as being uptight about the condition of the world. He is terribly

---

[2] Video published by KFA under the title "Pleasure".

concerned about it. I confess he is sometimes more concerned about it than I am. He has a notion about his responsibility for the character of the world condition that I don't share with him to the same degree. But he's not in anxiety about it. He hasn't got a neurotic attachment to getting rid of the disorder in the world. He is concerned because of his being the world and the world himself.

Student: If I am attending to the tree without thought, how do I remember later that I had the experience?

I take it you formulated the question because of what appears to be a strict relation between thought and memory. I get the impression from studying his books that what he calls thought is primarily calculative thought. Here again we might make a distinction. I can't imagine how thought is not present in a pure act of attention, but calculative thought doesn't dominate it. One can make a pure act of attention on a calculative problem. To say computation is the cause of anxiety is nonsense. Not so to say there is a relation to computation that was anxious, therefore we employ calculative thought as divisive. I can't imagine how calculative thought could be absent. Thought isn't suspended in a pure act of attention—it's given its proper rank. I was hoping when I mentioned St. Thomas he would discuss the notion of "distinguishing in order to unite." But he doesn't ever want to discuss further any quotations from Scripture or classical thought. I think that diminishes his possible influence.

Student: He speaks of a quiet state of mind, of death that brings life. This is the quietness of calculative thought?

Notice his phraseology—he says we need to go into this deeply. He never says think about this. He never employs thought in relation to making an inquiry. That suggests he believes in the distinction in the way he has made it.

Student: There must be some sort of thinking going on.

Let us examine our nature in relation to this problem. Calculative thought does not dominate a pure act of attention. One can make a pure act of attention upon a calculative problem, for example to the relation between means and ends. I must go in a certain direction and plot my course. Why is it a corruption to make a pure act of attention to a problem of means? I don't believe that it is a necessary corruption since I don't choose ends, I choose means—I desire ends. What I think he has done is collapsed two things which ought not to be collapsed. He has an extraordinary intuition of activity. Most people don't. They know consequences. They never make the distinction between activity and process therefore they have no present. Because he *grasps* activity, he is concerned about the present.

What is it Krishnamurti is collapsing? It seems to me he's collapsing truth judgments into the intuitive reception of beauty so that for him the distinction between them doesn't obtain within the process of intellection. At the first moment of intuiting essence one is affectively engaged. Feeling is much faster than thought. On the other hand, he does say that to make myself adequate to discern certain forms of danger I need instruction. That's interesting since he's been having such hard words about memory. What I'm trying to say: my affective relation which is immediate before what I confront is experienced by me as a wholeness. But now I think we can learn from St. Thomas. When St. Thomas says we distinguish in order to unite he is saying that the apprehension of the essence of the thing, no matter how ravishing it might be or how terrifying, is not yet to understand it as a whole. I'm not saying intuition is fragmentation, I'm saying that at the point of intuiting it, I haven't understood anything. I have to make a judgment about it—what confronts me has a way; that's where judgment of its particularity takes over. There is a difficulty with Krishnamurti's position. Given his rhetoric it's hard to see how the whole thing isn't reduced to an aesthetical experience.

Student: He used the example of reading a label.

That was an unfortunate illustration. Clearly one has to learn to read. What I'm trying to suggest here is that he seems not to grasp that human nature is incorrigibly deliberative. I've often thought it that if Keats had lived long enough to embark on the program of study he wished to take up, he might have thought more about his claim that, "beauty is truth, truth beauty this is all we know on earth, and all we need to know."

The trouble is not with saying that truth and beauty are convertible, but Keats left out the good. We also need to know the good. Keats wasn't completely insensitive to that. Read his development—you see he was cut off at a time when he was beginning to think deeply not simply about the relation between the beautiful and the true but about the hierarchy of values. Had he lived, I think he would have written more deeply and also more clearly.

I think it is better when talking about joy as Krishnamurti discusses it to say he would never want to undergo joy without the presence of concern. He's always talking about care. He's very devoted to the need to make a pure act of attention to the welfare of another. We could be wrong for want of sufficient practice in reading, to say nothing of learning some language! To put it hard, if one isn't careful, one is going to adopt a naïve attitude to the world with respect to receiving it sheerly aesthetically.

The upshot of the problem is that we learn Krishnamurti's vocabulary so we don't ask him to say things he has no intention of saying. We ought to try to learn his language. We would be remiss if we required him to say something which he doesn't see is there to be observed. None of us is omniscient. Notice when I told him how remarkable it was that he was capable of reading empathically our condition of anxiety, he said you don't need to become drunk... I stopped him saying there was a difference. He agreed but didn't say in what respect there was a difference. This exchange is helpful to us in recognizing a lacuna in his thought. It may have something to do with the way he has been in the world. He's had an unusual personal history, unusually free of material concerns. That does not imply that anyone freed from material want will become a Krishnamurti! But if one is sufficiently free of material concerns throughout one's term one doesn't learn what it means to cope with material needs. By that I mean coping with what it is to make something from beginning to the middle to the end. That I relate in some way to matter which requires me to grasp the way of the matter, and then I must continue if my work is to attain its end, I must stay with it, not as one making a pure act of attention in a state of wonder, but as one concerned throughout to perform the work of transformation on the material. So whether I am talking about writing a poem or making a cabinet or digging a well, I am involved in something which is going to put a strain on me in a way that talking about a pure reception of the world is not. I'm inclined to think that through that strain one funds some understanding that can't be attained to through any other means. I can tell you it is immensely more difficult to write a competent piece of verse than it is to talk about it. I don't care how brilliant the talk is or how deeply informed—it's tougher to actually write.[3]

Student: Do you include bringing up a child?

Yes attention must not only be on activity but on process.

Student: Is there a distinction between activity and process?

---

[3] According to a conversation with Prof. Anderson on this point: the examination of human nature should be rounded out by noting that human nature includes the possibility of making a pure act of attention in addition to being incorrigibly deliberative. He noted that clinically the possibility of making such a pure act of attention is small, nonetheless the possibility of being fully open in the present inheres in our nature. Next, he distinguished meditative thought from calculative thought. He noted that meditative thought, which includes Awareness, is present in a pure act of attention. On being asked to explain why he made the statement the way he did instead of saying "Awareness includes meditative thought," he said meditative thought includes something more, namely discrimination. It is discrimination which permits one to freely accord with Divine will and thus allows timely action to flow through oneself. There is no hint of agency.—Ed.

When one observes process one is observing movement therefore one has nothing but a specious present. All one sees by studying process is the quantitative division. Activity on the contrary is essentially timeless.

For example, the activity of the tree's bearing fruit as a function outlasts the organ we would call this tree because if it dies, there are other trees that bear apples, oranges and pears. The bearing of fruit doesn't stop with the death of this tree. Function always outlasts the organ, and points us therefore to the difference between activity and process. With process, one is always involved with coming to be and passing away. Where's the present in it? Our culture is besotted with process and progress therefore it has no present. Krishnamurti is serious when he tells us to turn our attention away from process and the temporal order, and learn what it is to interpret activity.

Student: How does this apply to the raising of a child?

In bringing up a child surely one must attend all the time to the activity of its human nature which is appropriate in its manifestation to the time, therefore we don't require the same embodiment of human activity in the three-year-old as we do in the seven-year-old. If you don't grasp human activity, you look around for process literature. So the poor babies are carved up into these categories. We get a strange norm.

Krishnamurti is correct in saying that unless we grasp activity we are always accelerating our illness. But what good is it to say it unless it can be heard and acted upon? Most do not grasp activity. Being future oriented only, we never undertake activity satisfied by its own exercise. So now you get the force of his saying we must not measure the present by the past. If we did something last week, and all we see is process, we would reach into the past and employ the same means. To have an abstract grasp of former means is bound to do violence to the present. On the other hand, we must be careful we don't find ourselves using language carelessly and ending up with notions that could corrupt our view of life in the world. He would apply to himself his own caution that the description is not the thing described.

Student: Why does he say, "I'm not a teacher"?

He doesn't want anyone to approach him as a clay tablet seeking an imprint. He is opposed to that educationally. His hard words for gurus and others who set themselves up as authorities are based upon that insight. The description is not the described and he's no exception to that. Let's do him justice and not make out as though his utterances are the tablets from Mt. Sinai.

Student: It seems he has done a marvelous job of resisting the adulation that has come to him as compared with Alan Watts.

It's very interesting if you look at the crises in each man's life. They have a bearing on their mode of relating. Krishnamurti's relation to the social order has always been austere. Alan Watts had a relation you might call incremental with respect to that. If you expand your social sphere not simply at the level of personal inclination to social contracts such as marriage, the acquisition of real estate—the need to support and attend to those things justly requires time. I don't mean one is required to go through life as abstemiously as Krishnamurti has done, but perhaps not as incrementally as Watts either given the vocation each had. If one had a vocation as a financier it's different—the chances are one would have to always put aside time for the study of making more money and not have all that much time for enjoying it. Such persons are *makers*, they make money. In principle that is no different from a maker of cabinets.

Krishnamurti's relation to his vocation in relation to his lifestyle is more prudent. The degree of austerity despite the millions bestowed on him is remarkable. Nevertheless he has always sustained that sort of support. Watts learned a great deal more that can't necessarily be gotten through empathy. They are two extremes.

I have the feeling that if Krishnamurti had lived his life in a more direct confrontation with the material order, he might have altered his rhetoric and might also have had a better appreciation of process in relation to activity and vice versa.

None of my remarks should divert us from grasping what he's pointing to! He's up to something important—it is nothing short of acquiring one's soul. There is no reason why one can't attend to both, giving the soul and intellect their due. Giving the intellect its due can't corrupt the soul since it's a function of the soul.

Student: Is acquiring one's soul an activity?

I don't know how to acquire my soul without a grasp of activity. You do have to take the risk of letting the motor run down to do that. Unlike Krishnamurti, I think an application to the tradition of canonical Scriptures, if applied to seriously, can do a great deal to instruct one. They also have the advantage of outliving us.

We have to try to move to center with respect to his thought while at the same time broadening our understanding of where and how we are to be in the world. We have not only to obtain to depth, but also to breadth.

Sorrow, Passion, and Beauty
March 27, 1979

On page 106 of *The Flight of the Eagle*: "I said, observe your reaction, do not call it good or bad. When you call it good or bad you bring about contradiction." This raises a problem. The questioner is concerned about making a judgment of value, and whether such a judgment can be based upon true possibility, namely without illusion. He wants to know whether good and bad can be distinguished. Krishnamurti says no, he didn't say all reactions were good, but he doesn't tell us what is good. Insofar as he is delivering to us a clinical description of our dysfunction (the way I relate to myself as an individual person in a dysfunctional manner), is he implying we should suspend philosophical inquiry into what has gone for centuries under the name of the problem of evil? That needs careful study. There's a great danger in assuming that a clinical description can stand in for a philosophical analysis. Is it a weakness in Krishnamurti's writings that there is an absence of genuine philosophical discussion? Is it a weakness to say, "The description is not the described"? Is it a weakness that he doesn't have an account of the dysfunction of the word (since he does talk)? What can we do about it? You have Lao Tzu, "those who know do not speak and those who speak do not know." Then Lao Tzu writes a book. It is easier to get out of Lao Tzu the function of the word than it is from Krishnamurti. What have I said about reality when I've said the description is not the described? I've said something is not but I haven't said what is. Is it a vice to attempt to say what something is?

This goes to the heart of what we ought to be doing in the activity we call education. If it is a vice to say what anything is—we're vicious.

There is another problem: can I take seriously that it is possible to learn something from another, or am I left simply to rely on my own self-inquiry? This also has to do with the problem of education. Is it a vicious posture to play the role of teacher? That is a very good question. If I dispense with it, how do I keep the role of student? I'm not attempting to confuse you. I'm simply forming certain questions that have to be engaged if we are to undertake to study Krishnamurti's thought adequately.

[Video—Dialogue IX: Sorrow, Passion, and Beauty[1]]

Student: Please elaborate on your earlier point about Greek sculpture.

The Romans grasped the efficient cause; the Greeks were bedazzled by the formal cause. When one looks at a Greek statue and compares it with a Roman statue, one is looking at an ideal rather than at an actual person. It seems to me the distinction is important. The Greek shows itself to be more contemplative toward an archetype. Had the Greeks achieved the balance between the contemplative and the Roman concern for the practical, it is unlikely the Romans would have conquered them. If the Romans had had a more intelligible grasp of the ideal while maintaining their genius for practical activity, it is hard to see how they would have declined. The decline of Rome with respect to the decline of Greece is interesting—each suffered from the want of the other's virtue. Roman sculpture is superior if one is thinking in terms of the power to represent personality. In Roman sculpture, we have an extraordinary introduction to suffering. In the Greek statue there is no sense of suffering, you get a sense of absorption, which is a different matter. The Roman at his best coped with the world with

---

[1] Video published by KFA under the title "Inward or True Beauty".

an astonishing amount of moral energy.[2] The Romans had a more sophisticated grasp of the efficient cause. It is strange to contemplate the two in relation to one another because each had so much to learn from the other and neither really mastered their lessons. The Roman grasp of the existential order was more efficient. And yet, the Romans didn't produce a Plato or an Aristotle. That's very important never to forget.

I get the feeling Krishnamurti could learn something from the Romans. The Roman is not satisfied with his saying, "action is just all of life," and "action is a movement that is ongoing." That's not what action is it is what activity is. A failure to distinguish between action and activity can be fatal when coping with the world. If I had made a response like that however, we wouldn't have 18 of these videos to listen to. What is important is not to have us deadlocked but to hear what he has to say. There is an aspect of his teaching that must be heard! The question you must ask is, is it enough? Here I come along and say "is it enough" and virtually everyone supposes they have grasped it. Don't imagine that! I'm saying that until one undertakes the activity he describes one can't ask the question. That would be an evasion. You must have a Roman (practical) and Greek (contemplative) approach to his discourses if you are to grasp them.

Student [rather angrily]: The whole question of action versus activity: is it not just labels?

I think you quite misunderstand. Let's move very carefully. A concept is not a label. We make a distinction between a name and a label. They aren't synonymous. The name discloses the essence. The label discloses what a thing is for, that's not the same as its nature. The label is on the side of utility; it has no respect for what the

---

[2] I suppose that's one of the reasons the British Empire lasted as long as it did—because it is primarily the Roman virtues the governing class learned early on in school. A similar want of a certain virtue in the British lost them the empire. I'm speaking somewhat from the inside to the outside, thinking of the literature I was brought up on. The accent was upon personal responsibility—that's much closer to the Roman ideal than the Greek.

thing is in itself, but for its instrumental sense. We label it because of its instrumental value to us. We name it out of a sense of wonder that we have discovered another being, whether or not that being is instrumental to us. It is a deficiency that he virtually assigns all language to label. His reason is clinical, but that's not all he knows. He's not incapable of relating to language at another level. It is crucial for us to study this; otherwise we are functioning as an ashram. I don't regard my role as being your guru, nor is it to rubberstamp what he's saying. That is why I say you must try on for size what he's saying.

Student: Is there a connection between Krishnamurti's clinical relation to language and art?

Gandhi once said that anyone who couldn't make a distinction between nature and art was deficient in sensibility. To make nature primary is to invert the proper order in relation to human beings and to beings we should refer to as natural beings which as far as can be determined do not function deliberatively. A work of art is, strictly speaking, a transfiguration of nature. It is undertaken as a work of clarification of our species' relation to nature, therefore art always possesses, when properly understood, a moral character.[3] The decadent notion of art for art's sake is the refusal to recognize the moral character of art as such. I don't mean to say art is a moral virtue as justice is, but the artist cannot perform a true work of art without a moral relation to his work. A work of art embodies the contemplative relation the artist undergoes in coping with the world as nature and therefore preeminently art is an intellectual activity and therefore cannot be simply a reaction—for reaction one only needs a perception, one doesn't need a conception. For a response to the world other than art one needs only cleverness. For example, in principle there is no difference between our arriving on the moon and the chimp banging fruit with his stick to knock it down since

---

[3] Prof. Anderson on the basis for this statement. "Art strives to realize the better and that places it in a moral context." –Ed.

the object of technology is always outside the activity. Not so with art. Artists are always a bit strange. When they are paid happily it is usually as a result of their representing the common mind. If it requires a high degree of intelligence to grasp a work of art executed today, chances are nobody is going to be bothered making the effort. When you figure the enormous amount of effort put into utilitarian activities you can see the difference.

The dreadful thing about our species is that we put most of our effort into unintelligent activity. Human intellectual activity is moral activity. To do as Krishnamurti does, to draw all his illustrations from nature, is to evade the issue. If the measure for one's action is the response one makes when on the edge of a cliff—that's dehumanizing. The two orders are not in correspondence. That's not what it is to be human. His dissolving the religious order in 1928 is not the same thing as walking too close to the precipice. If he is saying he had a vision and he did it, he is saying caprice is what orders his behavior. Patently that's not so. I think he hasn't thought it through. We must be careful we don't permit ourselves to accept every verbal explanation he brings forth. His action is vastly superior to what he says. I can't account for why he does it unless he has uncritically borrowed a prevailing way of understanding action which took powerful root in the 18th and 19th centuries. We have an example from literature, William Blake's *Tyger*. If you really read it, it puts the fear of God into you for the rest of your life. It raises a question which cannot be answered with finite intelligence, insofar as it opens out on the mystery that the Lord God tried to introduce Job to and which the Lord Krishna shows to Arjuna in the 11th chapter of the *Gītā*. There's something going on there that cannot be accounted for by one's own reason. If one didn't use that sentiment as a reason for understanding the poem, you would regard it as a bad poem because there is no definition to help us understand what the tyger is, what the lamb is. It opens out on something that transcends man and nature.

In the 19th century there was a good deal of sentimental poetry that represented nature. Wordsworth was capable of writing a great deal of sentimental stuff. There is no evidence that he understood what he was doing when he used nature as the measure of human action. You find Robert Frost in *The Road Not Taken* in which one gets the feeling that human decision is a matter of some crisis but the next thought is that maybe it isn't. There is no statement that qualifies anything. One is left with a vague feeling that arouses in us the sentiment for wondering on our pain when afflicted with having to make a decision. There is a profound absence of due attention to our deliberative nature in that, and in so far, the poem is not as good as it should have been. I'm not saying every poem should be didactic but Frost had an urge to write didactic poetry. When the distinction between the moral and the natural order becomes lost to our species, the very way we employ language becomes decadent. Most of the descriptions of Taoist thought come out of the same kind of impoverishment and sentimental posture to the point where it is now almost impossible to understand the *Chuang Tzu*. You can become so impoverished in your power to grasp rationally the subject matter that you explain a hard-nosed philosophy like the *Chuang-Tzu* on the basis of one's own caprice!

You cannot find a model for moral activity in nature. You can make analogies, but that's not good enough. Unless one possesses the moral capacity to distinguish between them, one will collapse and reduce one's nature to impulse. Those analogies are incapable of satisfactorily representing the moral order. Bright scientists are always saying not to go to them for moral counsel. So why does Krishnamurti use illustrations from nature to describe moral activity? He says stay with it. How would impulse support that? We have to be careful how we think about this. That I don't contradict him doesn't mean I haven't further thoughts. When I let him say it and try to relate it, it doesn't please him. It raises another question: is it sound to refrain from access to excellences in other persons and other things that could conceivably instruct us? If all I require is my own impulse, then of course I need only myself.

Student: What impulse funds the human act of liberation?

I wouldn't want to say impulse at all, but rather the energy supporting liberation is that which human nature conditions as the prism conditions light. Energy is refracted by human nature in such a way that we have the intuition at all times that we can violate our own nature (even if not conceptually represented to ourselves, it is available in correct sentiment). We sometimes experience it in conscience, but conscience is in part learned. Whatever it is that is refracting energy to support our sentiment for the possibility for violating our own nature, it never lets up. It is always present as the negative summons. One can negate one's natural bent as a species, which bent is to behave deliberately. If the capacity for self-betrayal were not present as a possibility, then we couldn't talk about deliberation; we would be back to simple perception and impulse. Rhetorically, that's where Krishnamurti leaves it with "perception is the action." One could infer from his rhetoric that he is an impulsive man, and yet, his conversation is not the conversation of an impulsive mind. He does have himself in a dreadful philosophical bind. On the one hand, as a clinical psychologist, he is telling us what not to do, but on the other, he is using an inadequate model to advise us. So we must do a work of therapy on his rhetoric else we are in grave danger of misunderstanding what he is saying.

Student: Was he as difficult to converse with in private?

We've had many delightful conversations. In one I pressed hard on his statement that "the perception is the action." By the end it was clear he wasn't throwing out deliberation.

The Art of Listening
April 3, 1979

Why have reductive descriptions of our nature always failed to satisfy, leaving us with the feeling that something has been left out? Even though Krishnamurti doesn't address himself directly to the question of human nature, his teaching raises the question. If one is to relate intelligibly to the claims he makes for our passage (that it is possible to go through the world without sorrow) I don't see how one can avoid the question of human nature.

I'd also like to clear up one thing I may inadvertently have left you with when I was talking about romantic poetry. I referred to Frost's *The Road Not Taken* in adverse terms. I wasn't speaking cavalierly and out of aesthetic preference of my own. It would be hard to find fault with the form of that poem. I was referring to the poem's content. I didn't mean to say that the poem's worth is properly measured by someone's idea of what the content should be. That would be perverse. A poem, like any work of art, is an aesthetic whole. I was speaking about a tendency in romantic poetry which I think undercuts the power to confront the moment decisively. I think one cannot completely divorce the character of the content from the work's overall excellence or deficiency. That is not the last word on Frost—in other works he makes a strong statement. I think Krishnamurti's disclosure would have been marvelously strengthened if he had followed up on his own questions. But that following up entails a commitment to a notion about reality which is on the side of embodiment. If one doesn't have that commitment, then the distinction between activity and process becomes blurred, and one can't help but fall into confusion.

[Video—Dialogue X: The Art of Listening[1]]

Student: Can you comment on the notion of consummation?

It's the old problem of being and becoming—process as such cannot consummate itself. Therefore, if one looks for consummation from process one is always disappointed. If process could consummate itself, everything would have been consummated long since. But that isn't the case. Process is found in the embodiment of activity. That is, when looking at embodiment, we are looking at the material representation of activity. But, of course, that material character you're looking at depends on activity for its movement since the material aspect as such has no power to move itself. I don't mean it doesn't contribute to movement, but the process of material embodiment cannot consummate itself. It cannot attain to its proper end in its own power. This is the great sorrow that attaches to potentiality. If potentiality could actualize itself, we'd have to give up potentiality as such—there would be nothing but actuality. That's not what we see—we see genuine change. If one is going to be in the condition of the realized Vedanta, one is consummated upon each instant because of one's relation to activity, not because one is part of a process. Becoming does not create being—it embodies it. When St. Paul says that patience energizes experience and then goes on to say that experience energizes hope [Rom 5:4], what he's saying is unless I am patient within process I'll be unable to try out my relation to it. I'm unable to try out my relation to becoming because I'm literally unconscious of it, since I'm mindlessly a part of it. This collapse into becoming or process is the ordinary mind of which it is Krishnamurti's burden to rid us. Krishnamurti does not seek to annihilate the ordinary mind, it too has its place, but he doesn't want us to understand ourselves as the prisoners of the ordinary mind.

---

[1] Video published by KFA also under the title "The Art of Listening".

The mark of being a prisoner to it is to be unaware of it, hence to be unaware of what imprisons one. It simply hurts—but one doesn't know what is causing it. I am melancholy while on my high because I'm anticipating the end. We say I wish it could never end.

Student: Why is there this craving for anxiety? We feed it.

We don't deliberately feed anxiety. We are already anxious to start with because without a genuine present, we expect the future to provide the occasion for satisfying us. If someone says in 15 years you will inherit $1 million—you have a jolly hard time living your life in the meantime. Everything done is measured by the future prospect. It never occurs to you that you might die in the next moment. Your reality is the promise. Well, you say, we're not in the same case. But what we are leaning on is a possibility of better times ahead. All our passage is measured by that prospect. If that is the way we are going through the world, we'll never overcome anxiety. That's why Jesus says, "don't be over anxious" that is, in a condition of anxiety. "Sufficient unto the day [is] the evil thereof." [Mt 6:34] Things are bad enough today without worrying about catching up tomorrow. As a farmer plants his crops he rests in a reasonable hope that the movement of the seasons will not let him down in relation to the crop to come. But "don't count on the harvest while plowing" as we're told in the *I Ching*.[2] So we don't really feed our anxieties at all. We become anxious that we're anxious and we'd rather not be but we don't know what to do about it. We don't prefer not to be anxious strongly enough to do something about it. So this maudlin notion about the dreadful condition of the world has to be taken with a grain of salt. Nothing can possibly be done about it until the individual wants badly enough to change. That's rare. It becomes decreasingly likely as the individual gets older because with the passage of years the sense of wonder decreases. What generates desire for self-change is the felt conflict between the profound sense of wonder and what appears to be the mechanical character of existence which is always

---

[2] Cf. Hexagram 25 line 2.

failing it. There's a marvelous sense of beauty and the horror that nothing stays. If one has a sense of wonder, one feels his sorrow that nothing stays. The greater the tension, the more pain until either one shoots oneself (literally or figuratively), or one starts getting to work on annihilating one's attachment to one's present self-understanding. So if someone claims he's not getting on with it, and doesn't know why—he is babbling. He doesn't want to. In this case pain increases, not between wonder and horror, but due to the sense of decreasing vital power.

Student: That is also a horror.

Yes but it is incomparable. As one senses a loss of vital power one finds ways of palliating it. That's why we have happy hour. We gain the illusion we have regained youth. We can even extend the hour by becoming increasingly blotto. Of course we have tranquilizers too. While on them we are not suffering extreme tension. To put oneself on drugs is a sign one has not suffered enough—that one isn't going to follow through with psychological stress. Just dull it, not come to terms with it.

So now you can see the force of his relating beauty and sorrow. He isn't interested in responding to beauty simply aesthetically. He wants to respond to it with self-knowledge. If all I can do is respond with an aesthetical sensibility, I'll never come to self-knowledge. In fact I suppose one of the reasons for the pathological attempt in some Puritan persuasions to remove occasions for rejoicing and beauty is a fear one will capitulate to the pleasure it brings and not become serious about one's passage. I call it pathological because it isn't the solution to the problem.

I don't think we should say we're consciously feeding our anxiety, though we do so unconsciously. We don't know what we're doing when we're embedded in process. "Father forgive them for they know not what they do." [Lk 23:34] They ought to have known, else why forgive them? But he doesn't add "and help them to know." There isn't a sentimental line in the gospel.

Student: Is pain associated with beauty because most people's eyes can't see beyond its embodiment?

They are unable to see beauty as activity. They confuse beauty with its embodiment which cannot stay.

Student: It is embodied in different ways.

It cannot be reduced to embodiment. If you grasp that intuitively you won't be impatient while waiting for what properly draws you, nor when presently enjoying something.

I remember when in graduate school I was studying mythology where the tension of the awareness of life and death is brought into magnificent dialectical play—suddenly it occurred to me that the only place worth being was between life and death and if one wouldn't take his stance there, one would always be turbulent. To have seen that was, at the level of apprehension, an immense relief. Apprehending the possibility of abiding between life and death is fine as far as it goes. There remains, however, the small problem of relating to that apprehension on every instant so as to be prepared to die but equally prepared to live. So the whole business of life-and-death is no longer a problem. When one is self-bound within the movement of process, there is no way to see it. The question can't arise. The question arose for me at that time because I was concerned to wonder on the difference between living the life of a hero and that of a saint. The life of the hero entails being caught up in external affairs, exercising great strength and courage; while the life of the saint tends to remind us continually that there is no special virtue in being caught up in the life of the everyday. So the whole thing struck me very dramatically as an occasion for meditating on "life is a battle." The saint relates one way and the hero another. What is the battle? I saw the importance of voluntarily internalizing the battle with myself rather than projecting it in the world. This meditation led me to see that the only stance worth taking is the one between life and death. I have often smiled to recall how many times I forgot

I had seen that. As the number of times I forgot increased, I became increasingly anxious about not seeing it again. If I forgot, I might never remember again—and what advantage would it have been to see it? That scared me witless: to realize that at any point along the line I could fail. One never builds up momentum in the order of spirit. Momentum is always on the other side, the side of process. That shook me to the marrow. I began to get an enormous concern for the instant. I knew that each succeeding instant presents that battlefield anew. If that's the case, you can see how terribly alert one must be? Each instant is an occasion for spiritual demise.

Student: Does the recognition of the possibility of one's spiritual demise each instant make one anxious?

One is not anxious in the instant, but one is aware of the possibility of failing.

Student: Would awareness of the possibility of failing impinge on seeing?

No. While greeting the instant, one is not forgetting that one cannot let up in self-examination. It is coincident with seeing. Krishnamurti agreed two or more times with the notion that one must not bolt, must not run away. Well obviously there is a moment which offers the occasion for bolting. If he really means that, then each instant presents one with the possibility for behaving badly, which for him would mean allowing oneself to be collapsed into mechanical momentum. What he doesn't provide in his analysis is the structure of one's relation to what I've been calling activity in contradistinction to process. That's what we must pay attention to.

In Keats' letter to Benjamin Bailey[3] he says, "It is unfortunate: men should bear with each other; there lives not the man who may not be cut up, aye, lashed to pieces, on his weakest side. The best of men have but a portion of good in them—a kind of spiritual yeast

---

[3] January 23, 1818.

in their frames, which creates the ferment of existence—by which a man is propelled to act, and strive, and buffet with circumstance."

Now, if Keats really believed that, he would not have had such a drive to study philosophy—by which I think he means the wisdom tradition. I think he must have had a question about it. The good doesn't drive us but draws us. To be is good, so existence embodies the good. But simply to exist is not yet to have reached one's humanity. It is our failing of the good that gives rise to a momentum that drives us. The good energizes us in our movement forward, impels us at the level of being, but doesn't compel or propel in the order of becoming ourselves. It is interesting that Keats would use the expression, "yeast which creates a ferment of existence." That's not very tranquil. He sees something but he hasn't got it worked out as to the distinction between activity and process. In that half-light he has given more value to natural process than is just. His sense of wonder is making up the difference between mechanism and spirituality—a typical romantic illusion. The reason I brought him forward is that he shows signs of growth; he makes a profound effort to get clear. His literary genius is coming up with stuff which requires further therapy. It is hard to think he wouldn't have continued with that task. Each of us has to set out to do that. It's hard to remember to keep at it.

Our nature has the power to violate itself and precisely on that account requires that each human individual person consciously accept the burden of becoming increasingly aware of that nature. It is a nature that for its realization requires self-awareness—but nothing in the world will coerce that self-awareness. A nature that requires to grasp itself cannot be coerced else it would have realized itself long since. There is a material possibility within it which human nature is capable of not realizing. That is full of dread and the reason timeliness is so crucial.

Student: Are we naturally aware of this need for realizing our nature?

You could say we have a nature which provides the power of knowing that we are crucially related to ourselves, but our nature doesn't coerce us to relate functionally to that knowledge. Krishnamurti says negation is involved. He doesn't push that far enough. It may be temperament—he might not be interested to do it. It isn't necessary to his clinical program. If we are to undertake a study of the structure of our nature in terms of its proper operation, we must press beyond that. There is not one negation but two.

Next time I think you will begin to see why he never answers in content the questions he raises on the side of principle. When he raises the question of activity, he never gives its content. There's a good reason and a bad reason. We have to understand the former to see what he's doing. We also must understand the bad one else we will not see when he fails to engage the relation between activity and process. What he says in pointing to activity as primary seems sound. Notice the manner in which he proceeds rhetorically. He asks what is learning, he then tells us in terms of mechanical process. He doesn't tell us the essence or activity of learning. There's a good reason for that, and we have to learn it. The bad reason applies to his want of relating activity and process in the totality of the act. He's not unaware of it. In this tape he said one is seeing and hearing while involved in the mechanical activity of learning. So he is aware of the nexus, but he doesn't open it up. He doesn't discuss the character of that nexus which I think can be discussed. I hope you will be able to infer what that might consist in. Ultimately, the real problem for our self-understanding is found in the nexus between activity and process, being and becoming. The whole drama takes place in the middle. When we explore what we've called the double negation we will get a sense of activity and its relation to the process of our own responses and the character of our activity in that nexus. If we can grasp that, I can't imagine we'd fail to see what he's striving so heroically to help us to grasp. Notice how sometimes you feel you've just apprehended something and feel irradiated for the moment? How can I abide there? I think that can be discussed and inferred from what he says. We need to do two things. First, develop the sensitivity to these moments—never forget we've enjoyed them. And second, press on to the further question of what is the activity that maintains one in that relation? What a marvelous introduction: sorrow, passion and beauty.

Being Hurt and Hurting Others
April 17, 1979

What can we make of Krishnamurti's notion that we must be severed from the past? I don't believe he wants us to sever absolutely the past since he reminds us that thought has a role to play. I can't overstress that fact because his iconoclastic style provides an occasion for lazy hearing. One can say he's given the past bad press and written it off, but it seems to me he's saying that memory has a function. The problem is not with memory but with my relation to memory. The natural function of memory, if interfered with sufficiently, can bring us to such a wretched point that we can't navigate. Is he asking us to become amnesiacs? No. He's concerned to say that anxiety produces an evaluation of the past which is pernicious. Whose fault is that? The evaluator's fault. One of the first steps to becoming truly aware is to grasp that one is in relation to oneself, to grasp it in actuality. One then must be in relation to oneself at two removes. First one must recognize that one is in self-relation and then consciously relate to oneself. So we must actively relate ourselves to ourselves. Kierkegaard in the *Sickness Unto Death* notes that when this is not done, despair is the upshot. Despair is the condition of our species when it is not aware or awake. Krishnamurti would agree. We're not simply unaware. So there are two things: the first is a natural screening process which must obtain because we can't take in such an abundance, that's taken care of at the instinctual level. Second and what is not instinctual is the evaluation we make. If I will not relate consciously to that, there is despair.

[Video—Dialogue XI: Being Hurt and Hurting Others[1]]

Quite difficult questions attended my mind concerning this dialogue. Do you have questions?

Student: Hurts arise and then get lost. How does one understand things buried beneath the conscious level?

Student: There are enough conscious hurts to keep us busy.

Student: How can we be hurt unconsciously?

Student: Hurt it is an emotion. You aren't your emotions, therefore there is a distance there.

Student: What is the relation between hurt and growing pains?

I think the notion of unconscious hurt which seems illogical could be understood in this way: what at the time is suppressed is in time, forgotten. For instance, we become angry. The basis of that anger is a sense of personal deprivation caused say by another person. For various reasons, we suppress our anger. Then we forget that incident but the mechanism of our total being does not forget it. So at the point where it is forgotten but is still registered, it is being repressed. Repressed emotion, though forgotten, continues to be expressed. Our responses to the environment are upon us faster than we can bring rational analysis to bear on them. Gurdjieff and Ouspenski are emphatic about the difference in speed at which feeling and thoughts operate. The response I make based on earlier hurt is upon me before I have consciously chosen it. I begin to identify as my nature a cluster of such expressions. Therefore, a great deal of behavior we take for granted is based on repression. It goes back to the point about an unconscious layer from which arises this patterned behavior.

---

[1] Video published by KFA under the title "Nature of Hurt".

Student: How do we know when we're acting from self-image formed from repressed emotions?

I think we can usefully make a distinction between the expression of contaminated nature and an expression of real nature. There is a great conflict as a result of being unsure of the relation of the one to the other. I want to admit of the role of repression as a springboard for our action. One might say that depth psychology which is so bound to personal history is on the right track. Still, it doesn't follow that if one goes about some method to excavate repressed emotion that that will be sufficient to free one from continuing to behave in the patterned way. One has a conscious investment in that behavior which also must be dealt with. There is also a tremendous investment on the part of others towards me—they depend on my patterned way. If one changes, one causes disruption. It is not, as is naïvely thought, that if I become better, the situation is going to become more pleasant. Others have a vested interest in the status quo.

Maybe it is the case, as Jesus said that, "there is nothing hid but what shall be revealed." [Lk 8:17, Lk 12:2, Mk 4:22, and Mt 10:26] If one reads that against the concern for self-transformation, when one becomes seriously ordered to self-change, it is astonishing what bubbles up to memory that might never have come up otherwise. You can make a strong argument for not undertaking it—there have been so many casualties historically. One can go about undertaking self-change just as imprudently as one was living before. The price, however, is much greater. The whole of society is supporting the unconscious imprudence. Society has an economic investment in it. You see how much trouble you can get into if you start interfering?

Student: How can he say he's never been hurt?

I don't know. I was equally amazed.

Student: You can't take those statements seriously. It is a device.

It would be interesting to ask if he meant what he said. I find it difficult to believe he is using such a device consciously. There would be enormous risk to undertake that and make such a fuss about truth.

Student: He's being playful.

Student: There is a distinction between grief and hurt. Why would he be speaking playfully? He's trying to be understood.

Student: He's talking about the whole structure, not individual hurts.

That's a reasonable interpretation. One could grasp in principle that one has no business getting hurt, yet to attain to freedom, one has to meet hurt a step at a time. If we make a clear case for the adequacy of this point at the level of confronting the whole of hurt, one must recognize that in confronting the hurt, at this juncture, one is nonetheless addressing all hurt. The next hurt you record is just as vociferously concerned that you relate to it as soundly. You're not, upon relating once, freed from the existential task of taking it one step at a time.

But be careful of what is meant by understanding. Either we grow or we don't. At the level of insight, one can discern the possibility of growth, perhaps even identify concrete steps which could facilitate that growth. The embodiment of that revelation is another matter. In fact, thought is not coincident with its object. There is a hiatus which is a condition of the finite mind. So whereas I can participate in the infinite precisely at the point where I am informed by it, I am not on that account transformed for the next moment. There is one small detail. What am I going to do? Between seeing and doing, nothing I've heard him say applies. Either I am incapable of understanding, or I do understand and have discerned that he hasn't said it all. If it is the case that one should take equally seriously the relation between process and activity as we take activity, we can't overlook the problem of growth. One is simply not changed for all time by insight alone.

Student: Perhaps Krishnamurti is referring to hurt feelings when he says he has never been hurt. I haven't been hurt in that way for 10 years.

I'm not quite sure what Krishnamurti means. It seems he's well aware of hurt. But it is a sensitive point for him. I tried at least three times to draw him into a discussion of human nature distinct from the nature of animals. He didn't want to do it. I think it would have made his discussions stronger. Each time he began to speak fast and he didn't deal with it. The whole issue becomes crucial for understanding human nature. It is not sufficient to say there was a time when humans behaved innocently and the priests corrupted that innocent relation to the environment by instilling fear. We must discover what aspect of our human nature permits us to become corrupted.

Student: With respect to the analogy from the field of art etc. you can't teach understanding.

The problem with the analogy from art is that when one undertakes any form of art, it is primarily for the sake of having one's power as an artist pass over to material that is external. One can't do it exclusive of the concern for oneself of course, but when the criticism of "not a true performance" is made, that is a moral judgment in the interest of an aesthetical judgment. When one undertakes to live one's life well, it is a performance, which in the doing, perfects the doer. I think Krishnamurti grasps that, but I wonder if he grasps that one's intentions are embodied in the material vehicle that attends it. At the level of the material vehicle, the analogy from art works. But at the level where one has to get together one's intentions with the material vehicle in prudential relation, one must deal with both orders together. I think he is sensitive to the possibility of human persons indefinitely resisting Love. I don't know if he has thought it through. He has felt it because he says don't bolt. But I doubt he has addressed himself in thought to that.

Student: Is he a romantic?

Yes.

Next time we need to consider what is the therapeutic possibility of dealing with hurt that is consciously present.

Love, Sex and Pleasure
April 24, 1979

There is an aspect of Krishnamurti's thought that is compatible with genuine nonsense. Genuine nonsense is not nonsensical. There is very little genuine nonsense literature around. I never asked what he thought of *The Owl and the Pussycat*. I don't know why I failed myself so seriously that I didn't ask. English is virtually the only language in which there is a deposit of nonsense literature. There are a few poems in German, but that's about it. Genuine nonsense erupted in the 19th century in Lewis Carroll and Edward Lear. What it expresses is that aspect of the world in which the opposites we discern somehow on every instant find a way of dwelling together. That things hang together at all cannot but be a source of wonder for anyone with a sense of existence. I don't think anyone can appreciate nonsense without a sense of existence. That the *Owl and the Pussycat* put out to sea together for a year and a day! The whole poem would be ruined if they sailed away for a year. The whole thing is beyond the pale of respectability; it's beyond the pale of Aristotelian common sense. It shows a feature of the world that is abidingly present. Everything that ought not to get along is somehow abidingly present. It happens on every moment. If it were left up to us, nothing should have lasted half an instant. When Krishnamurti talks about order breaking through and intelligence breaking out, I think he is consciously speaking about the non-possible. The non-possible is always actualizing itself and we don't see it.

You see when one reads that marvelous poem by Edward Lear about the Jumblies who put to sea in a sieve you know that it happened. To attempt to say that poem should not be taken seriously is to say you haven't read it yet. Nonsense is serious (not in an academic sense) but serious about existence. Existence is bursting at the seams with the non-possible, with Divine excess. Existence is bubbling over all the time with what from our own perspective cannot be the case, but it is the case. Krishnamurti is advising us to accept that it is, to allow room for it in our hearts. But we are too afraid. The little child isn't afraid to look on the non-possible, but he looks without knowing that he is, nor does he know what he is looking at. If we can have the courage of a little child to look upon the non-possible without blinking, knowing without demanding we be able to explain it, our IQs would make a quantum leap. When Krishnamurti talks about order and beauty, listen with respect to his invitation to that sort of receptivity. If you so listen, academic problems will fall into perspective.

[Video—Dialogue XII: Love, Sex and Pleasure[1]]

Student: How is eating vegetables not killing?

I get the impression that had he a sister who was under attack and had his defense required killing the rapist, he would have. So the difficulty is that his rhetoric is sometimes imprecise. I think the argument would be that it is possible to eat an adequate diet without killing animals. But what the Eskimos would do I don't know. Perhaps he'd argue he wasn't talking about fringe situations. For most of us he would say it is possible. If we could manage, then it would be hard to argue for the destruction of animals.

About killing as such: I don't think he means he is a pacifist, at least not an absolute one. He is highly sensitive to the unnecessary harm we do to other life. I think he's right about that—we don't go out of our way to live well with lower creatures. I saw a movie recently in which a father was taking his two young boys duck hunting. What is really going on? What is the sense in it? Why teach them

---

[1] Video published by KFA under the title "Love and Pleasure".

to kill birds? When killing becomes a sport, I think we can argue we become diseased. I don't think that it is a sentimental argument, a sound economy would require I not kill needlessly.

Student: Doesn't Scripture tell us that man has dominion over the earth?

I've always been impressed that in the Bible there is the invitation to Adam in the garden to eat plants but none to eat meat. That's from a tradition which had no scruples about eating meat. There is no word from Jesus although he is obviously eating animal flesh at the Passover. Out of this tradition came the remarkable first two chapters in Genesis. I don't think Krishnamurti is saying he will not kill, but wherein we do not require to kill we should not.

Student: I guess I still want to ask if eating vegetables is killing?

When you come to it, you must decide that a certain degree of our living as a process collides with the life space of other creatures. For instance, it collides with vegetables. Leave that alone. Sentimentality takes over where it begins to be in bad faith with the essential. Look at the enormous amount of trouble we've gotten into by exterminating lions and wolves because we feel so sorry for their prey.

1. Be prepared unsentimentally to discern what necessities attend existence and what do not.
2. We never live in peace if we do not in good faith live up to all the light we have. We should still not have exhausted all the light, therefore we must face it that a certain area in our going well will of necessity encroach on the life space of others, and probably I am in ignorance about unnecessarily encroaching. If I become neurotically anxious about it, I lose even the grasp of essential nature I had, and so I will behave more badly than I need to. If we follow his counsel

we are thrown back on ourselves as individuals. If we don't take this counsel seriously we're in a corrupt relation to it.

Student: If eating involves killing and if killing is wrong, are we really saying it is better not to exist at all?

I think the point is instructive. It shows what happens when we apply an abstract principle and take it to its logical conclusion. Is it possible though to live well while doing as little unnecessary harm to the life space of other creatures, while at the same time accepting that a fair degree of harm is going to be done even so? One ought not to conclude that since one must effect harm, there is nothing the matter with indiscriminate harm. That is fallacious. It confuses principle with operation. To say we ought not to harm others has to be understood. I think he showed himself wise when he said it is the individual's responsibility to make up his mind at any instant. When one lives outside the decision within the instant, and then starts codifying decision into rules, etc., you have one of the greatest errors our species has committed: that of reducing individual behavior to a collective standard. Don't imagine it can ever work. We are different from the social insects and must find a way to proceed in making individual passage. Who is going to decide that for you?

Even within the social order vocational differences create a degree of instability and unnecessary harm. Most of us are not so chaste that we don't sustain hurt. Take the relation between student and teacher. Each teacher necessarily embodies a certain bent. Let us assume a student is in the room who has suffered some hurt from another personality who like me is prone to state things positively. If they were hurt, I don't even know the history of that person, but it is unlikely they would not take offense. Am I to undertake violence to my own nature to avoid their hurt? The one whose hurt I was being careful of will likely be the first to complain. We have to settle for it that while we remain with a history of hurt and don't take radical responsibility for that, we go on hurting one another. If you think it through it should be clear why I have not made flattering comments about five year plans for individual personal transformation. I don't mean we shouldn't apply to the social amenities, but none of it touches the root spiritual disease.

Student: In the talks did you feel intimidated?

If I did I must have been unconscious of it. I had a task to provide him with as much access as I could for stating what he had to say.

Student: It seemed like you were avoiding hurting him.

I was avoiding making it unnecessarily difficult for him to say what he wanted. There were many times when I wanted to press the point home dialectically, but I didn't. It was not out of timidity but had I pressed a point, the whole thing would have stopped. "Dialogue" with Krishnamurti isn't what we understand by that word.

Student: You brought up conscience and he consciousness. Did he misunderstand?

There are points where he deliberately did not follow up on my suggestion.

With respect to timidity, notice I didn't stop quoting. I was convinced from early on that though he didn't like it, he would continue to support it. I did it in an attempt to understand him. Sometimes he will speak positively about tradition. It is important never to give the impression he is simply iconoclastic.

Student: Maybe the gurus he laughed at or wrote about derisively are trying seriously to solve the same problems he is. How can a teacher laugh at a potential student?

My impression is that he is not laughing derisively except where the guru was by his own admission falling into self-contradiction. He is extremely keen in his sense of how we put ourselves on.

It is possible there is a wide area of human experience of living that he has no direct acquaintance with. It might be he would prejudge that. I never got the sense he was malicious. He has an extreme revulsion, that's not quite the same as pleasure in observing another's hurt. I never got the impression he was petty. I did get the impression from his sweeping pronouncements that some things were outside his having direct acquaintance with them. One has to make allowances for his rhetorical lapses and find what he is saying that is of positive worth.

Think seriously through the relation of possessing a chaste mind and no longer being subject to hurt. His whole notion of chastity is worth deep inquiry. Remember the words of Jesus: "Neither do I condemn thee: go, and sin no more." [Jn 8:11]

A Different Way of Living
May 1, 1979

J. V. Cunningham's poem *Song* has a quality of purity both in the way form is handled and in the lyric. It is a simple lyric two stanzas of four lines each. The meter is a trimeter. The content has an astonishing purity:

> I know not whence she came,
> Nor why she dowered on me
> Steadfast unblushing shame.
> Mature simplicity,
>
> Appropriate to her years,
> She came as clouds hung low,
> And from her eyes fell tears,
> As water falls from snow.

You couldn't get anything more pure than that. The way water falls and the moment when snow falls from the bough is uncontrived purity of motion. It is aesthetically beautiful. One always has the feeling that something miraculous has happened when form and content come together without jostling. The Chinese call it the 'Mean.' Krishnamurti would probably agree that the chaste mind is a mind that enjoys the relation between form and content without conflict. Of course for the calculative intellect, it appears impossible to attain to that magic manner of living. One is either so filled by desire for content one feels oppressed by form, or so insistent upon imprinting upon the world the form of one's vision that one feels opposed by the content or matter of things. One oscillates back and forth. Temperament plays a part. Those gluttonous for highs try to overleap the strictures of form. What a marvelous thing to do precisely the chaste thing at the time, in the place, with the person, toward the end.

You see, if we didn't resonate to that as a possibility, the room wouldn't be so quiet. It's quiet enough to hear the birds. I sometimes think it was such a thought which Jesus had when he says "I and [my] Father are one." [Jn 10:30] Where they meet is the locus of the chaste mind. It cannot be reduced to a code of rules, and so on that account, it gets into trouble with the establishment. Neither does it lust after better things, and therefore is in trouble with the zealots. The chaste mind must tread very carefully. The impressive thing about Krishnamurti, despite his warmth, even at the end when he virtually embraced me, there was still a sense that there was something in his person that could not be exhausted by any formal gesture. Not that he was withdrawn! One is terribly grateful that there is something left over. One would never think of Krishnamurti throwing himself away, but neither is he worried about protecting himself. That is a feature of the chaste mind. Think about the chaste mind and inaccessibility.

[Video—Dialogue XIII: A Different Way of Living[1]]

Student: Please expand on his notion that the highest education is the resolving of conflict.

First let's define education. Education is that activity which, *freely* undergone, raises one's level of existence. That would immediately distinguish it from training since training has always an end outside itself. Education has an end within itself. One is trained for something. Education is satisfied by its own exercise. So if we *together* undertook to look at what he calls conflict, education would

---

[1] Video published by KFA also under the title "A Different Way of Living."

be taking place. We would be looking as an end in itself. Seeing is immanent, training is not. I don't mean to divide the two by saying training doesn't occur within the activity we call education. However training need not include education. One can train a fish, but it would be difficult to say the fish had been educated. Education is essentially self-critical. To be aware of one's motions (as in training) is not the same as being aware of and critical of one's motives.

The educated person acts always for the sake of one activity. When education is reduced to training, we become increasingly barbarous. It becomes impossible to converse with educators about education. I suspect today you have trouble finding a majority of faculty who could tell what education is. The matter is critical for your own level of existence which is what I am concerned in, as I am my own. It should simply be required of any instructor that he should be able to answer the question in a way of representing its principle. Otherwise he isn't ready to teach a class in humanities. I'd make the same comment about the church. Any minister unable to discuss the first principles of transformation must be kidding himself. It is true that churches don't hire much other than social directors. But you see when Nicodemus comes and says, "How can a man be born when he is old? Can he enter the second time into his mother's womb, and be born?" Jesus says, "Art thou a master of Israel, and knowest not these things?" [Jn 3:1-10]

This leads to the heart of consciousness and content. If I don't know what I'm doing in the name of what I'm doing, what's going on? In the practical order, I either become educated or I don't. If in this course you've not been attaining to a higher level of self-understanding, you are not doing your work. I remember this was brought home with a fierce shock when I was studying Plato. Plato is patently interested first of all in the possibility of someone attaining to some light on themselves. But do you think I heard any discussion of that? No. Just: see if this argument holds together; or what sort of literary device is the *Republic*? It's fine to look at that but is that all there is? Why read Plato at all if we reduce our study to an historical grasp of it?

If you're going to get unconfused about education, you have to do a lot of work. There are centuries behind our common notions. Don't misunderstand, I don't feel sorry for you. Nobody helped me. I take seriously the question you've asked. Contemplate the distinction between training and education. Because if you don't, it's hopeless, absolutely hopeless. I am capable of grasping what it is to be in a free relation to myself or I am not. And if I'm not, I'm in radical self-bondage. And I believe in my self-bondage, how on earth can anybody reach me with any other suggestion?

I'm inclined to think that when one loses a grasp on education, training also begins to fall away. Literacy is declining. You can't get anybody to train for its own sake, so it is no wonder students ask why they're in school. There is no way to answer if the measure is training. They see that the question cannot be answered and therefore what does the student do? He does as little as possible. Information gets passed off as understanding. When a student asks me to talk down to them, I refuse since I am here to assist them to raise their level to mine. That is not looked on with favor. In the '70s, students regarded education as some sort of inoculation, as with drugs, it is something that when assimilated, coerces a result. Education is considered by some to be a contagious disease—you merely have to be around to pick it up. What can you do with a mind like that?

I don't think when Krishnamurti tells us to start by observing conflict that he assumes that will coerce anything. Yet he's willing to start. He has no illusions about the result. He just feels the likelihood of his listener awakening to activity performed for its own sake is slight. That's why he stresses seriousness. Seriousness requires a free movement on my part. There is a whole generation of students unable to conceive what it is to be in a free relation to oneself. It is simply accepted that education ought to be coercive. Either I am capable of understanding that or I'm not. If I am not I'm in radical self-bondage. If I believe in my self-bondage, how can anybody reach me?

Maybe this generation's lack of seriousness is the mindless result of the drug culture. They wonder why I can't be turned on like TV.

Years ago in the '60s I was invited to give a lecture on Taoism. I said one couldn't compromise with Tao. Afterwards a young woman turned to her classmate and said, "What a turnoff!" What was the turnoff? There is no mushy place between me and Tao. That's one thing in Krishnamurti—there is no mush point. You've heard me be critical of his rhetoric, but that has nothing to do with the point I'm making. In the practice of self-change there is no mush point. He recognizes that. He says consciousness is its content and content is the consciousness. Philosophically that's difficult. In the practical order there is no way out of it. Face it: what are we talking about? Performance. And so, as long as one's performance issues from self-identification, Krishnamurti's comment makes sense: the unenlightened consciousness is totally identified with its object. Of course theoretically and at the level of enlightenment it is absurd to say consciousness is its content since there would then be no possibility for becoming aware. Awareness, (not "awareness of" but simple awareness) is free of all identifications. Consciousness irradiated by awareness is no longer collapsed into its content. Krishnamurti has made the distinction between simple awareness and "awareness of" but you can't get that distinction together with "consciousness is its content." Before we say he doesn't understand, see if there might not be two orders of discourse. On rare occasions Krishnamurti will make a theoretical statement—for example being aware and being aware of. Most of the time, however, he talks simply in terms of the performance of the person who is in conflict or self-bondage.

Student: By ego does he mean conceptual knowledge which mediates between awareness and what is out there? Even so it is bounded by time and space.

I don't think the ego is bounded. Ego is simply a focus of the seeing. When I say there isn't one who is doing the seeing, ego is not seeing. I don't mean there is no such thing as entity. We are fashioning ego all the time by our shifting focus. When we identify with that activity of focusing, or with what it focuses on, then there are indefinite numbers of egos. If I dwell continually in the activity of being aware, I never identify myself with my focus or its object, while enjoying or suffering both. Otherwise you have the difficulty of collapsing the activity of being aware into the ego; and collapsing the subject into that ego. By definition the subject 'I' cannot be grasped, by definition the subject cannot be gotten behind. When you try to turn the subject into an object, you have lost the self. Therefore one ought not to worry about self as an object.

The difficulty with depth psychology, except where by natural gift the person is a healer, is that it generates an inordinate concern for subjectivity. But the subject, in a radical sense, can't become an object. When we make it so, the subject slips out.

Student: I understand all that! Even if one is not generating a concern for the subjective, isn't the nature of existence in the physical world bounded? And doesn't the fact of our being bounded place limitations on seeing? It's not really either/or.

To say that our "seeing" or awareness is finite is simply to say that it opens out on content which is subject to change. Awareness, when fixed by an object is what we refer to as consciousness and as such, awareness is conditioned by what it opens out on. Bringing God into consciousness is to objectify God as a symbolic representation. That symbolic representation is itself subject to change. But God is not an object; God is ultimate subject. I can no more get behind God than I can self.

The talk of killing the ego is foolish. Ego is a necessary function. What is meant (if anything sane is meant) is that I must not be identified with either the activity or object of ego. But, of course, once I have learned that I need not be identified with the object of my focus, I have not yet learned not to be identified with my focus itself. I don't understand anything about what has been keeping me in bondage if I don't stop identifying myself as the agent or performer.

Let's go back to the issue of consciousness and content. There are two radically different notions of the way to go about self-change: 1) the psychological posture; and 2) that of Scripture. The two can never be ultimately accommodated, but they are not incapable of reflecting one another at their respective levels. In depth psychology one has for one's object one's subjectivity and one proceeds to chase down pathology. There is an endless chasing after self. I don't mean one doesn't see dysfunction, but to see it is not the same as to be healed. To identify it as a species isn't the same as to be freed from its dysfunctional hold.

The scriptural position (of all Scripture) is contrary in principle to the psychological position. The scriptural position does not invite us to run around looking for subjectivity by examining its products. (That inverts Krishnamurti's description of how one attains to a sense of beauty.) It is sufficient to look sincerely and seriously without having any purpose outside of that. Psychology is a utilitarian means of becoming healthy. There is nothing utilitarian in Scripture.

In the Christian Scripture there is all this fuss about surrender. In my teens that used to drive me up the wall. I didn't understand that it does not mean throwing oneself away. I wasn't interested in surrender but in *victory*. God, king and country doesn't include surrender! At best surrender is expedient, not an ultimate move. But properly understood surrender is an ultimate move. Grace picks up the tab and bam, I'm free.

Surrender is an ultimate move. I will or will not be sincere and serious about my intention to quit making excuses for myself, to quit referring to my pathology, my personal history. To quit saying, "I have this tic because my mother was frightened by a moose when she was carrying me!" Scripture says all that has to go. I simply have to face it that I'm in terrible shape. No amount of finding causes will make any difference to my being in this shape. I must begin by examining whether I am sincerely prepared to stop making excuses. Let's take an example. I once knew someone who wanted to quit smoking. He quit for a week and then started smoking again.

Something happened at the point where he started smoking again. He could not be serious for one half hour at a time.

I'm talking about sincerity of intent and the seriousness with which it is carried out. Scripture says if that is present, the rest is taken care of by the energy generated out of that. So Scripture is correct psychologically when it talks about grace. I do not through an act of will crank up will. Any time I'm truly sincere and totally serious, the energy in which the performance is carried out is available to me, enabling me to quit smoking for example. Krishnamurti's position in the order of performance is precisely that. If I look at it seriously, what is generated is passion. And what is passion? The power to move. In Biblical language, grace is enabled to effect the change for me if I'm serious.

The scriptural position is ultimate. If one is sincere and serious enough, energy is also present. The minute I chase the tails of my thoughts, my subjectivity, I am in deep trouble. I replace one compulsion with another. The reformed alcoholic is free from alcohol; but he is not free 'for' or 'in' the use of alcohol. Scripture, on the other hand, talks about getting cured. You can now see why Krishnamurti makes a fuss about the word 'total.' He's not saying there is no such thing as growth, but he is speaking about the performance and psychology that attends it.

There is no utilitarian motive in self-change; else we would be in bondage to an image of success. I have no other responsibility than sincerely, seriously undertaking the work of self-change. Never mind what's on the other side.

Anyone with normal intelligence recalls moments of sincerity and seriousness and wonders why they didn't last. The review of those moments cannot be comprehended by the finite mind but it is a mistake to assume in a self-congratulatory manner that it can't be apprehended. Jeremiah says, "The heart [is] deceitful above all [things], and desperately wicked: who can know it?" [Jer 17:9] How did he account for our monumental capacity for self-deception? Scripture never makes the claim that we are coerced to deceive ourselves. I can start with an examination of my thought. I can't start at the level of performance, by then I'm too far gone. But I can start at the level of my motivation and I can recognize whether there is a shift in my intention. If the smoker mentioned above had really undertaken an examination of his motivation, he would have seen a shift in intention wherein he was no longer serious about quitting. We willfully condemn ourselves. I'm not talking about guilt. At the point where one's intentions are mixed, one has lost hold on self-examination. The energy is drained away. There is no longer energy left to oppose the momentum of habit. As our smoker's intentions became mixed, he could no longer choose not to smoke. One ought to be able to choose. Everything we do ought to be subject to the power to choose otherwise I am in self-bondage.

Death, Life and Love Are Indivisible— the Nature of Immortality
May 8, 1979

[Video—Dialogue XIV: Death, Life and Love Are Indivisible—the Nature of Immortality[1]]

One of the claims of modern thought (not modern in the sense of bondage to years) is that it is bewitched and bedazzled by subjectivity. One of its overweening claims is that it has discovered subjectivity. It is not the case that the ancients were unaware of subjectivity. Take a look at classical Indian thought for example. The awareness of subjectivity is so pressing that there is a whole analysis of life in the world based on content called self. The whole is ordered to disengage the fascination with subjectivity.

In modern thought, something eminently stupid has been done: we've tried to make an object out of subjectivity. When we address ourselves to a subject, we necessarily point to a contemplation of content. If the content weren't there, there would be no subject. We relate to our own subjectivity only on a phenomenological level. Analysis is not of subjectivity but of the subject's phenomenology; an analysis is of the subject's expression. One can only do it if one mistakes one's own phenomenology as subject because by definition, subject is always behind. How can you reach it since you need it to do the reaching? Therefore to imagine I could make subjectivity an

---

[1] Video published by KFA under the title "Death".

object is to do a vain thing, so I should stop kidding myself that I am in a fair way toward chasing myself down.

At a certain point, the analysis as practiced in depth psychology and the scriptural approach are mutually exclusive. The essentially religious approach never requires us to chase down our subjectivity. Last time I quoted Jeremiah, "The heart [is] deceitful above all [things], and desperately wicked: who can know it?" [Jer 17:9]

To take a wicked heart to find the saintly heart is to begin from a point of departure which is already corrupt. If I give myself airs that in my own strength of intellectual probing I can find my subjectivity as such, I am according to the religious approach, kidding myself.

I think you have to take seriously Krishnamurti's point that analysis, as an activity, requires for the next session the subject of the last. The fundamentally religious approach is never bothered with that impediment. When you get to that level, you have to say there is an absolute distinction between the medical model and the spiritual model. Unfortunately there is really no way to describe or convey the religious activity of self-change until one has begun it whereas one can write tomes about analysis. There is no methodology in the spiritual model but there are courses offered on psychoanalysis, books and so on. You can't describe the religious understanding of it. You can only say there is something to be done and in the doing of it, you will find out.

You must make up your own mind whether to take the word 'subject' seriously. When you do it can never be an object. If it were, then you would need another subject to contemplate it. I'm not trying to play a philosophical game although it is a pretty little syllogism. Just look at it and you come up with the clear inference that it's silly.

Student: "By their fruits you shall know them."[2]

As Kierkegaard points out, it doesn't say *you* will be the one who knows. It is a terrifying thing to admit to oneself that one is a mystery

---

[2] Mt 7:20

to oneself and will remain so. The artful dodge is to prefer to think we discovered our subjectivity by exploring its private symbolism. On the contrary—I don't know myself at all on having studied all that. The review of it occurs after it has taken place but I don't know the one who is looking now.

Student: if I can't know myself, how do I avoid violating my nature?

If we will for once stop attempting to get our manipulative paws on what we imagine to be our subjectivity, the intuition of what is fitting for me is present to me upon that instant. We call it self-knowledge loosely; it is the intuition of my relation to the environment. I should not confuse myself with the relation.

It is embarrassing to have an intellect capable of confusing myself with my relation to the environment. But I also have the possibility of being aware, on any instant, of this collapse. I am warned of my pending mis-relation to myself at the level of primal intuition. Aware of what I am not, I must remain open to receive what insight might be provided. But we want a set of maps. People always look for a set of directions to help them find out how to tinker with themselves. Fine, so somebody has written a book on "how to tinker with myself." Why don't they tell me where myself is? I've got a set of plans for something which isn't evident. When I say it is simple, I mean it isn't complicated in the least. It is balderdash to tell us we are complicated. Our phenomenology is complicated—true. But truth isn't complicated in the least—it isn't bowls of spaghetti, cans of worms or aquaria of eels.

We're talking about truth. Either it is or it isn't true. The attempt to devise a roadmap to subjectivity is a dreadful invention based upon the dread of having to give up the notion that I can find my radical self. I can't stand the thought that I am being lived through by an energy which is not my private possession. I don't want to believe it, it renders me insignificant. On the other hand, what an extraordinary thing to be at all! Why should I be? So it seems I haven't lost any sense of worth. I can't give any good reason why life chose me. This should continually remind me how truncated my notions of power are.

Student: How are we to avoid repeating ourselves?

How could you *not* repeat yourself if your view of yourself never changes? It is the view of oneself that one protects ardently and hysterically. We regard that it changes when it grows by increment, but that is not the *essential* change which is required. It is a dreadful thing to say what is needed: this "emptying of the content of consciousness" is full of dread. Notice how grave he became when I said, "that's where the terror begins." He said in a low voice, "Yes sir!" The chances of not bolting are practically nil because nobody wants to die. It is a death.

Student: Please explain what he means when he says beauty is not in the field of consciousness.

Beauty is a non-dying thing which informs all things which do die. That energy isn't in my possession. He would give beauty as one of its names. The English word 'loveliness' expresses it—it has a touch of the ephemeral to it. One could refer to a woman as beautiful, but not lovely, and vice versa. We know least of what we mean when we use the word 'lovely.' If we see a beautiful woman, attention is directed primarily on the form, such things as the planes of the face are attended to, etc. For an artist to render beauty, he must look for just the right woman. To render loveliness he can choose any woman, if the light falls just right and she is a person who can reflect that light so that one senses something which is not subject to coming-to-be and passing-away. We're talking about a phenomenon which is the most elusive of all. Tread a little carefully around it. It is basically holy ground. If you meditate upon that term it would be helpful. We don't even think it is a necessarily enduring quality, as we would think of a beautiful form. We don't give loveliness a term. Either it is present or it isn't. And it might not be in the next moment. That is worth a long thought—it helps raise the attention above the phenomenological order.

Student: How can the intellect relate to mystery?

Leave it unless one is intelligent enough to say, "My Lord and my God!" The proper object of thought is being.

Student: Please explain the statement that the fall of man began at the point of imagination.

Strictly the fall of man is a product of the misuse of imagination—an effort to make it stand in for actuality.

Student: After emptying consciousness of its content, what keeps it from cluttering up again?

It is cluttered up with what one identifies with. The activity of being in act is effortless but resolution is required to maintain watchfulness so that one doesn't start re-identifying. You see, our pathological way of going through the world is to make the most extraordinary effort to manipulate what is external to us in the interest of having that which we've manipulated increase our power to further manipulate. The reason we do it is because we want to be able to undergo pleasure at will rather than wait upon it. Pleasure is the result of an external agency doing the stroking. If we're powerful enough, we think we can make a raid on all those agents and keep them in stock. We need power to get pleasure. Attaining to this has become institutionalized. Consider the extraordinary efforts we go to! And we pay no attention to our own enlightenment. So new effort is maniacally exerted out there. That is no way to have abiding satisfaction. When one truly turns attention to the transformation of consciousness so that one no longer makes that effort, there is nothing left to prove. One simply drops it. It is a profound shock to the system. Also, it is the point where one is most likely to bolt.

Now where does the effort lie? In maintaining a firm resolve not to bolt. Once one maintains oneself in that condition one's timing becomes correct. If one's timing is correct one can always get done that which one must do. So I drop all that external application of effort and turn the energy inward. If I do that I'll have no trouble, for example, in finding a parking place. It is not that the parking place is waiting for me but that I won't show up until there is one. There are these places. If I am in correct relation to myself, at any moment I am in one of them. I never have to worry about subjectivity in a condition of that sort. I'm always discovering myself, and discovering what it is disclosing in a timely way. I'm not running around taking notes about myself! If I am I can't keep my attention on the magical space. If one sees a book on how to do this, you know the condition of the author. It is obviously a case of rank self-deception.

There is another reason why there is no phenomenology of going well: there is no way to know in advance what it is like. It is all virgin territory completely a way of surprise. Each of our lives is lived in that order uniquely. I don't think it is ever possible to write seriously about how to go well. You can say how to go ill, that's dreadfully monotonous, dreadfully alike. The other is not. It is filled with perpetual wonder and surprise.

Student: If we write about it do we fall out of act?

One can render an aesthetical overview, but not a how-to. If that were not true how could you account for great poems, or scientific discoveries? A fine piece of verse is essentially miraculous. Something else is going on otherwise it would read dreadfully.

Student: What does Krishnamurti mean when he talks of dying?

Dying means really dying. In the ordinary sense it is just a moment in a process that is rotten. In a non-ordinary sense of dying, there's something absolute about the instant in which it occurs. If I remain firmly resolved, power is made continually available to me. When this happens every moment is unprecedented.

The ancients felt it was better never to get born if being born meant simply to be a part of this rotten process. It is difficult to tell younger persons that because they still are suffering a degree of shock in having been hurled into existence. The wind whistles past their ears so fast it is easy to confuse the shock with the wonder and therefore give oneself the idea that things will get better. They won't. Even if you don't undertake self-change, things get worse because your load of disappointments is larger than the vessel you have to carry them. Walk downtown and look at the faces over 30. Don't fail to have a long thought, that will be your face soon enough. In the '60s young people got the idea that they were created out of whole cloth as though each was an absolute event. Now you find many of them living in penthouses. That too is worth a long thought.

Take Krishnamurti seriously when he says the change must be total.

Religion, Authority and Education—Part I
May 15, 1979

If we are still groping for what Krishnamurti is about this should clarify much of our confusion. He feels his notion of meditation is fundamental to what he's about. We must understand in principle what he feels he's up against in trying to communicate it.

[Video—Dialogue XV: Religion, Authority and Education, Part I[1]]

Student: Why is Krishnamurti considered an authority?

There is a lust after security, and there is also some laziness at work. If one will not get on with self-examination one will likely give authority to someone else.

Student: Does Krishnamurti consider himself an authority?

Krishnamurti would echo the Buddha's imperative that one "Be a lamp unto yourself." So the ordinary notion of authority would not apply for Krishnamurti, but it applies etymologically. The root meaning of 'authority' is to enlarge, to increase. In Sanskrit the idea of growth is also included. In this deep meaning of authority Krishnamurti is authoritative. But it must be emphasized that in self-examination one doesn't slip out of the obligation to oneself to operate according to what light one has at the time. One is absolutely responsible for acting on what light one has.

---

[1] Video published by KFA under the title "Religion and Authority, Part 1".

Student: Is it necessary for a person to rely on another to enable him to detach from lies?

We must not simply act on what someone advises on the basis of intellect. We must make a volitional movement. We might truly believe their counsel is better than our own understanding, not because they have advised it but because of the quality of their counsel. The measure is whether we take responsibility. If we pass off responsibility we have acted badly. That easily becomes habitual. There is no way to avoid anxiety when one does it. The deeper layers of the self reject it. We never come to peace. This tape, Dialogue XV, runs to the heart of the character of education both as one undergoes it and as the ideal.

Student: Why do we so seldom act on what light or understanding we presently have?

Our species tends not to behave at the time in relation to what light it possesses. What makes it difficult to behave according to the light one has is that this behavior, measured by the collective, appears eccentric. One is unique and every circumstance has something unique in it. There is a temptation to disregard the uniqueness of oneself and the situation and act rather on the basis of some formula. It is risky to act on the basis of what differentiates oneself from others. Reducing the situation to essence, one will ask what another person would do in this situation. We are always attempting to validate the worth of our performance on the basis of a class or essential reference and we don't behave according to the character of the time. I'm not describing situational ethics! There is a proper character of the time; I am part of a situation but I can distinguish myself in the situation. I have to act according to what light I have at the time. The price I pay for not living up to the light I have is anxiety. I don't have anxiety living the other way. I have alertness. Now, there may be discomfort if my timely behavior makes the collective unhappy. Notice Krishnamurti stressed how we choose not to examine ourselves by the quality of our existence. Instead we use an outside measure provided by others. We are deeply ingrained with the notion that that's the way to go. We have years of momentum behind us. In this environment we may say I will watch, but the momentum of the past is so weighty I fall into it again. It is easy to get discouraged, but that's not a sufficient reason for not keeping at it.

Student: It's easy to lapse into self-pity. How do we figure out how to get more light?

Not by looking exclusively at disorder. Krishnamurti's fundamental conviction is that most disorder reflects order. Classically that is not correct; evil is the privation of order. When we are so disordered that nothing is left to feed on, disease overcomes us and the organism perishes.

Student: I'm puzzled by the fact that Krishnamurti set up schools.

One can question that. One wonders about the quality of the teachers in the school. Would they not unwittingly be a model for students to emulate?

Student: Is there a prescription for eliminating the distinction between work and play?

Doesn't the distinction become oppressive early on? Play must be earned. So we have to undergo toil so as to merit the pleasure the future holds in trust. We are attached to the notion of performance and reward. If you do this you get what you want. We are never introduced to observing that virtue is its own reward. Children must accept be encouraged to take responsibility for the activity itself. The distinction between work and play becomes pernicious when I do not accept responsibility for the character of the moment. We become victims of the past and must undertake contrivances and work overtime to get out of it. I spend the present funding the power to coerce relief later. It is dreadful to work 11 months and have a heart attack on vacation. I think the mythology of religion encourages this utilitarian relation between work and play. We behave while we're here so we can get the goodies later. That is pernicious and contrary to the gospel. The Kingdom of Heaven is present but it doesn't force itself on us. Unless we are chastely related to the present we always forfeit heaven.

Student: How does Krishnamurti refer to the Father?

In St. John [14:11] Jesus says he is in the Father and the Father in himself. He doesn't reduce the Father to himself and so on. In Krishnamurti's context, 'Father' would represent the source of intuition which operates on the instant and which cannot be identified with intellect. 'Father,' for Krishnamurti is the source of energy. Never forget that Krishnamurti makes the claim that if I am correctly related to the present, the energy for my passage is present. In that sense his understanding is no different from the classical doctrine of grace. You see we have it turned around when we make a distinction between work and play. We feel we have to do something to get up the energy. He feels if we are incorrectly related to authority we cannot be correctly related to the present instant.

This incorrect relation to authority and so to the present instant is the same position as Adam was in after his eating of the fruit of the knowledge of good and evil [Gen 3:9-10]. As God walked through the garden in the cool of the evening, he asked Adam, "Where art thou?" Since Adam was in miss-relation to the present he didn't know where he was. All he could muster for an answer was, "I was afraid and I hid." When asked, "Where art thou?" he should have answered, "Wherever you are, I am." He would then have been stanced as was Jesus, "in the Father." To use Krishnamurti's language, he would have been stanced in the source of intuition. We have an essential place, but we exist out of place. We don't know where our space is that's why there is so much violence. We are always getting in each other's way.

Student: Can what you're pointing to really be discovered by reading a book?

He did agree when I said the word has the power to disclose. But, if I don't relate correctly to the page no communication takes place. The chances of communication occurring may be greater in dialogue because I can say no that's not what I meant. In part, that's the psychological basis for his not being overly impressed with books. Consider the enormous amount of reading done to get through school. How adequately are we really reading those books? What is going on? We are not concerned to have a dialogue with the book but rather to regurgitate it on demand. What has that to do with a genuine dialogue with book? The word's power to disclose is not coercive.

Meditation and the Sacred Mind[1]
May 22, 1979

[Video—Dialogue XVIII: Meditation and the Sacred Mind[2]]

On the question of will: Will implies direction and direction points to one space among others. Therefore any space will opens out on must be finite, so it is one among others and on that account up against limit. And since the activity takes place in time it is involved in succession. It seems clear that when we are required to formulate activity we have a beginning, middle and an end and that we need to be skillful. Will is the power that is needed for moving through the whole field of knowledge. Now when Krishnamurti speaks of meditation he's talking about will that is really will-lessness. Meditation must inform everything, it is not one thing among others. I can't imagine that he means anything else by meditation than the sensitivity to one's quality of being at any time under any circumstances, in any place. That is why he does not wish to relate will to meditation. Will is directional while, for him, meditation ultimately is pure attention.

Krishnamurti seems to understand by meditation what the Chinese Taoist referred to as *wu wei*[3] or not doing. Meditation, as with *wu wei*, entails a self-monitoring against identification, mixed motives or an agenda that would negate the energy of the present to

---

[1] The semester was too short to allow all the videos to be shown. Dialogues XVI and XVII were omitted.
[2] Video published by KFA under the title "Meditation, Part 2".
[3] Allan W. Anderson, *Reflections on the I Ching*, p. 94.

inform and transform one. It is not a direct action. Growing a will is based on the capacity to attain to not doing. Now Krishnamurti doesn't want to say along with G. I. Gurdjieff that, "Patience is the mother of will," yet Gurdjieff's statement is consistent with both Krishnamurti and the Taoist. Krishnamurti himself says there cannot be essential effort in the field of knowledge.

The American philosopher John Dewey makes a distinction between change *in* will and change *of* will.[4] Thus when we walk down the hall there is no question of direction. We suffer a change *in* will when we turn right. We suffer a change *in* will all the time providing we are moving soundly. Change *of* will refers to my reception of the world. If I am related to it in an essentially manipulative way I have never learned what it is to be quiet and at peace. I must learn what it is to become receptive. It is a totally different orientation in being from before. It cannot be reduced to a series of directions as I move through physical space. To avoid the use of the word 'will' applied to meditation is to avoid the notion one meditates on the basis of contrivance. Still, there are distinctions to be made in the function of will. Will is always operating.

He expects one to sustain a choiceless awareness. He doesn't expect it will be sustained by energy one generates oneself. On the contrary, it is sustained by energy that is cosmic. But one does require to make a movement that is correct otherwise we will not learn what it is to be choicelessly aware. It would have been better if he had analyzed it analytically and seen the double negation. We must negate our refusal to allow the energy to inform us. Ultimately that is the proper use of will, the proper condition of the heart. How would the well-ordered person perceive the world? As it is, in its Suchness. They see the Kingdom of Heaven within and among us and therefore remain tranquil under any circumstance whether joyful and sorrowful. They never shift from center. They could never forget that all things pass, so they are not clutching. Action would always be timely. Things would happen magically because no one

---

[4] John Dewey, *A Common Faith*, p. 17.

would be interfering with the Way as the Way ought to be undergone by us. The Way is never frustrated but we can frustrate ourselves by getting in the way of the Way because the Way's operation is always its own rule. As soon as our operation is its own rule we know the Way is having in all respects for ultimate Good its way in us. It will have its way anyway. The difference between us and the Way centers on the fact that the Way has no need for thought and care while we have need of both. True care is a loving act. True thought minds its own business.

We have come to the end of our class. I enjoyed being with you. There is a spirit that is unusual. It's a very rare experience to share in such a spirit. I'm grateful for what in the order of spirit you brought to your work.

Works Cited

_____. *Acts of Phillip,* http://wesley.nnu.edu/biblical_studies/noncanon/acts/actphil.htm

_____. *Bhagavad Gītā. Sanskrit Text and Translation.* Tr., Franklin Edgerton, Harvard Oriental Series, vol. 38, Cambridge: Harvard University Press, 1952.

_____. *Bhagavad Gītā.* Tr., Radhakrishnan, S. New York: HarperCollins College Div., 1973.

_____. *Bṛhadarāṇyaka. Upaniṣad.* Tr. Swami Krishnananda, http://www.swami-krishnananda.org/brhad_00.html

_____. *Mundaka Upaniṣad.* See Shearer and Russell (below).

Blau, Evelyne. *Krishnamurti: 100 Years.* New York: Stewart, Tabori, & Chang (ABRAMS), 1995.

Castaneda, Carlos. *A Separate 'Reality, Further Conversations with Don Juan.* New York: Simon and Schuster, 1971.

Chuang Tzu. *Basic Writings.* Tr. Burton Watson. New York: Columbia University Press, 1964.

Confucius. *Analects, Great Learning, and Doctrine of the Mean.* Tr. James Legge. New York: Dover Publications, Inc., 1971.

Coomaraswamy, Ananda K. *Hinduism and Buddhism.* New York: Philosophical Library, undated.

Dewey, John. *A Common Faith.* New Haven and London: Yale University Press, 1934.

Frank, Erich. *Philosophical Understanding and Religious Truth.* London, N.Y., etc.: Oxford Univ. Press, 1959.

Grimm, George. *The Doctrine of the Buddha.* Berlin: Akademie-Verlug, 1958.

Grohe, Friedrich. *Beauty of the Mountain: Memories of J. Krishnamurti.* Ojai: The Krishnamurti Foundation, 2004.

Heimann, Betty. *The Significance of Prefixes in Sanskrit Philosophical Terminology.* Hertford: Royal Asiatic Society Monographs, Vol. XXV, 1951.

Hogan, Linda. *Dwellings: A Spiritual History of the Living World.* Beaverton: Touchstone Press, 1966.

Hsi, Chu and Lu Tsu-Ch'ien. *Reflections on Things at Hand: The Neo-Confucian Anthology.* Tr. Wing-Tsit Chan. New York: Columbia University Press, 1967.

Kierkegaard, Søren. *Fear and Trembling and The Sickness Unto Death.* Tr. Walter Lowrie. Garden City, New York: Doubleday, 1954.

_____. *The Sickness Unto Death.* Tr. Howard & Edna Hong. Princeton: Princeton University Press, 1983.

Kingsley, Charles. *The Water-Babies: A Fairy Tale for a Land-Baby.* Boston: Adamant Media Corp., 2003. (Facsimile of the 1907 Macmillan edition.)

Krishnamurti in dialogue with Professor Allan W. Anderson. *A Wholly Different Way of Living.* London: Victor Gollancz Ltd., 1991.

Krishnamurti, Jiddu. *Awakening of Intelligence*

_____. *Flight of the Eagle.* New York: Harper & Row, 1971.

———. *Inward Revolution*. San Francisco: Shambhala, 2006.

———. *Krishnamurti's Notebook*. Ojai: Krishnamurti Publications of America, 2003.

———. *Total Freedom: The Essential Krishnamurti*. New York: HarperOne, 1996.

Lao Tzu. *The Way of Lao Tzu (Tao Te Ching)*. Tr. Wing-tsit Chan, Indianapolis and New York: Bobbs-Merrill Co. Inc., 1963.

Lee, Mark. *Under the Pepper Tree*. Soon to be published.

Maharaj, Sri Nisargadatta. *I Am That*. Tr. Maurice Frydman. Durham: Acorn Press, single volume edition 1988.

Maharshi, Sri Ramana. *Supplement to 40 Verses on Existence*, #39. *Ramana Maharshi and His Philosophy of Existence* by T.M.P. Mahadevan. Triuvannamalai: Sri Ramanasramarn, 1959.

Martin, Raymond. "Why isn't Krishnamurti accepted at the University?" KFA *Newsletter*, Fall, 1998.

Masson, Jeffrey Moussaieff and Susan McCarthy. *When Elephants Weep: The Emotional Lives of Animals*. New York: Dell Publishing, 1996.

Neruda, Pablo. *100 Love Sonnets: Cien Sonetos de Amor* Tr. Stephen Tapscott. Austin: University of Texas Press, 1986.

Nishitani, Keiji. *Religion and Nothingness*. Berkeley: University of California Press, 1982.

Ortega y Gasset, Jose. *Meditations on Quixote*. Tr. Evelyn Rugg and Diego Marin. New York: W. W. Norton and Co. Inc., 1969.

———. *Some Lessons in Metaphysics*. Tr. Mildred Adams. New York: W. W. Norton and Co. Inc., 1969.

Pagels, Elaine. *Adam, Eve, and the Serpent*. New York: Vintage Books, 1989.

Partridge, Eric. *Origins: A Short Etymological Dictionary of Modern English*. New York: Greenwich House, 1983.

Plato. *Plato: The Collected Dialogues*. Ed. Edith Hamilton and Huntington Cairns, Bollingen Series LXXI, Princeton University Press, 1961.

Schürmann, Reiner. Meister Eckhart Mystic and Philosopher. Bloomington: Indiana University Press, 1978.

Shearer, Alistair (Tr.) and Peter Russell (Tr.). *The Upanishads*. Easton: Harmony, 2003.

Swinburne, Algernon Charles. *A Selection of Poems by Algernon Charles Swinburne*, ed. H. Treese. London: The Grey Walls Press, 1948.

———. *Atalanta in Calydon and Lyrical Poems*. Selected by William Sharp. Boston: Adamant Media Corp., 2001. (Facsimile of the Tauchnitz 1901 edition.)

Waley, Arthur. *The Analects of Confucius*. London: George Allen Unwin Ltd., 1964.

Wilhelm, Richard (Tr.). *The I Ching or Book of Changes*. Tr. to English, Cary F. Baynes, 3rd ed. Princeton: Princeton University Press, 1967.

Index

A

abyss, 108

academic life, journey through forest of abstractions, 15

acquired conditioning, 118, 121

action
  according to the light I have, 230
  essence of, 103, 108
  essential, 102
  field of, 102
  fruit of, 43
  gross and subtle, 102

activity
  intellectual, 185
  moral, 185
  satisfied by its own exercise, 84, 177

Acts of Phillip ch IX:140, 91

actuality, not a concept, 160

agency, 176. See illusions

agency of God, 115

alienation, 85, 117, 167

aloneness, 11, 16, 52, 97

Analects, bk IX.30, 42

anxiety, 97, 175, 191, 199, 230

anxious worry, 48, 51, 120

aphorisms, "nothing was divided and there is nothing to unite", 35, 69, 107

Aristotle, 93, 148
  four causes, 139

art, 184

Atalanta in Calydon, 108

Ātman, xix

attachment, 67, 110, 152, 173
   to egoic activity, 103
   to inaction, 43

attention
   as negation, xvii
   two orders of, 65

attention, pure act of, xvii, xviii, xx, 6, 17, 64, 81
   calculative thought in, 173
   immune from possibility or actuality of self-misunderstanding, 102

attitude, 47, 66, 82, 106
   choice and decision follow from, 101
   free for, 47
   meditational, xx, 48, 74
   relieves one of attending to successive instants, 102
   that frees from self-betrayal, 72

attunement, 120

authority, 155

awakening of intelligence, defined, 134

aware
   defined, 158
   of being aware, 150

awareness, 6
   and consciousness. *See* distinctions
   and knack, 100
   apprehended not comprehended, 103
   as choiceless watcher, 6
   as pure witness, 103
   between and beyond instants, 35
   choiceless, 8, 14, 82, 236
   described, 103
   etymology of, 98
   ever aware of consciousness, 104
   function of on near and far sides, 105
   relation to ultimacy, 104
   two aspects of, 98

B

battle, 193

bearing, 71, 78
  compared with language, 93
  drama of career, 110
  first encounter with, 86
  given to us in advance, 93
  near and far sides of, 107
  radical character of, 88
  role of, 84
  taking it seriously, 86

beatitude, 110

beauty
  not in the field of consciousness, 224
  sense of, 217

becoming, 190

being, proper object of thought, 134, 225

being and becoming, 190
  intersection between, 88

Bhagavad Gītā, 82, 113
  ch 2:47, 43
  ch 4:18, 102
  ch 7, 113
  ch 11, 185

Blake, William, 185

Blau, Evelyne, xv

Bohm, 139

bolting, 83, 194, 203, 224, 226

Book of Changes. See I Ching

books, correct relation to, 233

Bṛhadāraṇyaka Upaniṣad, 43, 51

Buddha, 30, 69, 81, 141, 229
  "all becoming is suffering", 32
  "Ananda, be a lamp unto yourself", 127
  Deer Park sermon, 151
  translation of name, 116

Buddha nature, 30, 35

C

Carroll, Lewis, 205
Castaneda, Carlos, 119
catharsis, 162
change
  independent of knowledge and time, 129
  of heart, 102
  total, 227
choice follows from attitude, 47
choiceless awareness. See awareness, choiceless
Chuang Tzu, 14, 186
cleft, 108
  between eternal and time, 109
  between infinite and finite, 109
  between necessary and free, 109
collapsing
  into abstract disembodied consciousness, 89
  into authority, xv
  into becoming, 190
  into content of thought, 14
  into ego, 216
  into external conditions, 114
  into imaginary future liberation, 33
  into Krishnamurti, 126
  into mechanical momentum, 194
  into object experienced, 102
  into the eternal, 49
  into the past, 65
comparison, invidious, 156
conflict, 214
  resolving of, 212
conflict of motives, xvii, xviii, 6, 119, 169
Confucius, 8, 42
confusions

essence and existence, 137, 147
principle and operation, 208

conscience, 187

consciousness, 103
and awareness. *See* distinctions
and content, 213
cannot be conscious of awareness, 104
desired goal of, 104
emptying content of, 224
etymology of, 103
extraordinary vs rectified, 157
inherent duality in, 103
not self-correcting, 15
strength of, weakness of, 106

consummation, 190

contradiction, existential, 91

Coomaraswamy, Ananda K., 35

courage, 16, 107
moral and spiritual, 62

cross, 96

Cunningham, J. V., 211

D

daimon, xix, 118

death, 224
and creation, 6
of yesterday, 10
psychological, 9, 14, 62

deliberation, 187

depth psychology, 201
absolutizes consciousness, 15
chief liability of, xvi
difficulty with, 216
pillars of, 5

Descartes, 85

desire, 14

despair, 199

destiny, 43
  a matter of living time, 118

detachment. See non-attachment

Dewey, John, 111, 236

dialogue, genuine, 94

disease, spiritual, 209

disorder
  defined, 150
  reflects order, 231

distinctions
  action and activity, 183
  action, gross and subtle, 102
  activity and condition or state, 158
  activity and process, 171, 176, 190
  alteration and transformation, 111
  anxiety and concern, 172
  anxiety and fear, 163
  aware and aware of, 156
  awareness and awareness of, 215
  awareness and consciousness, 15, 98, 107
  change in and change of will, 111, 236
  creation and novelty, 134
  ecstasy and enstacy, 157
  education and training, 212
  essence and existence, 150, 160
  hero and saint, 193
  medical and spiritual models, 222
  meditative thought and calculative thought, 176
  moral and natural orders, 186
  name and label, 183
  necessary and sufficient, 141
  patience and endurance, 10, 72
  peak experience and intuition of Ultimacy, 157
  primal intuition and instinct, 95, 119
  psychological and philosophical orders, 140
  quality and quantity, 94
  speech and chatter, 95
  truth judgments and intuitive reception of beauty, 174

   un-attached and non-attachment, 41
   waiting for and waiting on, 93
   wisdom and understanding, 146
   wonder and awe, 157

distinguish in order to unite, 174

Dōgen, 32

doing your own thing, 168

dragon's pool and the tiger's lair, 116

dreams, 155

dropping of body and mind, 32, 115

drugs, a sign one has not suffered enough, 192

E

ear
   ear and eye, 94
   favors the qualitative, 94

earnestness, 107

education
   character of, 230
   defined, 212

ego
   as external to the self, 64
   described, 215
   destruction of, 83
   functions of, 83
   killing of, 216

either/or, 144, 146
   enlightened or unenlightened, 135
   liberated or in bondage, 135
   saved or lost, 135

Eliot, T. S., 109

embodiment, principle of, 87

emptiness, 8, 49, 63
   creation born out of, 75
   home of Silence, 95
   of the mind as foundation of meditation, 20

without a centre, 11

Endymion, 50

enlightenment, *135, 141*
  defined, 117
  experience, 116
  not a termination but a consummation, 118
  occasion for, 149
  roadblocks to, 82
  true, 116

Enlightenment, the, 116

enstacy, 169

essence
  apprehended first, 150
  defined, xvi, 136

estrangement, 95

eternal, 10, 11, 17, 39
  home of, 68

eternal and the temporal
  functional cleft between, 109

eternal life, 68, 69

eternal now, 49, 51

eternity, 39
  defined, 68
  instant as atom of, 100
  losing, 43

evil, 19
  defined, 231

existence
  always has the first move, 71, 83
  described, xvi, 136
  mothers us, 87
  sense of, 205

experiencer and the experienced, 101

eye
  and ear, 94
  favors the quantitative, 94

F

fall of man, 225

Father, Krishnamurti's view of, 232

fear, 16
  as cause of violence, 67
  attends self-inquiry, 47

fear and trembling, 41, 51

feeling
  faster than thought, 174, 200

feelings of
  opposed by matter, 212
  oppressed by form, 211

forms, 163

Frank, Erich, 71

free will, xviii, 47
  fatal twist on doctrine of, 32

freedom
  from having to choose, 90
  is not having to choose, 101
  of choiceless awareness, 82

Frost, Robert, 186, 189

fruit of action, 43

Fu, Charles, 27

futility
  sense of, 120
  sentiment of, 33

G

Gandhi, 184

goddess of speech, 45, 51

Goethe, 32

Good
  beyond being surpassing it in dignity and power, 88, 104
  beyond conceptualization, 89
  beyond good/evil, 88

   Form of forms, 89
   intersection with Being and Becoming, 88
   not this, not that, 89

good, draws us, 195

Gospel, 113

grace, 218, 232

Groundless Ground, 84

Gurdjieff, G. I., 200, 236

H

habits
  momentum of, 31
  superimposing image from the past on the present, 67

hearing, not letting anything interfere with seeing, xix, 93

heaven and earth, man stanced between, 40

Heraclitus, xv
  "You cannot step in the same river twice", 134

hero, 193

hexagrams
  h 11 - Peace, 89
  h 15 - Modesty, 40
  h 25 - Innocence, 191
  h 41 - Decrease, 120
  h 51 - The Arousing, 41

Hogan, Linda, 86

holiness, 167

Holy Spirit, xix

human condition, 119

human nature, 17, 46, 77, 111
  able to violate, 187
  as essentially meditative, 4
  can violate itself, 195
  capacity for self-betrayal, 47
  counter tension in, 71
  deliberative, 175, 186
  discovering, 101

essential promise of, xv
  has something that eludes scientific measure, 30
  in Genesis, 80
  in the I Ching, 80, 83
  not reducible to biology, 28
  possibility of self-betrayal, 51
  primal intuition, 100

Hume, David, 21

hurt, 201

hypomonē, 11

I

I, who and what is, 64

I Ching, 40, 79, 83, 87, 94, 120

Idealism, 73

ideals, 136, 148, 163

identification, 101
  and ego, 215
  with personality, 31

illusions
  adversity produces fine character, 89
  agency, 31, 89, 216
  agency in leap from self-misunderstanding to self-awareness, 103
  anxiety in human nature, 17
  death of ego releases one from self-bondage, 83
  ego is an independent substance in being, 63
  essential alienation of human nature, 117
  essential progress, 32
  estrangement in human nature, 17
  intellect and will can impose themselves on intuition and instinct, 79
  one is the center of one's world, 70
  one is the doer of the action, 108
  original nature is a private possession, 5
  potentiality can actualize itself, 190
  self-inquiry and introspection are the same, 63
  sense of self-presence is ego, 64

we have the power to save ourselves, 79

image, 149

imagination
  abuse of, 67
  Achilles' heel of, xv

inaccessibility, 212

inevitability, 48, 52, 161

infinite, 39

infinite and the finite
  functional cleft between, 109

inquiry means self-inquiry, 137

insight is not enough, 202

instant, 10, 11
  as atom of eternity, 69
  bears within it the unexpected, 24
  character of, 14
  creation and destruction in, 49
  though timeless seems to be a matter of time, 10

instinct, distinguished from primal intuition, 95

intellect
  a function of the soul, 179
  vocation of, 119

intellect and intelligence
  confusion between, 119

intelligence, 10
  character of which supports self-inquiry, 64
  etymology of, 48
  mark of, 119
  root meaning, 74

intent, sincerity of, 218

introspection, 131

intuition, primal. See primal intuition

intuition, supra-relational, 108

inward man, energized by spirit, 31

J

Japanese art of flower arrangement, 41

Jesus, 8, 64, 69, 81, 91, 113, 137, 152, 191, 201, 207, 210, 212, 213, 232

Job, 185

Jōseki, Gasan, 34

journal, reason for, 131

joy and concern, 175

Jumblies, 205

Jung, Carl
 four functions, xix
 grasped existence at 40, 160

K

karma, 33

Keats, 175
 "A thing of beauty is a joy forever", 50, 161
 letter to Bailey, 194

Kierkegaard, 25, 69, 78, 84, 100, 199

killing, 206

Kingdom of Heaven, 236

Kingsley, Charles, 33

knack, xvi, 99
 of obedience to the necessary, 101

know that I know, 150

knowing
 distinguished from knowledge, 68
 three orders of, 68

knowledge
 and time, 66
 etymology of, 66

Krishnamurti
 how to understand him, 130
 significance of teachings, 4

Krishnamurti Center, 19

Krishnamurti quotes
  "change must be total", 227
  "consciousness is its content", 5, 215
  "Creation is born out of this emptiness", 14
  "emptying of the content of consciousness", 224
  "For two years I have been thinking about this, slowly, carefully, patiently ", 10
  "I am not a teacher", 178
  "I am the world and the world is me", 24, 126, 158
  "ideals are idiotic", 136, 148
  "In attention there is no exclusion, no resistance, and no effort. And therefore no frontier, no limits", xvii
  "learning is always in the active present", 171
  "[meditation] opens the door to the incalculable, to the measureless", 15
  "observing without the observer", 22, 102
  "perception is the action", 6, 24, 163, 187
  "[silence] in which and from which all things flow and have their being.", 11
  "the description is not the described", 127, 178, 181
  "the first step is the last step", xviii, 9, 11
  "the observer is the observed", 21, 147
  "the very seeing of what is false is the truth", xvii
  "There is a 'thinking' born out of the total emptiness of the mind", 7, 49, 51, 75, 95
  "truth is a pathless land", 61

Kriṣna, 43, 82

L

Lakshmi, 151

language, grounded in intuition of actuality, 161

language of myth
  Earth, 87
  Heaven, 87

Lao Tzu, 95
  ch 25, 84
  ch 28, 99
  ch 37, xx, 84

ch 56, 181
ch 70, 8, 22
ch 71, 71

leap, 92
  from self-misunderstanding to self-awareness, 103

Lear, Edward, 205

learning, 196
  activity and process of, 172

liberation, 135
  of St. Paul, 32
  secular, 28, 30
  ultimate, 29, 32, 33, 35

life
  lived meditatively, xviii
  lived out between the timeless and time, 74
  lived well, 74
  lived without a why, xix

life and death, abiding between, 193

light unto oneself, 76, 127, 141, 229

listening
  and bearing, 94
  with the spiritual ear, 94

Locke, 86

loneliness, 95

love, 108
  and death, 10, 14, 49, 75, 95

Love
  possibility of resisting, 203
  source of creation, 5

Love and Death, one who is both, 35

loveliness, 224

M

Maharaj, Sri Nisargadatta, 35, 69, 105

manipulation, 89, 93, 121, 136, 152, 225, 236

Martin, Raymond, 21

Masson and McCarthy, 85

me mistaken for the I, 63

Mean, Chinese notion of, 211

meditation, 5, 15, 16, 17, 21, 47
  as will-less-ness, 235
  labors in the field of self-inquiry, 62
  opens to the incalculable, 15
  thought necessarily operates in, 48

Meister Eckhart, xix, 167

memory, relation to, 199

middle, 196
  creatures of, 40

mind and image, 149

mind, chaste
  described, 211
  locus of, 212

moksha, 137

momentum, 5, 31, 231
  none in the order of spirit, 194

Mundaka Upanishad, 169

mystical activity, defined, 157

mysticism, test of, 157

N

narrow pass, 108

nature
  being true to one's, 71
  Original, 30
  ultimate, 87

necessary and the free
  functional cleft between, 109

negation
  and transformation, 143
  double, 196, 236

negative summons, 187. See primal intuition

Neruda, Pablo, 96

New Age, 116

New Testament
  Mt 6:33, 157
  Mt 6:34, 38, 191
  Mt 7:13-14, 92
  Mt 7:14, 113, 168
  Mt 7:20, 222
  Mt 10:16, xvii
  Mt 10:26, 201
  Mt 11:6, 91
  Mt 11:15, 137
  Mt 13:13-14, 102
  Mt 23:23, 141
  Mt 26:39, 152
  Mk 4:12, 102
  Mk 4:22, 201
  Lk 7:23, 91
  Lk 8:10, 102
  Lk 8:17, 201
  Lk 11:42, 141
  Lk 12:2, 201
  Lk 23:34, 192
  Jn 1:1, 160
  Jn 3:1-10, 213
  Jn 8:11, 210
  Jn 10:30, 212
  Jn 14:11, 232
  Jn 16:12-13, 8
  Jn 17:3, 68, 69
  Rom 5:4, 190
  Rom 6:2, 138
  Rom 7, 32
  Rom 7:19, 31
  2 Cor 3:18, 168
  Gal 2:20, 31
  Heb 5:8, 96
  Phil 4:7, 48, 169
  1 Jn 4:16, 161

Newton, 86

Nicodemus, 213

nirvāna is samsāra, 28

non-attachment, 37, 38, 41, 42, 44
  correlative virtue, 43
  occasioned by, 89
  returns us to origin, 89

Non-being
  condition for relating viscerally to, 89
  out of which Being arises, 95

non-possible, 205

non-rational
  examples of, 118
  highest expression of, 116

nonsense, genuine, 205

not doing, 235

not misunderstanding, xvii, 77
  and timing, 66

now, 126

O

obedience
  etymology of, 96
  foundation of bearing, 120
  to suasions of Heaven, 90

offense, 208

offer, etymology of, 106

Old Testament
  Gen 3:9-10, 232
  Ps 46:10, 156
  Ps 51:10, 115
  Prov 4:7, 146
  Eccl 1:9, 33, 134
  Jer 17:9, 86, 218, 222

omega point, 32

opposites, co-operation not coincidence, xx

oracle, 40

order, from seeing disorder, 166

original innocence, 90

original nature, 5, 11, 79, 117, 118
  has us, 5
  not a private possession, 5

original sin, 32

Ortega y Gasset, xv, 73
  "the death of what is dead is life", 67

Ouspenski, 200

P

Pagels, Elaine, 32

Pan, 164

parking place, finding, 226

Pascal, 113

passion, defined, 218

past, the, 142

patience, 16, 44, 72, 93
  correlative virtue to non-attachment, 43
  distinguished from endurance, 10
  etymology of, 72
  mother of will, 236

pause
  intemporal, 24

peace
  defined, 89
  that passeth all understanding, 28, 93

perceiver and perceived, 15, 17

perception, without the perceiver, 15

perfection, 113

performance, 215

perseverance, 107

persona, 6, 14, 31, 63, 79

   disappears, 63
   mistaken for the self, 63

personality and experience, 63

perspective, intuitive and meditative, 87

Phaedrus, 164

philosophy, absolutizes consciousness, 15

place, essential, 232

Plato, 8, 65, 163, 213
   "The Good is beyond being surpassing it in dignity and power", 88, 104

Pleasure, 225

poems
   "Before the beginning of years ", 108
   "Driftwood returns to the abandoned shore..." 26
   "I know not whence she came", 211
   "It is ninety-one years", 34
   "She lived unknown, and few could know", 162
   "That time was like never, and like always", 96
   "The flowery branch of the wild cherry", 42
   "When all the world is young, lad", 34
   "Who can wander for a lifetime", 90
   Between, 90
   The Owl and the Pussycat, 205
   The Road Not Taken, 186, 189
   Tyger, 185
   Young and Old, 33

poetry, and necessity, 161

potentiality cannot actualize itself, 190

present, 133
   why we don't have a, 138

primal intuition, xix, xx, 10, 74, 75, 77, 93, 99, 113, 118, 223
   and spiritual ear, 95
   opens out on the unprecedented, 95
   voice of original innocence, 102

principle, abstract
   taken to logical conclusion, 208

prisoner, mark of, 191

process, 49
progress, idea of, 114

Q

quality, differentiated from quantity, 94
questions, rhetorical, 164

R

rational empiricism, 116
rational, irrational and non-rational, 116
Realism, 73
Reality
  hallmarks of, 106
  neither event nor experience, 63, 116
reality and fantasy, 108
realization, requires constant testing, 105
rebirth, 41
receptivity, 236
reducing things to the past, 137
relation, to myself, 129
relationships
  beauty and sorrow, 192
  deep listening and bearing, 96
  knowledge and freedom, 139, 141
  necessity and freedom, 134
  offering and receiving, 106
  principle and corrective, 166
  process and activity, 202
  structure and process, 140
repression, 200
Republic, 6.509C, 104
resolution, 107, 225
responsibility, 230, 231
restlessness, 120

reversal, 121

rhetoric, proper use of, 9

Rig Veda, 45

S

sacred, 46

sacrifice, 41, 89

sage, description of, 101

sageliness, 19, 29, 87

saint, 193

St. Augustine, 32

St. Thomas Aquinas, 173
 "we distinguish in order to unite", 94

salvation, 135

samsāra, 33
 is nirvāna, 27, 28

science, experimental, 29

sculpture, Greek and Roman, 182

seeing
 seeingimmanent, 213
 seeingmanifests in action, 6

self
 hiddenness and manifestation of, 79
 neither objectifiable nor cognizable, 31
 not my private possession, 223
 not reducible to body and soul, 64, 65

self-awakening, 69
 and the instant, 14
 defined, 69
 indispensable condition for, 102
 pre-requisite for, 105
 suffering in, 89

self-awareness, mark of, 103

self-betrayal, 5, 47, 71, 187
 possibility of qualifies us as a species, 168

self-bondage, 31, 62, 78, 82, 214

self-change
  desire for, 191
  ways of, 217

self-corruption, possibility of, 162

self-deception, in Jeremiah, 218

self-examination, 131

self-identification, 14, 85, 215

self-identity, 83

self-inquiry, xv, 5, 6, 15, 17, 21, 47, 62, 63, 78
  abiding pressure of bearing draws us toward, 85
  and introspection, 63
  beginning of, 16
  contrasted with conventional religion and applied secularity, 81
  independent of outward and inward authority, 97
  kept alive by the passionate few, 81
  only intelligence is required for, 64
  price of, 9
  reason for fear in, 138
  thought's role in, 8

self-liberation, 62, 78

self-misunderstanding, xv, 5, 6, 27, 31, 69, 75, 79, 82, 88
  and the instant, 14
  basic character of, 97
  beginning of, 85
  belongs to the self, not the ego, 83
  how it arises, 84
  invited by apparent continuity, 10
  possibility of, 101

self-monitoring, against identification, 235

self-pity, 89, 231

self-presence, sense of, 64

self-transformation. See transformation

seriousness, 25, 41, 46, 214, 218
  defined, 144

shock, 162
  of fate, 41

  of heaven, 41
  of the heart, 42
  possibility in, 138

Siddhartha, lost self-misunderstanding, 117

Smith, Huston, 169

Socrates, xix, 64, 74, 77, 81, 95, 99, 118, 127, 164
  "an unexamined life is not worth living", 65
  Apology, 65
  "I know that I do not know", 104

soul, 91
  acquiring, 179
  awakening to exaltation and humility, 71
  defined, 88

speech, 95

spirit, 31
  conditioned, 87
  freedom of, 5
  has no agenda, 71
  health of, 71
  unconditioned, 87
  vocation of, 91

spiritual disease, 4

spirituality, 61
  defined, 75

spiritual life, 37
  biblical vs. mistaken views, 92

standing, we bear our humanness in, 88

subjectivity, 221
  cannot be made an object, 221

Suchness, xix, 236

suffering, 89
  attributed to moral guilt, 32
  over suffering, 89

surrender, 217

Swinburne, Algernon Charles, 108

T

Tao, 87
  is a turning back, 84
  the One as the many, 84

Tao Te Ching. See Lao Tzu

tê, 99

technology, 106

temperament, 212

tension between
  unfolding and fall, 107

terror, 224

tethlimménē, 92

theology, 46

thinking
  calculative, 173
  calculative and meditative, xix, 3
  healthy role of calculative, 4
  meditative, 87

thought
  not coincident with its object, 202
  proper object of, 225

thought and knowledge
  proper uses of, 7

timeliness, xvii, 10, 48, 51, 52, 74
  defined, 89

timing, 226

transformation, 91
  defined, 78
  independent of knowledge and time, xvi, 19, 61, 63, 65, 76, 143, 172
  instantaneous, 75

transition is unintelligible, 129

trust, 120
  radical, 16

truth goodness and beauty, 164

truth, the seeing of what is false, xvii

U

Ultimacy
  is awareness, 104
  radical intuition of, 157

Unconditioned is one's real self, 97

unconditioned self cannot be an object, 103

uncontrivance, xviii

understand, 11

understanding
  and timelessness, 66
  distinguished from knowledge, 70
  etymology of, 70
  open to intelligence, closed to calculative reason, 70

unenlightenment, defined, 117

unexpected, 88

unfulfilled promise, vague sense of, 81

unprecedented, 65, 74, 88, 95
  opens on the eternal, 10

Upaniṣads
  "It cannot be attained by the weak", 169
  "The full outflows from fullness", 44, 51

V

vacant mind, 9

Vedanta, 190

vegetarianism, 206

virtue, its own reward, 231

vocation, universal human, 88

Voltaire, 86

W

Warytko, Sandra, 27

watchfulness, 225

Watts, Alan, 178

way
  that leads to destruction, 92

Way, 237
  see Tao, 87

wholeness, 61
  defined, 75
  no evolution to, 132

wild animal, alert as, 133

will, 111, 235
  change of, 118
  proper use of, 236

wisdom, 29, 108, 115

wisdom, primordial, 64

wonder, 205
  sense of, 105, 191

word
  pregnant silence in, 95
  primordially, 160

Wordsworth, 161, 185

wu wei, 235

www.ingramcontent.com/pod-product-compliance
Lightning Source LLC
Chambersburg PA
CBHW030136170426
43199CB00008B/83